3D
iOS Games
by Tutorials

By Chris Language

3D iOS Games by Tutorials

Chris Language

ISBN: 978-1-942878-16-2

Dedication

"To my wife Corné and my daughter Marizé.
Thank you for your patience, support, belief,
and most of all, your love.
Everything I do, I do for you."

— *Chris Language*

About the author

Chris Language is a seasoned coder with 20+ years of experience. He has fond memories of his childhood and his Commodore 64; more recently he started adding more good memories of life with all his iOS devices. By day, he fights for survival in the corporate jungle of Johannesburg, South Africa. By night he fights demons, dragons and angry little potty-mouth kids online. For relaxation he codes. You can find him on Twitter @ChrisLanguage. Forever Coder, Artist, Musician, Gamer and Dreamer.

About the editors

Chris Belanger was an editor for this book. He spends his days developing real-time industrial control applications; he fills the rest of his time with writing, editing, travelling, composing music, enjoying the great outdoors and appreciating the finer things in life. He's excited to have worked on yet another book with the great raywenderlich.com team and can't imagine life without this crazy, wonderful bunch.

Wendy Lincoln was an editor for this book. By day, she manages complex content development projects and by night she escapes into the world of iOS. Before all this, she produced a cooking show named Hot Kitchen, wrote a cookbook and taught cooking classes. A few years ago she realized her love for writing, editing and playing with computers; she's never looked back. Once in a while, her husband manages to tear her away from the computer for trips to the beach and random home improvement projects.

Toby Stephens was a technical editor for this book. has over twenty years of software development experience, and is currently Head of Mobile Development at inplaymaker in London. Toby has a passion for gaming and game writing. He also writes music and enjoys a spot of bread baking. You can find him on Twitter: as @TJShae and on his website: tjshae.com

Ray Wenderlich was the final pass editor for this book. Ray is part of a great team - the raywenderlich.com team, a group of over 100 developers and editors from across the world. He and the rest of the team are passionate both about making apps and teaching others the techniques to make them. When Ray's not programming, he's probably playing video games, role playing games, or board games.

Ken Woo was a technical editor for this book. He loves making mobile apps and games and have been doing professional for a number of years now. Currently, he's trying to spread the fun by teaching others how to code as well. You can follow his adventure on ikenwoo.com and on Twitter as @ikenwoo.

Table of Contents:

Introduction

This book will show you how to make iOS games in Swift using SceneKit, Apple's built-in 3D game framework.

You'd be forgiven for thinking that making 3D games is far more complicated than creating a classic 2D game. 3D games have a reputation for being notoriously difficult to program, usually involving a lot of complicated math.

However, that is no longer the case, thanks to the advent of SceneKit. The simplicity of SceneKit lets beginners create simple and stylish games in a short amount of time. Yet it's also powerful enough to satisfy the needs of advanced developers, who want to create the next FPS killer.

Hopefully this sounds awesome to you, but you might have a few questions about the technology used in this book. Here's the reasoning behind our choices:

- **Why SceneKit?** Apple's built-in framework for making 3D games on iOS is easy to learn, especially if you already have some SpriteKit, Swift or iOS experience.

- **Why iOS?** For a game developer, there's no better platform. The development tools are well-designed and easy to learn, and the App Store makes it incredibly simple to distribute your game to a massive audience — and get paid for it!

- **Why Swift?** Swift is an easy language to get started with, especially if you are a beginner to the iOS platform. In addition, we believe Swift is the way of the future for iOS development, so take this as an opportunity to develop your Swift skills early!

- **Why 3D?** As awesome as 2D games may be, 3D games have a greater appeal in the look and feel department. Creating modern artwork such as popular voxel-style graphics is easier than ever. With SceneKit, even the programming is far less complicated than ever before, and you don't need an advanced math or physics degree! :] All of this puts 3D firmly within your grasp.

So rest easy - with iOS, 3D games and SceneKit, you're making great choices!

A History of SceneKit

Making 3D games for iOS with SceneKit is easy - but it wasn't always that way. Historically, your only option was to use OpenGL ES, which (along with Metal) is the lowest-level 3D graphics API available on iOS. Unfortunately, OpenGL ES is quite the untameable monster, which often left puny little beginner game developers running with their tails between their legs, seeking for alternative options. Unity offered a great alternative, but did so at the cost of having to learn an entirely new programming paradigm.

To solve this, Apple introduced SceneKit to OS X developers with the release of OS X Mountain Lion back in 2012. Two years later, SceneKit made a surprise debut in iOS with the release of iOS 8.

At the time, iOS developers were already familiar with SpriteKit, Apple's graphics framework for 2D games. What makes SceneKit so attractive is the seamless integration between SpriteKit and SceneKit. Now, SpriteKit can easily incorporate 3D content into 2D scenes, and SceneKit can easily incorporate the 2D power of SpriteKit into 3D scenes, giving the developers the best of both worlds.

SceneKit sits on top of OpenGL ES; iOS 9 added support for Metal. This gives you the freedom to choose between Metal, to give your SceneKit game that "closer to metal" performance, or OpenGL ES if you still want to use the OpenGL ES API.

Just like SpriteKit, the SceneKit API is well-designed and easy to use — especially for beginners. Best of all, you can use it knowing it's fully supported by Apple and heavily optimized for 3D gaming on iOS.

From here on out, if you want to make a 3D game on iOS, tvOS, or MacOS X, we definitely recommend you use SceneKit rather than other game frameworks, with one exception. If you're looking to make a cross-platform game to run on Android or Windows as well as on iOS or OS X, SceneKit only serves Apple platforms so porting your game from SceneKit to those platforms would be easier in a tool that's designed for cross-platform games such as Unity.

If you want to make a 3D game for Apple platforms only, then SceneKit is definitely the way to go!

What you need

To follow along with the tutorials in this book, you'll need the following:

- **A Mac running OS X Mountain Lion or later**. This is so you can install the latest version of the required development tool: Xcode.

- **Xcode 7.2 or later**. Xcode is the main development tool for iOS; you'll need Xcode 7.2 or later to follow along with this book.

- **An iPhone or iPod Touch running iOS 9 or later, and a paid membership to the iOS development program [optional]**. For most of the chapters in the book, you can run your code on the iOS 9 Simulator that comes with Xcode. However, there are a few chapters later in the book that require a device for testing. Also note that SceneKit performs better on physical devices than it does in the simulator, so your frame rates will appear lower than expected when running your game in the simulator.

If you don't have the latest version of Xcode installed, be sure to do that before continuing with the book.

Who this book is for

This book is for beginning to advanced iOS developers. Wherever you fall on that spectrum, you will learn a lot from this book!

This book does require some basic knowledge of Swift. If you're not familiar with Swift, you can still follow along with the book as all instructions are in a step-by-step format. However, there will likely be parts that are confusing due to gaps in your knowledge. Before starting this book, you might want to go through our Swift Apprentice series, which covers the basics of Swift development:

- www.raywenderlich.com/store

How to use this book

There are two ways to use this book, depending on whether you are a complete newcomer to iOS game development, or an advanced developer with knowledge of other 3D game frameworks.

If you are a complete beginner

If you're a complete beginner to iOS game development, the best way to read this book is from cover to cover. We have arranged the chapters to introduce the material in the most logical manner to build up your skills one layer at a time.

If you are an advanced developer

If you're an advanced developer with knowledge of other 3D game frameworks, you will have an easier time adapting to SceneKit, as the core concepts and syntax will look very familiar.

Our suggestion is to skim through the early chapters and focus more on the later, more advanced chapters, or areas where you have a particular interest.

Don't worry — you can jump right into any chapter in the book, because we'll always have a starter project waiting for you!

What's ahead: an overview

3D iOS Games by Tutorials is split into four sections and moves from beginning to advanced topics. In each section, you will create a complete mini-game from scratch!

Let's take a look at what's ahead.

Section I: Hello, SceneKit!

This section covers the basics of making 3D games with SceneKit. You'll look at the most important techniques used in almost every 3D SceneKit game created, and by the end of this section you'll know enough to make your very own little 3D game: Geometry Fighter.

This is a *Fruit Ninja* style game, with colorful geometric shapes thrown up into the air for your pure destructive indulgence. Seek out your inner Darth Vader and use the force to destroy the colorful shapes with a single touch of death! :]

1. **Chapter 1, Scenes**: Start off by creating your very first SceneKit game project, and get to know the basics.

2. **Chapter 2, Nodes**: Learn how to use nodes, primitive geometry shapes and cameras to construct a basic 3D scene from the ground up.

3. **Chapter 3, Physics**: Unleash the power of the built-in physics engine, and learn how to add basic physics to the elements in your game.

4. **Chapter 4, Render Loop**: Learn all about the render loop within SceneKit, and how you can leverage it to update the elements in your game.

5. **Chapter 5, Particle Systems**: Create massive explosions for your game, by learning how to create and use the 3D particle system.

Section II: The SceneKit Editor

Xcode include a variety of standard built-in tools; in this section, you'll take an in-depth look at them. These tools will make building your 3D games with SceneKit easier, faster and even more fun.

Throughout this section you'll be making a game called **Breaker**, which is based on *Breakout*, but it adds a nice new 3D look and feel. Keep your paddle and ball close by, so you can go bust up some bricks! :]

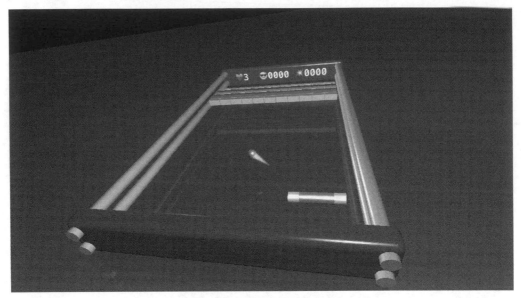

6. **Chapter 6, Scene Editor**: Get a hands-on introduction on how to use Xcode's awesome built-in SceneKit Editor.

7. **Chapter 7, Cameras**: Learn about the different types of cameras SceneKit has to offer.

8. **Chapter 8, Lights**: Learn all about the different types of lights, and how to properly set them up for your game.

9. **Chapter 9, Primitives:** Get your hands dirty and construct the entire game scene with just using the built-in SceneKit primitive shapes.

10. **Chapter 10, Basic Collision Detection:** Add physics to your game and learn how to handle basic collision detection.

Section III: Intermediate SceneKit

In this section you will create stunning a make belief world, with a shiny wooden relic awaits brave warriors with exceptional balancing skills to guide it through a maze high up in the sky. The game is called **Marble Maze**, and is somewhat based on the *Labyrinth* styled games with a twist.

11. **Chapter 11, Materials**: Learn about the different lighting models and the various material types supported by SceneKit.

12. **Chapter 12, Reference Nodes**: Learn how to start using reference nodes in your game.

13. **Chapter 13, Shadows**: Learn how to use and configure the darker element of light, known as shadows.

14. **Chapter 14, Intermediate Collision Detection**: Learn all about bit masks and how to make use of them for more intermediate collision detection scenarios.

15. **Chapter 15, Motion Control**: Add motion control to your game, and learn how to use the motion data to move the elements in your game.

Section IV: Advanced SceneKit

"The SceneKit Force is quite strong within you, young apprentice. (Read in a deep, heavy, asthmatic breathing voice. :])

In this section, you'll learn few more advanced techniques, as well as apply all the skills you've learned up to this point, to creating an awesome little voxel style game. By the end of this section, you'll know enough to take on the big *Hipster Whales* out there with your very own game: Mr. Pig.

This is a *Crossy Road* style game with stunning voxel graphics, a catchy tune and some cool sound effects.

The premise: Mr. Pig is out-and-about scouting for lost coins in a nearby park while waiting for his late afternoon tea to heat up on the stove. Unfortunately, some big bad wolf decided to build a massive mall nearby, resulting in a very busy highway straight through his lovely park.

Mr. Pig better watch his step, or he'll end up as pulled pork in the road. :] Our hero can carry quite a few coins with him, but to score, he has to deposit them at his little house.

No need to get your tail in a twist or ham it up — we'll walk you through every step of building the game!

16. **Chapter 16, Transitions:** Create multiple scenes and learn how to transition from one to the other.

17. **Chapter 17, Advanced Reference Nodes:** Start building more complex scenes by leveraging the power of reference nodes to make scene-building child's play.

18. **Chapter 18, Actions:** Learn how to add basic animation to the elements in your game by using Xcode's built-in action editor.

19. **Chapter 19, Advanced Collision Detection:** Learn how to use more advanced collision techniques to solve certain scenarios.

20. **Chapter 20, Audio:** Harness SceneKit's built-in sound capabilities to play music, sound effects and ambient sounds.

Book source code and forums

You can get the source code for the book here:

- www.raywenderlich.com/store/3d-ios-games-by-tutorials/source-code

Some of the chapters have starter projects or other required resources that are also included, and you'll definitely want to have these on hand as you go through the book.

We've set up an official forum for the book at raywenderlich.com/forums. This is a great place to ask any questions you have about the book or about making games with Sprite Kit, or to submit any errata you may find.

PDF Version

We also have a PDF version of this book available, which can be handy if you ever want to copy/paste code or search for a specific term through the book as you're developing.

And speaking of the PDF version, we have some good news!

Since you purchased the physical copy of this book, you are eligible to buy the PDF version at a significant discount if you would like (if you don't have it already). For more details, see this page:

- www.raywenderlich.com/store/3d-ios-games-by-tutorials/upgrade

License

By purchasing 3D iOS Games by Tutorials, you acquire the following license:

- You are allowed to use and/or modify the source code provided with 3D iOS Games by Tutorials in as many games as you want, with no attribution required.

- You are allowed to use and/or modify all art, music and sound effects that are included with 3D iOS Games by Tutorials in as many games as you want, but must include this attribution line somewhere inside your game: "Artwork/sounds: from 3D iOS Games by Tutorials book, available at http://www.raywenderlich.com".

Acknowledgements

We would like to thank many people for their assistance in making this book possible:

- **Our families**: For bearing with us during this hectic time as we worked all hours of the night to get this book ready for publication!

- **Everyone at Apple**: For developing an amazing 3D game framework and other helpful APIs for games, for constantly inspiring us to improve our apps and skills, and for making it possible for many developers to have their dream jobs!

- And most importantly, **the readers of raywenderlich.com and you**! Thank you so much for reading our site and purchasing this book. Your continued readership and support is what makes this all possible!

Section I: Hello, Scene Kit!

This section covers the basics of making 3D games with Scene Kit. You'll look at the most important techniques used in almost every 3D Scene Kit game created, and by the end of this section you'll know enough to make your very own little 3D game: Geometry Fighter.

This is a *Fruit Ninja* style game, with colorful geometric shapes thrown up into the air for your pure destructive indulgence. Seek out your inner Darth Vader and use the force to destroy the colorful shapes with a single touch of death! :]

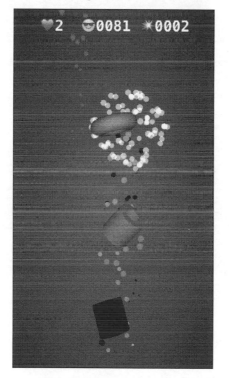

Chapter 1: Scenes

Chapter 2: Nodes

Chapter 3: Physics

Chapter 4: Render Loop

Chapter 5: Particle Systems

Chapter 1: Scenes

Chris Language

Getting started

In order to better understand the concepts behind Scene Kit, you can draw some mental parallels between a Scene Kit scene and a typical Hollywood movie scene.

- A movie scene has basic components such as lights, cameras and objects used to build the sets, as well as actors and actions for the actors to perform when the director shouts "Lights! Camera! Action!"

- When you build a Scene Kit scene from scratch, you'll add the same types of components as you build up your project. Scene Kit organizes these components into a node-based hierarchy known as the **scene graph**. A scene starts with a root node that defines the coordinate system; you add content nodes underneath the root node to form a tree structure. These content nodes are your basic building blocks for the scene and can include elements such as lights, cameras, geometry or particle emitters.

Consider the image below which shows a typical scene in Scene Kit:

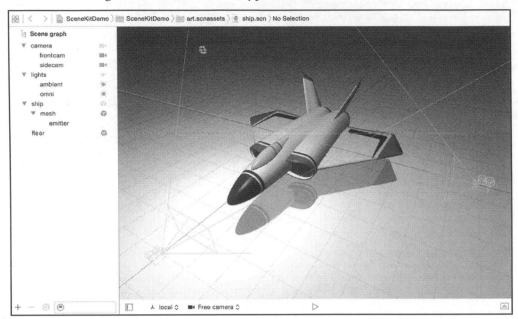

Note the node-based hierarchical structure on the left; it serves as a good example of the tree-like scene graph you'd construct within Scene Kit. This particular screenshot is of Xcode's built-in Scene Kit editor; hopefully this whets your appetite for things to come! :]

Working with your game project

Now that you've covered a few basic concepts of Scene Kit, you'll learn best if you dive right in and create your first Scene Kit project. The sections below will take you through the process of creating a project using Xcode's built-in project template.

Creating your Scene Kit game project

Open up Xcode and select **File\New\Project** from the main menu. If you want to become an Xcode ninja, use the shortcut command: ⇧⌘N.

Select the **iOS\Application\Game** template and click **Next** to continue:

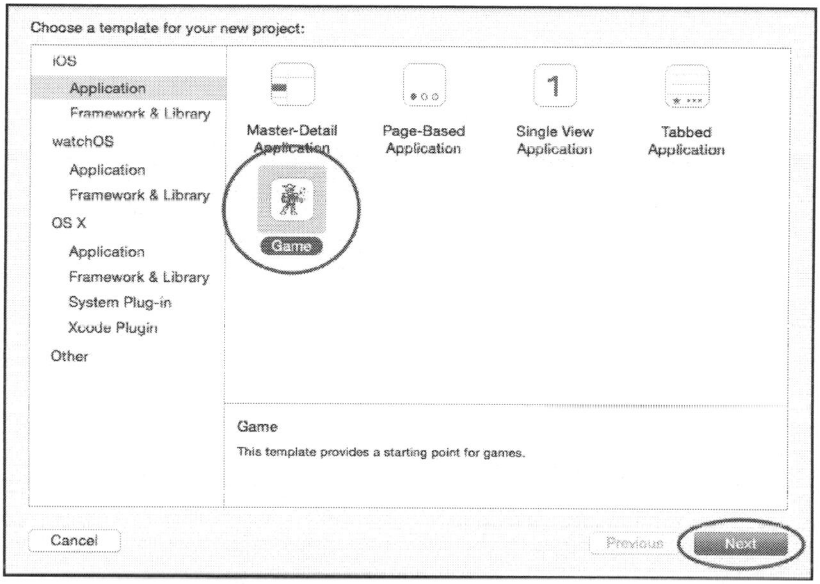

Now you need to provide some basic details about your project. Enter **GeometryFighter** for the Product Name, select **Swift** for Language, **SceneKit** for Game Technology, **Universal** for Devices, uncheck the unit tests and click **Next**:

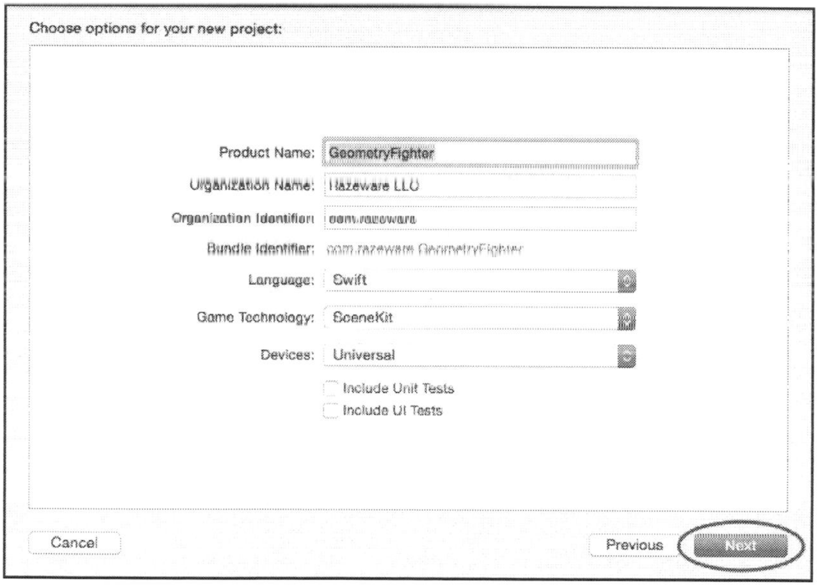

The final step is to choose a convenient location to save your project. Pick a directory and select **Create**; Xcode will work its magic and generate your project.

Building your Scene Kit game project

Now that you've generated your Scene Kit game project from the template, you'd probably like to see it in action! :]

First, choose the **iPhone 6** simulator from the toolbar, then press the **Play** button at the top to build and run your project. Xcode ninjas can simply press ⌘R:

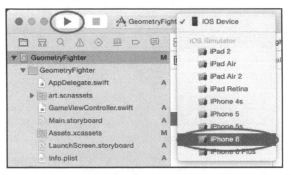

You'll see the simulator spin up, and your first 3D Scene Kit game will appear. You can rotate the view of your 3D spaceship in the game. Simply drag around the screen in different directions to change the camera angle:

Cool! It's okay to take a moment and do a little happy dance in your seat, then continue on with the rest of the chapter.

Challenge - deciphering supporting files

It's time for your first mini-challenge! Before you move on, have a read through the game template project. Pay careful attention to the following key files and folders under the project navigator:

- **art.scnassets**
- **ship.scn**
- **GameViewController.swift**
- **Assets.xcassets**
- **LaunchScreen.storyboard**

You might not understand how everything works at the moment, but try to figure out what you think each file might do at a high level. You'll be cleaning up the project in the next section, so take a look at the files and folders while they're still around. :]

Cleaning up your game project

There are a few components you need to remove in order to start with a clean Scene Kit game project. Don't worry; you'll re-create all the content from scratch so you can learn where it comes from.

Removing unnecessary folders

The first thing to get rid of is the **art.scnassets** folder. Right click the folder, select **Delete** and then click **Move to Trash**:

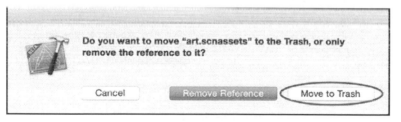

> **Note**: Don't worry too much about the purpose of the **art.scnassets** folder now. Just know that the Xcode Scene Kit game template generated **art.scnassets** for you automatically. It's always a good idea to keep your project free of any cruft.

Cleaning up the main project files

The **GameViewController.swift** file is a key component of your game; it's where all your game logic and code will live. Before you can start coding, you need to purge all the code the Xcode Scene Kit game template created for you.

Replace the contents of **GameViewController.swift** with the following:

```
import UIKit
import SceneKit

class GameViewController: UIViewController {

  override func viewDidLoad() {
    super.viewDidLoad()
  }

  override func shouldAutorotate() -> Bool {
    return true
  }

  override func prefersStatusBarHidden() -> Bool {
    return true
  }
}
```

The old code generated the spaceship; you've replaced that code with an empty slate. `shouldAutorotate()` handles device rotation and and `prefersStatusBarHidden()` hides the status bar.

Setting up Scene Kit

Earlier, you learned how Scene Kit uses the scene graph to display content on the screen. The `SCNScene` class represents a scene; you display the scene onscreen inside an instance of `SCNView`. Your next task is to set up a scene and its corresponding view in your project.

Setting up your project's view

Add the following property to **GameViewController.swift**, just above `viewDidLoad()`:

```
var scnView: SCNView!
```

Here you declare a property for the `SCNView` that renders the content of the `SCNScene` on the display.

Next, add the following function just below `prefersStatusBarHidden()`:

```
func setupView() {
  scnView = self.view as! SCNView
}
```

Here, you cast `self.view` to a `SCNView` and store it in the `scnView` property so that you don't have to re-cast it ever time you need to reference the view. Note that the view is already configured as an `SCNView` in **Main.storyboard**.

> **Note**: `SCNView` is a subclass of `NSView` in OS X, and a subclass of `UIView` in iOS. So whether you're working with OS X or iOS, the same `SCNView` provides a view specifically for Scene Kit content.

Setting up your project's scene

It's time to set up your scene. Add the following property to **GameViewController.swift**, just below the `scnView` property:

```
var scnScene: SCNScene!
```

Here you declare a property for the `SCNScene` in your game. You will add components like lights, camera, geometry, or particle emitters as children of this scene.

Now add the following function below `setupView()`:

```
func setupScene() {
  scnScene = SCNScene()
  scnView.scene = scnScene
}
```

This code creates a new blank instance of `SCNScene` and stores it in `scnScene`; it then sets this blank scene as the one for `scnView` to use.

Adding finishing touches

Now that you've created functions to set up instances of `SCNView` and `SCNScene`, you'll need to call them from somewhere during the initialization step. A good place to do that is just after the view finishes loading.

Add the following lines to `viewDidLoad()`, just after the call to `super`:

```
setupView()
setupScene()
```

For the final finishing touch, you'll add an app icon to your game. Take a look under the

Resources folder; you'll find app icons of various sizes in there for your use.

To set an image as the icon for your game, open the **Assets.xcassets** folder, select the **AppIcon** entry and drag each file from the **Resources** folder to the appropriate spot. Your AppIcon pane should look like the following when you're done:

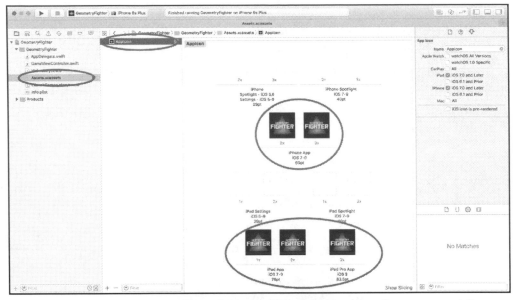

Build and run your project, and stand in awe of the black screen of opportunity! :]

In all fairness, this might not seem very impressive at first, but you've come a long way already:

- You've created a basic Scene Kit game project that uses built-in Scene Kit game template.

- You also learned how to clean out the project by removing unnecessary folders such as **art.scnassets**.

- Finally, you learned how to initialize an SCNView with a blank SCNScene.

Now that you have a blank slate to start with, keep reading to get started making your first SceneKit game!

Chapter 2: Nodes

Chris Language

In the previous chapter, you learned that Sprite Kit organizes the components of your game into a hierarchy known as the **scene graph**.

Each element of your game (such as lights, cameras, geometry, or particle emitters) is called a **node** and is stored in this tree-like structure.

To illustrate how this works, think back to a nursery rhyme you might have heard in your childhood...

♫ *The hip bone's connected to the back bone* ♫ *The back bone's connected to the shoulder bone...* ♫

You're right, it's the classic song *Dem Dry Bones*! Bonus points if you can think of a classic video game that makes particularly good use of this ;]

With those lyrics in mind, take a look at the following anatomically-correct structure of a rare four-fingered skeleton:

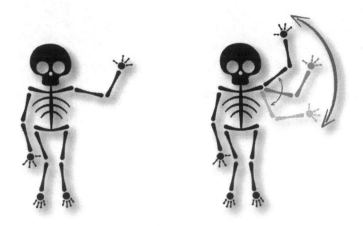

To help illustrate how you could construct a node-based hierarchy from this skeleton, think of each bone in the skeleton as a **node**.

As the song points out, the shoulder bone's connected to the back bone. So consider the back bone as the **parent** node of the shoulder bone, and the shoulder bone as the **child** node of the back bone.

To add the shoulder bone to the scene, you add it as a child of the back bone. You can continue to construct the whole arm in this way, adding child bones to parent bones, right up to the little pinky.

To position a bone, you position it relative to its parent. For example, to wave the skeleton's left arm, you simply rotate the shoulder node back and forth as indicated by the little blue arrow. All child nodes of the shoulder node will rotate along with their parent.

Congratulations! You just passed skeleton anatomy 101! :]

From a technical perspective, a single node is represented by the `SCNNode` class and represents a position in 3D space relative to its parent node. A node on its own has no visible content and is invisible when rendered as part of a scene. To create visible content, you have to add other components such as lights, cameras or geometries (such as bones) to the node.

The scene graph contains a special node which forms the foundation of your node-based hierarchy: the **root node**. To construct your scene, you add your nodes either as child nodes of the root node or as a child of one of the root node's descendants.

In this chapter, you will start to work with a few simple nodes in Scene Kit, such as camera and geomtetry nodes. By the end of the chapter, you'll have rendered a simple 3D cube to the screen!

> **Note**: The next sections continue on using the project as you left it in Chapter 1. If you didn't follow along, no sweat – you can simply use the starter project for this chapter.

Getting Started

Once you're a successful and rich 3D game designer, you'll have enough money to hire your very own graphics artist and sound engineer, which will free you up to focus on the game code alone. :] The **Scene Kit asset catalog** has been designed specifically to help you manage your game assets separately from the code.

An asset catalog lets you manage your game assets in a single folder; to use it, simply add a folder with the *.scnassets* extension to your project and save all your game assets in that folder. Xcode will copy everything in your catalog to your app bundle at build time. Xcode preserves your assets folder hierarchy; this gives you full control over the folder structure.

By sharing your assets folder with your artists, they can quickly fix any issues, such as a not-quite-so-scary cross-eyed monster and have it ready for the next build – without having to copy the changed assets back into the project.

Now that you understand what the asset catalog is all about, you'll add one to Geometry Fighter.

Drag and drop the **GeometryFighter.scnassets** folder from the **resources** folder into your game project in Xcode. In the popup that appears, make sure that **Copy items if needed**, **Create Groups**, and your **GeometryFighter** target are all checked, and click **Finish**.

Choose options for adding these files:

Destination: ☑ Copy items if needed

Added folders: ⦿ Create groups
⦿ Create folder references

Add to targets: ☑ 🔲 GeometryFighter

Cancel   Finish

Select the **GeometryFighter.scnassets** folder in your Project Navigator and note you can see some settings unique to the asset catalog in the right hand pane. Expand the GeometryFighter.scnassets folder and sub-folders to see more detail about your assets:

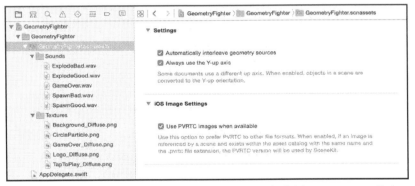

There are two folders inside the asset catalog: the **Sounds** folder contains all the sound assets you'll need for your game, while the **Textures** folder contains all the images you'll need. Feel free to take a sneak peek of what's inside.

Adding the launch screen

Now that you've imported the asset catalog, you'll take care of some basic housekeeping steps and add a proper image to the launch screen.

First, click **Assets.xcassets** in the project navigator. Drag and drop **GeometryFighter.scnassets\Textures\Logo_Diffuse.png** into the assets, below the **AppIcon**.

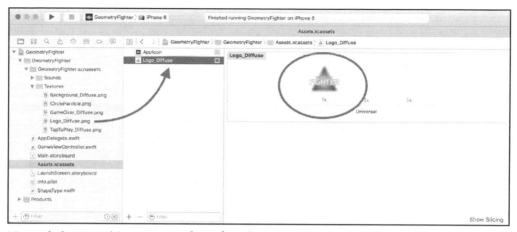

Next, click **LaunchScreen.storyboard** in the project navigator. Select the main view and set the **Background** property to a dark blue (or some other color you like):

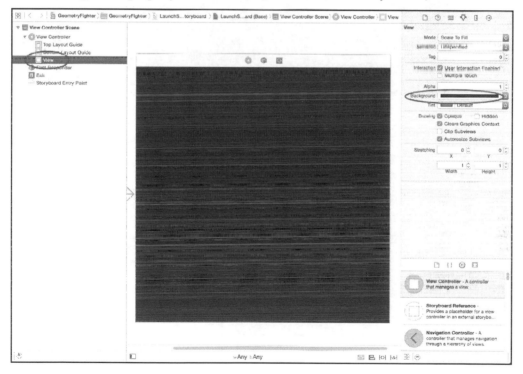

Next, drag the **Logo_Diffuse** image from the **Media Library** into the center of the view. Set the **Mode** property of your new image to **Aspect Fit**:

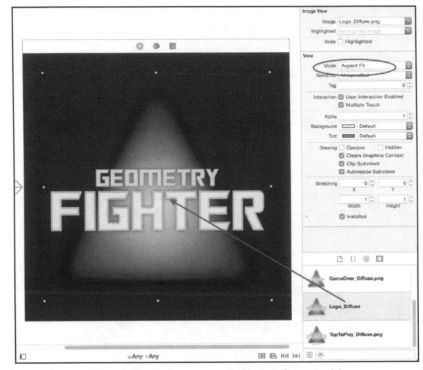

You're almost done with your launch screen; all that's left is to add some constraints so that the splash image will work on all devices. Click the **Pin** button at the bottom, toggle the constraints on for all four edges and click **Add 4 Constraints** as shown below:

You're done setting up your launch screen! Build and run your app; you'll see your shiny new launch screen appear:

Adding a background image

Once your splash screen disappears, you're dumped back to the black screen of opportunity. Time to add a nice clean background so you don't feel like you're staring into a black hole.

To do this, add the following line of code to the bottom of `setupScene()` in **GameViewController.swift**:

```
scnScene.background.contents = "GeometryFighter.scnassets/
Textures/Background_Diffuse.png"
```

This line of code instructs the scene to load the **Background_Diffuse.png** image from the asset catalog and use it as the material property of the scene's background.

Build and run; you should now see a blue background image once the game starts:

You've finished all the basic housekeeping tasks for your project. Your game now has a flashy app icon, a splash screen, and a pretty background that's all ready to display the nodes you're about to add to the scene.

The Scene Kit coordinate system

Before you can start adding nodes to the scene, you first need to understand how Scene Kit's coordinate system works so you can position your nodes where you want them.

In a 2D system such as UIKit or Sprite Kit, you use a point to describe the position of a view or a sprite on the x and y axes. To place an object in 3D space, you also need to describe the depth of the object's position on the z-axis.

Consider the following simple illustration:

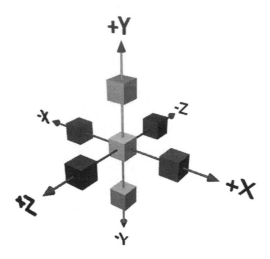

Scene Kit uses this three-axis system to represent position in 3D space. The red blocks are placed along the x-axis, the green blocks along the y-axis and the blue blocks along the z-axis. The grey cube in the very center of the axes indicates the **origin**, which has coordinates of (x:0, y:0, z:0).

Scene Kit uses the SCNVector3 data type to represent coordinates in three dimensions as a three-component vector. Here's how you create a vector in code:

```
let position = SCNVector3(x: 0, y: 5, z: 10)
```

This declares the variable position with a vector of (x:0, y:5, z:10). You can easily access individual properties of the vector like so:

```
let x = position.x
let y = position.y
let z = position.z
```

If you've worked with `CGPoint` before, you can easily draw comparisons between it and `SCNVector3`.

> **Note**: Nodes added to the scene have have a default position of (x:0, y:0, z: 0), which is always relative to the *parent* node. To place a node at the desired location, you need to adjust the position of the node relative to its parent (local coordinates) — not the origin (world coordinates).

Working with cameras

Now that you understand how to position nodes in Scene Kit, you're probably wondering how to actually *display* something onscreen. Think back to the analogy of the movie set from Chapter 1: to shoot a scene, you'd position a camera looking at the scene and the resulting image of that scene would be from the camera's perspective.

Scene Kit works in a similar fashion; the position of the node that contains the camera determines the point of view from which you view the scene.

The following illustration demonstrates how a camera works in Scene Kit:

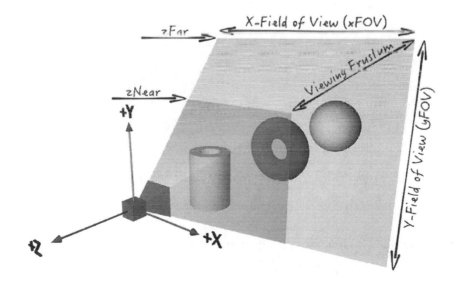

There are a couple of key points in the previous diagram:

- The camera's direction of view is always along the negative z-axis of the node that contains the camera.

- The **field of view** is the limiting angle of the viewable area of your camera. A tight angle provides a narrow view, while a wide angle provides a wide view.

- The **viewing frustum** determines the visible depth of your camera. Anything outside this area – that is, too close or too far from the camera – will be clipped and won't appear on the screen.

A Scene Kit camera is represented by SCNCamera, whose xPov and yPov properties let you adjust the field of view, while zNear and zFar let you adjust the viewing frustum.

One key point to remember is that a camera by itself won't do anything unless it's a part of the node hierarchy.

Adding the camera

Let's try this out. Open **GameViewController.swift** and add the following property below scnScene:

```
var cameraNode: SCNNode!
```

Next, add the following method below setupScene():

```
func setupCamera() {
  // 1
  cameraNode = SCNNode()
  // 2
  cameraNode.camera = SCNCamera()
  // 3
  cameraNode.position = SCNVector3(x: 0, y: 0, z: 10)
  // 4
  scnScene.rootNode.addChildNode(cameraNode)
}
```

Taking a closer look at the code:

1. You first create an empty SCNNode and assign it to cameraNode.

2. You next create a new SCNCamera object and assign it to the camera property of cameraNode.

3. Then you set the position of the camera at (x:0, y:0, z:10).

4. Finally, you add cameraNode to the scene as a child node of the scene's root node.

Finish things off by calling the method you just added in `viewDidLoad()`, right below `setupScene()`:

```
setupCamera()
```

There's no need to build and run at this point in time, as you won't see that anything's changed. Even though your scene now has a camera, there's still nothing to look at. To fix this, let's add some actors to this scene.

Working with geometry

In order to create visible content, you need to add a geometry object to a node. A geometry object represents a three-dimensional shape and is created of many points known as **vertices**.

Additionally, a geometry object can contain material objects that modify the appearance of a geometry's surface. Materials let you specify information such as the color and texture of the geometry's surface and how the geometry should respond to light along with other visual effects. A collection of vertices and materials is known as a **model** or a **mesh**.

Scene Kit includes the following built-in geometric shapes, also known as **primitives**:

In the front row from the left, you have a cone, a torus, a capsule and a tube. In the back row from the left, you have a pyramid, a box, a sphere and a cylinder.

Note: You can provide your own custom geometry data, but you'll cover this in later chapters.

Adding ShapeTypes

Before you start adding geometric shapes to the scene, create a new Swift file to define a ShapeType enum for the various different shapes you'll use in the game.

Right-click on the **GeometryFighter** group and select **New File...**. Select the **iOS \Source\Swift File** template and click **Next**:

Name the file **ShapeType.swift**, make sure it's included in your project, then click **Create**.

Once the file's been created, open **ShapeType.swift** and replace its contents with the following:

```
import Foundation

// 1
public enum ShapeType:Int {

  case Box = 0
  case Sphere
  case Pyramid
  case Torus
  case Capsule
  case Cylinder
  case Cone
  case Tube
```

```
// 2
static func random() -> ShapeType {
  let maxValue = Tube.rawValue
  let rand = arc4random_uniform(UInt32(maxValue+1))
  return ShapeType(rawValue: Int(rand))!
}
}
```

The code above is relatively straightforward:

1. You create a new public enum ShapeType that enumerates the various shapes.

2. You also define a static method random() that generates a random ShapeType. This feature will come in handy later on in your game.

Adding a geometry node

Your next task is to create a method that spawns the various random shapes defined in the **ShapeType** enumerator.

Add the following method to **GameViewController.swift**, right below setupCamera():

```
func spawnShape() {
  // 1
  var geometry:SCNGeometry
  // 2
  switch ShapeType.random() {
  default:
    // 3
    geometry = SCNBox(width: 1.0, height: 1.0, length: 1.0,
  chamferRadius: 0.0)
  }
  // 4
  let geometryNode = SCNNode(geometry: geometry)
  // 5
  scnScene.rootNode.addChildNode(geometryNode)
}
```

Taking each numbered comment in turn;

1. First you create a placeholder geometry variable for use a bit later on.

2. Next, you define a switch statement to handle the returned shape from ShapeType.random(). It's incomplete at the moment and only creates a box shape; you'll add more to it in the challenge at the end of this chapter.

3. You then create an SCNBox object and store it in geometry. You specify the width, height, and length, along with the chamfer radius (which is a fancy way of saying rounded corners).

4. This statement creates an instance of SCNNode named geometryNode. This time, you

make use of the `SCNNode` initializer that takes a `geometry` parameter to create a node and automatically attach the supplied geometry.

5. Finally, you add the node as a child of the scene's root node.

You now need to call this method from somewhere. Add the following line to `viewDidLoad()` below `setupCamera()`:

```
spawnShape()
```

Build and run; you'll see a white square displayed onscreen:

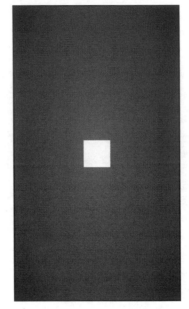

There's a few things to observe here:

- The box node is the default shape from `spawnShape()`, and sits at (`x:0, y:0, z:0`) in the scene.

- You're viewing the scene through your `cameraNode`. Since the camera node lives at (`x:0, y:0: z:10`), the box is smack dab in the center of the camera's viewable area.

Yes, it's not very exciting (and hardly three-dimensional looking), but fear not – the next section will change all that.

Using built-in view features

SCNView comes with a few out-of-the-box features that help make your life easier.

Add the following lines to setupView() in **GameViewController.swift**, just below the current implementation:

```
// 1
scnView.showsStatistics = true
// 2
scnView.allowsCameraControl = true
// 3
scnView.autoenablesDefaultLighting = true
```

Here's what's going on in the code above:

1. showStatistics enables a real-time statistics panel at the bottom of your scene.

2. allowsCameraControl lets you manually control the active camera through simple gestures.

3. autoenablesDefaultLighting creates a generic omnidirectional light in your scene so you don't have to worry about adding your own light sources for the moment.

Build and run; things should look a little more exciting this time around!

You can use the following gestures to control the active camera in your scene:

- **Single finger swipe**: Rotates your active camera around the contents of the scene.

- **Two finger swipe**: Moves, or *pans* your camera left, right, up or down in the scene.

- **Two finger pinch**: Zooms the camera in and out of the scene.

- **Double-tap**: If you have more than one camera, this switches between the cameras in your scene. Of course since you have only one camera this won't don that. However, it also has the effect of resetting the camera to its original position and settings.

Working with scene statistics

Find the statistics panel at the bottom of the screen:

```
+  ▭▭▭▭▭     GL 53fps          ◆3 ▲72 ✳ ▮
```

Here's a quick breakdown of what each element means:

- **fps**. Stands for *frames per second*. This a measurement of the total amount of consecutive frame redraws done in one-second. The lower this amount, the poorer your game is performing. You typically want your game to run at 60fps, which will make your game look and feel smooth.

- **◆**. Stands for *total draw calls per frame*. This is typically the total amount of visible objects drawn per single frame. Lights affecting objects could also increase the amount of draw calls of an object. The lower this amount, the better.

- **▲**. Stands for *total polygons per frame*. This the total amount of polygons used to draw a single frame for all the visible geometry. The lower this amount, the better.

- **✳**. Stands for *total visible light sources*. This is the total amount of light sources currently affecting visible objects. The Scene Kit guidelines recommends not using more than 3 light sources at a time.

Click on the + button to expand the panel and see more detail available to you:

```
-  ▭▭▭▭▭     GL 3fps           ◆3 ▲76 ✳ ▮

        ╭──────╮         ■ Animations    ■ Delegate
       │        │        ■ Physics       ■ Rendering
       │22.3 ms │        ■ Constraints   ■ GL flush
        ╰──────╯         ■ Particles     ■ 2D
```

This panel provides you with the following information:

- **Frame time**. This is the total amount of time it took to draw a single frame. A *frame time* of 16.7ms is required to achieve a *frame rate* of 60fps.

- **The color chart**. This provides you with a rough frame time percentage breakdown per component within the Scene Kit rendering pipeline.

From this example, you now know that it took 22.3ms to draw a single frame of which ±75% was used for *Rendering*, and ±25% was used for *GL Flush*.

> **Note:** The Scene Kit rendering pipeline will be discussed in more detail later on.

You can click the - button to minimize the panel again.

And that's it! Congratulations, you've learned about quite a few concepts in this chapter:

- **Asset catalogs**: Helpful when managing your various game assets and working with your artists.

- **Coordinate system**: Now you know your up from your down and your left from your right – and most importantly, what backwards and forwards means in Scene Kit.

- **Geometry**: You've covered the built-in primitive shapes in Scene Kit and learned how to add geometry to a node to create visible content.

- **Skeleton Anatomy**: You should now able to identify a four-fingered skeleton, should one cross your path someday! :]

Challenges

It's important for you to practice what you've learned, on your own, so many chapters in this book have one or more challenges associated with them.

I highly recommend giving all the challenges a try, because while following a step by step tutorial is educational, you'll learn a lot more by solving a problem by yourself. In addition, each chapter will continue where the previous chapter's challenges left off, so you'll want to stay in the loop!

If you get stuck, you can find solutions in the resources for this chapter—but to get the most from this book, give these your best shot before you look!

Challenge 1

There's only one challenge in this chapter, but it's a fun one.

Your challenge is to improve the `switch` statement inside `spawnShape()` to handle the remaining shapes in the enumerator.

Use Apple's official Scene Kit documentation as a guide to the various geometric shapes. Also take a look at the `ShapeType` enum to see which shapes are left to create; their names should give you a good idea of where to start.

Don't worry too much about the sizes to use; just try to make them about the same relative size as the box you made earlier.

If you get this working, congratulations, you are getting a firm grasp of some of the most fundamental concepts in Scene Kit! :]

Chapter 3: Physics

Chris Language

Getting started

In this chapter, you'll use Scene Kit's physics engine to add physics to your game.

Scene Kit's physics engine is powerful, yet easy to use. You simply tell Scene Kit on which objects you want to apply physics; the engine will take over from that point and simulate things such as gravity and collisions for you.

Before you dive into integrating physics in your game, you'll first need to add some some game utilities to your project.

> **Note**: This chapter's project continues on from the previous chapter. If you didn't follow along, or if you want to start fresh, you can find the starter project for this chapter under **/starter/GeometryFighter/**.

Adding game utilities

The game utilities were created especially for you to make your life a little easier. These utilities include a bunch of helper methods that handle the complicated bits in your game to let you focus on the gameplay.

To add the game utilities, simply drag and drop the **GameUtils** folder into your project under the **GeometryFighter** group folder:

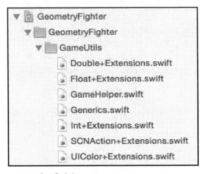

Leave all the settings at their defaults and click **Finish**:

This imports the entire **GameUtils** folder into your project as a group. Expand this folder and have a quick look at some of the helper methods, but don't worry too much if some of the code doesn't make sense to you yet.

Introducing physics

Time for a quick status check of the current state of your game. Run up the game; a cool random geometric object spawns out of thin air like some kind of dark magic. This might not seem like much right now, but things will definitely start to "shape" up soon! :]

The freshly spawned object just hangs there in an empty space and doesn't do much. Sure, you can rotate the camera around it and zoom in and out, but that's about it. It's not much of a fun game. To pump up the excitement level, it would be nice if the object at least moved around a little.

Now, you *could* take the long way around and manipulate the object's position and rotation over time so that it spins and moves around. You'd soon realize that although it's possible to animate objects in this manner, it requires a lot of coding effort, especially when you add other features like realistic collisions and interactions between objects to the mix.

Thankfully, the developers at Apple have already thought about this; to this end, they integrated a very powerful 3D physics engine into Scene Kit. To make use of this built-in physics engine, you simply need to make the engine aware of your object.

In the same way you attach geometry information to your node, you can attach a **physics body** to your node. The physics body describes all the physical properties of your node, which includes things such as shape, mass, friction, damping and restitution. The physics engine takes all this information into account when it simulates the real-world physics interactions of your objects. This includes things such as gravity, friction and collisions with other bodies within the physics world.

The next section details some of the important characteristics of a physics body.

Working with physics body types

One of the key properties you must specify when creating a physics body is its **type**. The physics body's type defines how the body interacts with forces and other bodies in the simulation.

There are three types used in Scene Kit:

- **Static** bodies don't move: while other objects can collide with these bodies, the static bodies themselves are unaffected by any forces and collisions in the simulation. You could use this type for things like walls and massive immobile boulders.

- **Dynamic** bodies are affected by forces and collisions; you could use this type for things such as movable chairs, tables and cups.

- **Kinematic** bodies are similar to static bodies, in that they are also unaffected by forces and collisions. However, you can move these types around and they can also collide with dynamic bodies. You could use this type of body for things such as moving elevators or a door that can open and close.

Working with physics shapes

In addition to the type of the body, another import property you must specify when creating a physics body is its **shape**. The physics shape defines the 3D shape used by the physics engine during collision detections. While the geometry defines the *visuals* of the node, the physics body defines how the node *interacts* with other objects in a physics simulation.

To let the physics simulation run as fast as possible, you should make use of simple geometries to define the physics shape. You'd typically set the physics shape to a simple bounding box, sphere, or one of the provided primitive shapes that roughly matches the node's visible appearance like so:

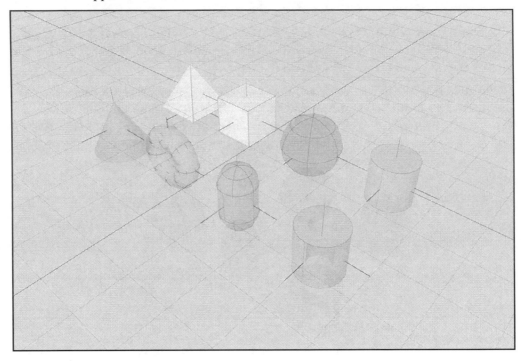

Adding physics

Now that you've learned the theory behind the physics, it's time to start using these concepts to move things around in your game.

In Scene Kit, all the physics bodies are `SCNPhysicsBody` objects. You can then assign the bodies to the `physicsBody` property of the `SCNNode` instance that will use that physics body. Once you've assigned the physics body, the physics engine can then simulate the physics for you. It's that simple! :]

Open **GameViewController.swift** and add the following after the line of code that creates `geometryNode` in `spawnShape()`:

```
geometryNode.physicsBody = SCNPhysicsBody(type: .Dynamic, shape:
nil)
```

This line of code creates a new instance of `SCNPhysicsBody` and assigns it to the `physicsBody` property of `geometryNode`. When you create a physics body, you specify the type and shape the body should have. If you pass in `nil` for the physics shape, Scene Kit will automatically generate a shape based on the geometry of the node. Neat, huh?

If you want to add more detail to the physics shape, you could create a `SCNPhysicsShape` and use that for the shape instead of passing in `nil`.

Build and run your game; a random shape spawns into the scene, and then drops out of the air with all the grace of a dead bird, falling out of sight:

You can even pan the camera to watch the object fall into oblivion. What you're witnessing here is the effect of gravity acting on the object. A scene in Scene Kit has gravity turned on by default. Now that the spawned object has a physics body, the physics simulation will apply simulated forces such as gravity to the object.

Working with forces

Think about objects in real life for a moment: to make something move, such as a spoon on top of a table, you have to apply some sort of physical force on it. Unless you're living inside the Matrix, your name is Neo, and there isn't even an actual spoon to begin with. :]

The Scene Kit physics engine does a pretty good job mimicking real-life physics, so just as you'd apply a force to move an object in real life, you'll need to apply a force on your physics body to move it around.

When you apply a force to a physics body, you use `applyForce(_: atPosition: impluse:)` and pass in an instance of `SCNVector3` for both the force and the position where you want to apply that force, along with whether or not the force will be applied as an impulse. The force that you apply will affect both the linear and angular acceleration of the physics body.

An impulse applies the force only once to the physics body, such as when you kick a ball. Forces that *aren't* impulses are applied at each step in the physics simulation. Scene Kit will add up all applied forces on the object and accelerate the physics body according to the net result of those forces. This can simulate something like a booster rocket, where the force is continuous.

Earlier you learned that a force is a vector with an x, y and z component. But what does that mean? Take a look at the diagram below:

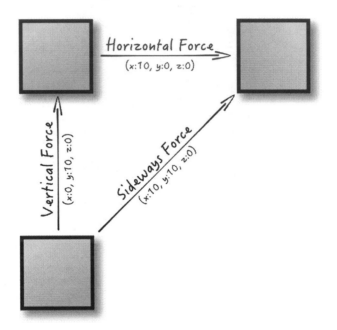

A force has both magnitude and direction, so the vector determines the magnitude of the force for each individual axis. In the example above, applying a force with a vector of (x: 0, y:10, z:0) moves the body upwards with a vertical force.

To apply a horizontal force, you would only specify the magnitude of the force on the x axis using a vector of (x:10, y:0, z:0). To move the body left instead of right, you would apply a negative magnitude of force on the x axis. When you combine various vectors together like (x:10, y:10, z:0), you can control exactly how you want the body to move – in this case, diagonally.

Forces can also be applied at a specific position on a physics body to produce different movements:

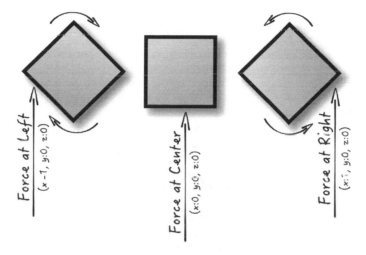

Again, it helps to think of real-life examples. If you had a block in front of you and pushed it, the block would move differently depending on the spot you applied the push. Applying the same force to the left or right of the body's center of mass, for example, at (x:1, y:0, z:0) would cause it to spin. Applying the force directly in line with the center of mass at (x:0, y:0, z:0) won't produce a spin.

Applying forces

Roll up your sleeves — it's time to apply some force! :]

Add the following code after the line where you create the physics body for geometryNode inside spawnShape():

```
// 1
let randomX = Float.random(min: -2, max: 2)
let randomY = Float.random(min: 10, max: 18)
// 2
let force = SCNVector3(x: randomX, y: randomY , z: 0)
// 3
let position = SCNVector3(x: 0.05, y: 0.05, z: 0.05)
// 4
geometryNode.physicsBody?.applyForce(force, atPosition:
position, impulse: true)
```

Taking each commented line in turn:

1. This creates two random float values that represent the x- and y-components of the force. It uses an extension on Float from the utilities you added earlier in this

chapter.

2. Next, you use those random components to create a vector to represent this force.

3. This creates another vector that represents the position the force will be applied to. The position is slightly off-center so as to create a spin on the object.

4. Finally, using all those components, you apply the force to `geometryNode`'s physics body using `applyForce(_: atPosition: impluse)`.

Build and run; as the object spawns out of thin air, some magical force kicks it up into the air instead of dropping like a dead bird:

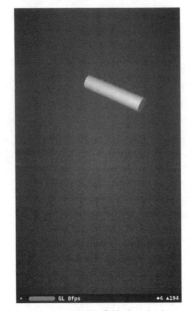

As gravity takes its toll, the object eventually falls back down.

Working with torque

Torque is another rotational force you can apply to a body using `applyTorque(_: impulse:)`. Torque only affects the angular momentum of the physics body, not the linear momentum. Applying torque causes an object to spin around its center of mass.

To see how torque affects a physics body, take a look at the following illustration:

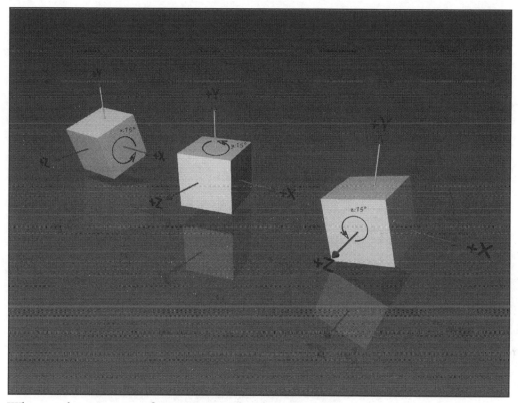

When applying a torque force, you specify a four-component vector using `SCNVector4` rather than a three-component vector as you do with forces. The x-, y- and z-components determine the rotation axis, while the w-component determines the rotation angle, that is, the magnitude of the torque.

Just as you do with `applyForce(_: atPosition: impulse.)`, you can choose whether or not to apply the torque as an impulse, which affect how the physics engine treats the vector.

If the torque is an impulse, the directional vector is treated as an instantaneous change in the angular momentum. Think of spinning a basketball on your finger; to keep the ball spinning, you have to quickly flick the side of the ball with you hand, which applies an a impulse with each flick that instantaneously increases the angular momentum of the ball.

When a torque is not applied as in impulse, it's applied after each physics simulation step. Scene Kit will sum all applied forces and torques and accelerate the angular force of the physics body according to the net effect of those forces. Think of this as a planet spinning at a constant speed around its own axis.

> **Note**: The Scene Kit physics simulation uses the International System of Units (SI) for measurements: **Kilograms** for units of mass, **Newtons** for units of force, **Newton-second** for units of impulse, and **Newton-meter** for units of torque.

Adding some flair

Now that you've got your geometric object moving, you may have noticed it spawns out of thin air right in the middle of the screen, which looks a bit awkward. To fix that, you'll shift the camera on the y-axis a bit so that the object spawns off-screen.

Positioning the camera

To move the camera position up, replace the line where you set the camera's position in `setupCamera()` with the following:

```
cameraNode.position = SCNVector3(x: 0, y: 5, z: 10)
```

Build and run, and you'll see that the object appears to spawn off-screen!

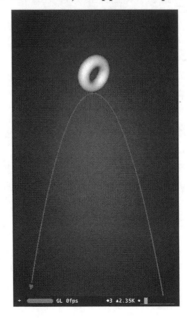

Adding color

As a final touch, you'll add a bit of variety to your randomly generated shapes.

Add the following lines inside `spawnShape()`, after the spot where you randomly create `geometry`, but just before you create `geometryNode`:

```
geometry.materials.first?.diffuse.contents = UIColor.random()
```

To color your random object, you modify `materials` on `geometry`; this line gets the first available material of `geometry` and sets the `diffuse` property's `contents` to a random `UIColor`. The `random()` method on `UIColor` is another helper defined as an extension inside the game utilities.

> **Note**: You'll learn more about materials and their properties in Section II of this book. The takeaway here is that you can assign a UIColor to the diffuse property's content in order to change the object's color.

Finally, build and run your game to see a beautifully colored object:

Wouldn't it be neat if you could spawn more than one object? You'll fix this...in the next chapter! :]

Where to go from here?

You're making excellent progress, and you're more than halfway through your first Scene Kit game! If you're flexible (unlike me), give yourself a pat on the back.

In this chapter you've learned about a number of things:

- **Scene Kit's physics engine** and how to leverage it for object animation.
- **Physics bodies** and how to attach them to a node to recreate real-world object behavior.
- **Physics shapes**, how to define them, and how to efficiently use simplified shapes for your complex geometry.
- **Forces and impulses** and how to use them to create linear and angular movement.

There's no challenge for this chapter, so keep reading for the next chapter, where you'll learn how to spawn multiple objects through the power of the render loop!

Chapter 4: Render Loop

Chris Language

In the previous chapter, you enabled basic physics for your spawned object and applied an impulse to kick it up into the air. Eventually, the object fell back down due to the simulated effect of gravity and disappeared into the abyss.

Although the effect is neat, it would be *so* much cooler to spawn multiple objects that collide with each other. That would certainly push the excitement factor up a notch!

Right now, your game calls spawnShape() just once. To spawn multiple objects you'll need to call spawnShape() repeatedly. Introducing...the **Render Loop**!

As you learned in previous chapters, Scene Kit renders the contents of your scene using an SCNView object. SCNView has a delegate property that you can set to an object that conforms to the SCNSceneRendererDelegate protocol, and SCNView will then call methods on that delegate when certain events occur within the animation and rendering process of each frame.

In this way, you can tap into the steps Scene Kit takes to render each frame of a scene. These rendering steps are what make up the *render loop*.

So – what exactly *are* these steps? Well, here's a quick breakdown of the render loop:

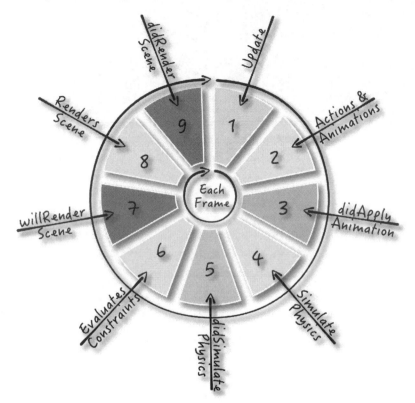

Is this *Wheel of Fortune*? :] No, it's simply a depiction of the nine steps of the render loop. In a game that runs at 60 fps, these steps run... you guessed it... 60 times a second.

The steps always execute in the following order, which lets you inject your game logic exactly where it's needed:

1. **Update**: The view calls `renderer(_: updateAtTime:)` on its delegate. This is a good spot to put basic scene update logic.

2. **Execute Actions & Animations**: Scene Kit executes all actions and performs all attached animations to the nodes in the scene graph.

3. **Did Apply Animations**: The view calls its delegate's `renderer(_: didApplyAnimationsAtTime:)`. At this point, all the nodes in the scene have completed one single frame's worth of animation, based on the applied actions and animations.

4. **Simulates Physics**: Scene Kit applies a single step of physics simulation to all the physics bodies in the scene.

5. **Did Simulate Physics**: The view calls renderer(_: didSimulatePhysicsAtTime:) on its delegate. At this point, the physics simulation step has completed, and you can add in any logic dependent on the physics applied above.

6. **Evaluates Constraints**: Scene Kit evaluates and applies constraints, which are rules you can configure to make Scene Kit automatically adjust the transformation of a node.

7. **Will Render Scene**: The view calls renderer(_: willRenderScene: atTime:) on its delegate. At this point, the view is about to render the scene, so any last minute changes should be performed here.

8. **Renders Scene In View**: Scene Kit renders the scene in the view.

9. **Did Render Scene**: The final step is for the view to call Its delegate's renderer(_: didRenderScene: atTime:). This marks the end of one cycle of the render loop; you can put any game logic in here that needs to execute before the process starts anew.

Because the render loop is, well, a *loop*, it's the perfect place to call to spawnShape() — your job is to decide where to inject the spawn logic.

Adding the renderer delegate

It's time to put this cool feature to use in your game.

First, make the GameViewController class conform to the SCNSceneRendererDelegate protocol by adding the following to the bottom of **GameViewController.swift**:

```
// 1
extension GameViewController: SCNSceneRendererDelegate {
  // 2
  func renderer(renderer: SCNSceneRenderer, updateAtTime time:
NSTimeInterval) {
    // 3
    spawnShape()
  }
}
```

Taking a closer look at the code above:

1. This adds an extension to GameViewController for protocol conformance and lets you maintain code protocol methods in separate blocks of code.

2. This adds an implementation of the renderer(_: updateAtTime:) protocol

method.

3. Finally, you call `spawnShape()` to create a new shape inside the delegate method.

This give you your first hook into Scene Kit's render loop. Before the view can call this delegate method, it first needs to know that `GameViewController` will act as the delegate for the view.

Do this by adding the following line to the bottom of `setupView()`:

```
scnView.delegate = self
```

This sets the `delegate` of the Scene Kit view to `self`. Now the view can call the delegate methods you implement in `GameViewController` when the render loop runs.

Finally, clean up your code a little by removing the single call to `spawnShape()` inside `viewDidLoad()`; it's no longer needed since you're calling the function inside the render loop now.

Build and run; unleash the spawning fury of your render loop! :]

The game starts and spawns an insane amount of objects, resulting in a moshpit of colliding objects — awesome! :]

So what's happening here? Since you're calling `spawnShape()` in every update step of the render loop, you'll spawn 60 objects per second — if the device you're running on can support your game at 60 fps. But less-powerful devices, which includes the simulator, can't support that frame rate.

As the game runs, you'll notice a rapid decrease in the frame rate. Not only does the graphics processor have to deal with increasing amounts of geometry, the physics engine has to deal with an increasing number of collisions, which also negatively affects your frame rate.

Things are a bit out of control at the moment, as your game won't perform terribly well on all devices.

Adding a spawn timer

To make the gaming experience consistent across devices, you need to make use of **time**. No, I don't mean taking more time to write your game! :] Rather, you need to use the passage of time as the one constant across devices; this lets you animate at a consistent rate, regardless of the frame rate the device can support.

Timers are a common technique in many games. Remember the updateAtTime parameter passed into the update delegate method? That parameter represents the current system time. If you monitor this parameter, you can calculate things like the elapsed time of your game, or spawn a new object every three seconds instead of as fast as possible.

Geometry Fighter will use a simple timer to spawn objects at randomly timed interval that any processor should be able to handle.

Add the following property to GameViewController below cameraNode:

```
var spawnTime:NSTimeInterval = 0
```

You'll use this to determine time interval until you spawn another shape.

To fix the continuous spawning, replace the entire body of renderer(_: updateAtTime:) with the following:

```
// 1
if time > spawnTime {
  spawnShape()

  // 2
  spawnTime = time + NSTimeInterval(Float.random(min: 0.2, max:
1.5))
}
```

Taking each commented line in turn:

1. You check if time (the current system time) is greater than spawnTime. If so, spawn a new shape; otherwise, do nothing.

2. After you spawn an object, update `spawnTime` with the *next* time to spawn a new object. The next spawn time is simply the current time incremented by a random amount. Since `NSTimeInterval` is in seconds, you spawn the next object between 0.2 seconds and 1.5 seconds after the current time.

Build and run; check out the difference your timer makes:

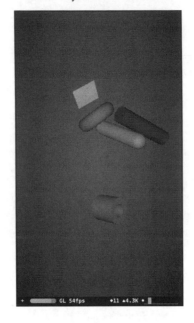

Mesmerizing, eh?

Things look a bit more manageable, and the shapes are spawning randomly. But aren't you curious about what happens to all those objects after they fall out of sight?

Cleaning up your scene

`spawnShape()` continuously adds new child nodes into the scene – but they're never removed, even after they fall out of sight. Scene Kit does an awesome job of keeping things running smoothly for as long as possible, but that doesn't mean you can forget about your children. What kind of parent are you?! :]

To run at an optimal performance level and frame rate, you'll have to remove objects that fall out of sight. And what better place to do this than – that's right, the render loop! Handy thing, isn't it?

Once an object reaches the limits of its bounds, you should remove it from the scene.

Add the following to the end of your `GameViewController` class, right below `spawnShape()`:

```
func cleanScene() {
  // 1
  for node in scnScene.rootNode.childNodes {
    // 2
    if node.presentationNode.position.y < -2 {
      // 3
      node.removeFromParentNode()
    }
  }
}
```

Here's what's going on in the code above:

1. Here you simply create a little `for` loop that steps through all available child nodes within the root node of the scene.

2. Since the physics simulation is in play at this point, you can't simply look at the object's position as this reflects the position *before* the animation started. Scene Kit maintains a copy of the object during the animation and plays it out until the animation is done. It's a strange concept to understand at first, but you'll see how this works before long. To get the actual position of an object while it's animating, you leverage the `presentationNode` property. This is purely read-only: don't attempt to modify any values on this property!

3. This line of code makes an object blink out of existence; it seems cruel to do this to your children, but hey, that's just tough love.

To use your method above, add the following line to call `cleanScene()` just after the `if` statement inside `renderer(_: updatedAtTime:)`:

```
cleanScene()
```

There's one last thing to add: by default, Scene Kit enters into a "paused" state if there aren't any animations to play out. To prevent this from happening, you have to enable the `playing` property on your `SCNView` instance.

Add the following line of code to the bottom of `setupView()`:

```
scnView.playing = true
```

This forces the Scene Kit view into an endless playing mode.

Build and run; as your objects start to fall, pinch to zoom out and see where they disappear into nothingness:

Objects that fall past the lower y-bound (noted by the red line in the screenshot above), are removed from the scene. That's better than having all those objects lying around the dark recesses of your iPhone. :]

Where to go from here?

You're making good progress on your game; the finish line is in sight and there's only one more chapter in this section!

This chapter covered some fairly complex Scene Kit concepts:

- **The Render Loop**: You've learned about the nine steps of the render loop, and you know you can inject game logic at certain points using `SCNSceneRendererDelegate`.

- **Timers**: You've learned how to use time to make your game behave consistently across devices.

- **presentationNode**: You've learned that all nodes under animation have a "copied" version called the `presentationNode` and that you can read real-time information from this node while the animation plays.

- **removeFromParentNode**. You've learned how to be a responsible parent and remove children nodes that are no longer needed.

Again, there's no challenge this time, so keep reading to spice up your game through the power of particle systems!

Chapter 5: Particle Systems

Chris Language

Picture yourself in the movie theatre, popcorn in hand; on the screen, a bad guy from *The Fast and the Furious* smashes his roaring, high-performance dragster into a highly volatile fuel tanker which explodes in a massive fireball of death and carnage. Yeah! ;]

Now think of that same scene, but without the massive fireball explosion: you can almost feel the collective disappointment of audiences around the world. :[

Just like a Hollywood blockbuster, your game needs special effects to amp up the excitement level; these special effects come in the form of what's known as **particle systems**. You can use particle systems for a multitude of effects, from moving star fields, to burning rocket boosters, to rain and snow, to metal sparks – and yes, even massive exploding fireballs!

Let's take a look at how you can add some of these neat special effects to Geometry Fighter.

SCNParticleSystem

In Scene Kit, `SCNParticleSystem` manages the creation, animation and removal of particles from the scene graph.

A *particle* is essentially a small image sprite. The particle system doesn't add the individual particles into the scene graph itself, so you don't have direct access to each particle - the particle system manages the particles and their look, size, and location.

However, you can influence the particle system by modifying various properties on it, such as:

- **Appearance**: Each particle of the system can be rendered as a single image, or an animated sequence of images. You can adjust the size, tint color, blending mode and other rendering parameters of the particles generated.

- **Life Span**: The system uses a **particle emitter**, which gives birth to each individual particle. The lifespan of the particle determines how long it stays visible in the scene.

- **Emitter behavior**: You can control various parameters of the emitter, such as where particles spawn and the spawn rate.

- **Variation**: Introducing variations into your particle system can make it look more, or less, random.

- **Movement**: You can adjust how particles move once they've spawned. Particles use a simplified physics simulation to speed up performance, but the particles can still interact with objects managed by the physics engine.

> **Note**: You can find the starter project for this chapter under the **/starter/ Geometry Fighter/** folder, or carry on with the completed project from the last chapter.

Getting started

Before you add a particle system to your game world, you'll need a group to house this particle system to keep your project organized. Right-click on the **GeometryFighter** group and select **New Group**, like so:

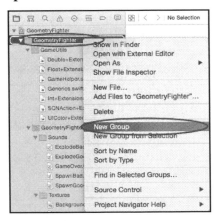

Name this new group **Particles**. Right-click on the group and select **New File**. Select the **iOS\Resource\SceneKit Particle System** template and click **Next** to continue:

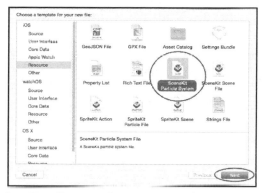

On the next screen, select **Fire** for Particle system template then click **Next**. Save the file as **Trail.scnp** and click **Create**. Once you're done, you should see the following in your scene:

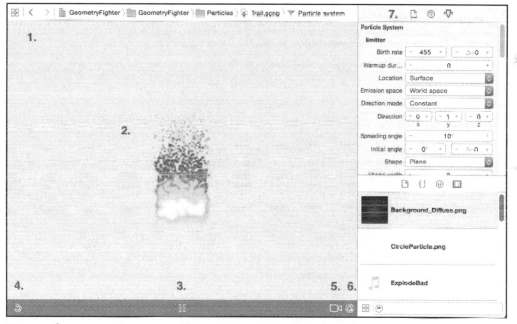

Hot stuff! :] Say "hello" to Xcode's built-in particle system editor.

Here's a quick overview of the various sections of the editor as annotated above:

1. **Center Stage**: The center holds a visual representation of your particle system. You can use this to get an idea of what the end result will look like.

2. **Gesture Controls**: You can use gestures to manipulate the camera view; it's similar to

how you'd move the camera around in a scene.

3. **Pause/Play Button**: You can pause your particle system simulation and inspect it in more detail. While paused, the pause button changes to a play button you can use to resume the simulation.

4. **Restart Button**: This lets you restart your particle simulation from the beginning.

5. **Camera Reset Button**: Use this to reset your camera view to its default position.

6. **Color Button**: This lets you set an appropriate background color for your editor; for example, it's easier to see snowflakes against a black background.

7. **Particle System Properties**: Selecting the Attributes Inspector reveals a host of properties which you'll learn about in the next section.

Configuring the trail particle system

In this section, you'll take an in-depth look at the particle system attributes on the right-hand side of the editor. As you go through each section, copy the values of each setting in the screenshots into your own particle system.

Keep an eye on the particle system editor as you change each attribute; you'll see how each parameter affects the behavior of the particle system. Later on, you'll use this particle effect in your game to create a trail of particles falling from your spawned objects.

Emitter attributes

The particle emitter is the origin from where all particles spawn. Here's the emitter attributes:

Emitter		
Birth rate	25	Δ=0
Warmup dur...	0	
Location	Vertex	
Emission space	World space	
Direction mode	Constant	
Direction	0 0 0	
	x y z	
Spreading angle	0°	
Initial angle	0°	Δ=0
Shape	Sphere	
Shape radius	0.2	

- **Birth rate**: Controls the emitted rate of particles. Set this to 25, instructing the particle engine to spawn new particles at a rate of 25 particles per second.

- **Warmup duration**: The amount of seconds the simulation runs before it renders particles. This can be used to display a screen full of particles at the start, instead of waiting for the particles to fill the screen. Set this to 0 so that simulation can be viewed from the very beginning.

- **Location**: The location, relative to the shape, where the emitter spawns its particles. Set this to **Vertex**, which means the particles will use the geometry vertices as spawning locations.

- **Emission space**: The space where emitted particles will reside. Set this to **World Space** so that the emitted particles are emitted into the world space, and not the local space of the object node itself.

- **Direction mode:** Controls how spawned particles travel; you can move them all in a constant direction, have them travel radially outwards from the surface of the shape, or simply move them in random directions. Set it to Constant, keeping all emitted particles moving in a constant direction.

- **Direction**: Specifies a directional vector to use when **direction mode** is constant. Set this vector to (x: 0, y: 0, z:0), setting the direction to nothing.

- **Spreading angle**: Randomizes the emitting angle of spawned particles. Set this to 0º, thus emitting particles exactly in the previously set direction.

- **Initial angle**: The initial angle at which to emit particles. Set this to 0º as this does not matter with a zero direction vector.

- **Shape**: The shape from which to emit particles. Set the shape up as a **Sphere**, thus using a sphere shape as the geometry.

- **Shape radius**: This existence of this attribute depends on which shape you're using; for an spherical emitter, this determines the size of the sphere. Set this to 0.2, which defines a sphere just large enough for what you need.

> **Note**: Note that some of the attributes have two input areas, one of which has a $\Delta=$ symbol next to it (see Birth Rate and Initial angle). The first input area contains the base value, and the $\Delta=$ input area contains the delta value. Each time a particle is spawned, it uses the base value plus a random value in the range (-delta value, +delta value). This allows you to get some random variance for these properties.

Simulation attributes

The simulation attributes manage the motion of particles over their lifetimes. This lets you manage their movement without having to use the physics engine:

Simulation		
Life span	− 1 +	− Δ=0 +
Linear velocity	− 0 +	− Δ=0 +
Angular velocity	− 0 +	− Δ=0 +
Acceleration	− 0 + (x)	− -5 + (y) − 0 + (z)
Speed factor	− 1 +	
Stretch factor	− 0 +	

- **Life span**: Specifies the lifetime of a particle in seconds. Set this to 1, so that a single particle will only exist for a total time of a single second.
- **Linear velocity**: Specifies the linear velocity of the emitted particles. Set this to 0, the particles are spawned with no direction or velocity.
- **Angular velocity**: Specifies the angular velocity of the emitted particles. Set this to 0, the particles will not be spinning.
- **Acceleration**: Specifies the force vector applied to the emitted particles. Set this to (x: 0, y: –5, z: 0), which is a downwards vector, simulating a soft gravity effect on the particles once spawned.
- **Speed factor**: A multiplier that sets the speed of the particle simulation. Set this to 1, running the simulation at a normal speed.
- **Stretch factor**: A multiplier that stretches particles in their direction of motion. Set this to 0, keeping the particle image un-stretched.

Image attributes

The image attributes control the visual aspects of the particles. They also govern how the appearance of those particles can change over their lifetimes:

Image		
Image	CircleParticle.png	
Color		
	☐ Animate color	
Color variation	− + (h) − + (s)	− + (b) − + (a)
Size	− 0.1 +	− Δ=0 +
	Custom animation	☼▾

- **Image**: Specifies an image with which each particle will be rendered. Select the **CircleParticle.png** image, giving the particle its primary shape.

- **Color**: Sets the tint of the specified image. Set the color to **White**, giving the particle system a base color of white.

- **Animate color**: Causes particles to change color over their lifetimes. Un-check this, because the particle color is not going to change at all.

- **Color variation**: Adds a bit of randomness to the particle color. You can set this to (h: 0, s: 0, b: 0, a: 0), because the particle color will not vary.

- **Size**: Specifies the size of the particles. Set this to 0.1, so that the emitted particles are small in size.

Image sequence attributes

To create an animated image for your particles, you arrange each frame of the animation into a grid on a single image (like a sprite sheet in a game). Then you simply use that grid image as the image for your particle emitter. The image sequence attributes let you control the basic animation properties of the particle:

- **Initial frame**: Sets the first zero-based frame of the animation sequence. The zeroth frame corresponds to the top left image in the grid. You're using a single frame image, so set this to 0.

- **Frame rate**: Controls the rate of the animation in frames per second. Set this to 0, it only applies when using an image containing multiple frames.

- **Animation**: Specifies the behaviour of the animation sequence. Repeat loops the animation, Clamp only plays once, and Auto Reverse plays from the start to the end, then back again. You can leave this on Repeat, it doesn't matter when using a single frame image.

- **Dimensions**: Specifies the number of rows and columns in the animation grid. Set this to (Rows: 1, Columns: 1), because you're using a single frame image.

Rendering attributes

The rendering attributes define how the render phase treats the particles:

Rendering	
Blending	Alpha
	☐ Enable black pass
Orientation	Billboard screen-aligned
Sorting	None
Lighting	☐ Enable lighting

- **Blending**: Specifies the blend mode of the renderer when drawing the particles into the scene. Set this to **Alpha**, which will use the image alpha channel information for transparency.

- **Orientation**: Controls the rotation of the particles. Set this to **Billboard screen-aligned**, which will keep the flat particles facing the camera view at all times, so you won't notice that the particles are indeed flat images.

- **Sorting**: Sets the rendering order of the particles. This property works in conjunction with the blend mode and affects how the blending is applied. Set this to **None**, the particle system will not make use of sorting.

- **Lighting**: Controls whether Scene Kit applies lighting to the particles. Un-check this, so that the particle system ignores any lights in the scene.

Physics attributes

The physics attributes let you specify how particles behave in the physics simulation:

Physics		
Particles	☐ Affected by gravity	
	☐ Affected by physics fields	
	☐ Die on collision	
Mass	— 1 +	— Δ=0 +
Bounce	— 0.7 +	— Δ=0 +
Friction	— 1 +	— Δ=0 +
Damping	— 0 +	

- **Affected by gravity**: Causes the scene's gravity to affect the particles. Un-check this, you don't want the particle system to participate in the physics simulation.

- **Affected by physics fields**: Causes physics fields within the scene to affect the particles. Un-check this, you don't want physics fields to have an effect on the particles.

- **Die on Collision**: Lets physics bodies in your scene collide and destroy the particles. Un-check this, you don't want particles to be removed when they collide with node objects in the scene.

- **Physics Properties**: Basic physics properties that control the physics behaviour of the particles during the physics simulation. You can leave all these at their default values, because the particle system will not make use of this.

Life cycle attributes

The life cycle attributes let you control the overall life cycle of your particle system:

Life cycle		
Emission dur.	− 1 +	− Δ=0 +
Idle dur.	− 0 +	− Δ=0 +
Looping	Loops continuously	

- **Emission Duration**: Controls the length of time that the emitter will emit new particles. Set this to 1, which will activate the particle emitter for a total length of 1 second.

- **Idle Duration**: Looping particle systems emit particles for the specified emission duration, then become idle for the specified idle duration, after which the cycle repeats. Set this to 0, the particle system will only emit once.

- **Looping**: Specifies whether the particle system emits particles once, as in an explosion, or continuously, as a volcano would. Set this to **Loops continuously**, so that the emitter emits for as long as it can before it is removed from the scene again.

Phew! There are a *lot* of attributes to consider for a single particle system, but this gives you a lot of control to get the exact special effect you're looking for.

If you diligently copied over the values from the screenshots to your particle system, you will have a system that represents the following effect:

If yours doesn't look like this, try rotating the camera. It might also help to change the background color to a dark blue like you see here to make the particle system easier to see.

Adding the trail particles

It's finally time to add the cool particle effect to your game. Add the following to your **GameViewController.swift** class:

```
// 1
func createTrail(color: UIColor, geometry: SCNGeometry) ->
SCNParticleSystem {
  // 2
  let trail = SCNParticleSystem(named: "Trail.scnp",
inDirectory: nil)!
  // 3
  trail.particleColor = color
  // 4
  trail.emitterShape = geometry
  // 5
  return trail
}
```

Here's what's going on above:

1. This defines createTrail(_: geometry:) which takes in color and geometry parameters to set up the particle system.

2. This loads the particle system from the file you created earlier.

3. Next, you modify the particle's tint color based on the parameter passed in.

4. This uses the geometry parameter to specify the emitter's shape.

5. Finally, this returns the newly created particle system.

This method helps you create instances of SCNParticleSystem, but you still need to add the particle systems to your spawned shape objects.

Note that createTrail(_: geometry:) takes in a color parameter and uses it to tint the particles. You will set the color of the particle system to be the same as the color of the shape.

Find the line in spawnShape() where you set the shape's material diffuse contents and split it up so that the random color is stored in a constant like so:

```
let color = UIColor.random()
geometry.materials.first?.diffuse.contents = color
```

Next, add the following lines further down in spawnShape(), just after you apply a force to the physics body of geometryNode:

```
let trailEmitter = createTrail(color, geometry: geometry)
geometryNode.addParticleSystem(trailEmitter)
```

This uses `createTrail(_: geometry:)` to create a particle system and attach it to `geometryNode`.

Build and run; take a look at your hard work in action!

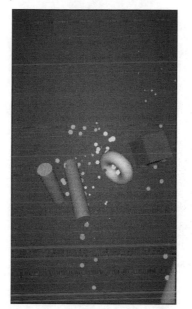

Woot! :] It looks great – but what would *really* make this shine is a heads-up display.

Adding a heads-up display

In this short section you'll use the *Game Utils* to quickly add a little heads-up display to show your player's remaining lives, best score, and current score. The code behind the scenes uses a Sprite Kit label and uses the output of the label as a texture for a plane.

> **Note**: You will learn more about Sprite Kit integration in Chapter 21, "Sprite Kit Integration". For now, we'll treat it as a black box.

Add the following new property to **GameViewController.swift**, right below `spawnTime`:

```
var game = GameHelper.sharedInstance
```

This lets you quickly access the `GameHelper` shared instance, which contains a set of methods to do the heavy lifting for you.

Add the following method to the bottom of `GameViewController`, below `createTrail()`:

```
func setupHUD() {
    game.hudNode.position = SCNVector3(x: 0.0, y: 10.0, z: 0.0)
    scnScene.rootNode.addChildNode(game.hudNode)
}
```

Here you make use of `game.hudNode` from the helper library. You set its the HUD node's position and add it to the scene.

Next, you need to call `setupHUD()` from somewhere. Add the following line to the bottom of `viewDidLoad()`:

```
setupHUD()
```

Now that you have a heads-up display, you need to keep it up to date. Add the following call to `game.updateHUD()` to the bottom of `renderer(_: updateAtTime:)`

```
game.updateHUD()
```

Build and run; you'll see your display at the top of the screen as shown below:

Your game now has a nifty little HUD with a life counter, the high score and the current score.

Okay, the heads-up display is nice, but it's high time to add some interaction to your game.

Adding touch handling

As is usually the case, enabling touch in your app isn't as straightforward as one would hope.

The first step is to understand how touch handling works in 3D. The image below shows a touch point in a side view of your scene and how Scene kit translates that touch point into your 3D scene to determine which object you're touching:

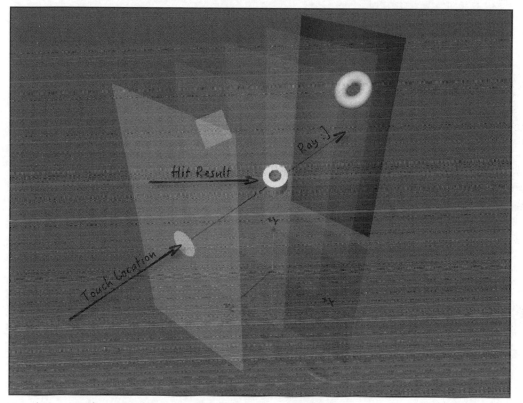

So what steps do you take to handle the user's touch event?

1. **Get Touch Location.** First, you need to get the location of the user's touch on the screen.

2. **Convert to View Coordinates.** After that, you need to translate that touch location to a location relative to the `SCNView` instance that's presenting the scene.

3. **Fire a Ray for a Hit Test.** Once you've established a touch location relative to the view, Scene Kit can perform a hit test for you by firing off a ray (No, not *that* Ray! :]) into your scene and returning a list of objects that intersect with the ray.

Naming nodes

Before you can activate the touch ray of death, you need a way to identify each spawned object. The simplest approach is to give them names.

Add following to `spawnShape()`, right after you add the particle system to `geometryNode`:

```
if color == UIColor.blackColor() {
  geometryNode.name = "BAD"
} else {
  geometryNode.name = "GOOD"
}
```

True to the spirit of the black-hatted villains of old Western movies, you assign the moniker `"BAD"` to black-colored objects and `"GOOD"` to all others.

Adding a touch handler

Next you need to write a method that you will later call when you detect that the user has tapped a particular node.

Add the following method to the bottom of `GameViewController`, below `setupHUD()`:

```
func handleTouchFor(node: SCNNode) {
  if node.name == "GOOD" {
    game.score += 1
    node.removeFromParentNode()
  } else if node.name == "BAD" {
    game.lives -= 1
    node.removeFromParentNode()
  }
}
```

This method checks the moniker of the touched node; good nodes increase the score and bad (black) nodes reduce the number of lives by one. In either case, you remove the node from the screen as it's destroyed.

Using the touch handler

To capture the user's touches, you'll use `touchesBegan(_: withEvent:)`, which is called every time the player touches the screen.

To implement your own version, add the following to `GameViewController`, right below `handleTouchFor(_:)`:

```
override func touchesBegan(touches: Set<UITouch>, withEvent
event: UIEvent?) {
  // 1
  let touch = touches.first!
  // 2
  let location = touch.locationInView(scnView)
  // 3
  let hitResults = scnView.hitTest(location, options: nil)
  // 4
  if hitResults.count > 0 {
    // 5
    let result = hitResults.first!
    // 6
    handleTouchFor(result.node)
  }
}
```

Taking each numbered comment in turn:

1. Grab the first available touch.

2. Translate the touch location to a location relative to the coordinates of `scnView`.

3. `hitTest(_: options:)` gives you an array of `SCNHitTestResult` objects that represent any intersections that hit ray starting from the spot inside the view that the user touched, and going away from the camera.

4. Check if there are any results from the hit test.

5. If there are, take the first result in the set.

6. Finally, you pass the first result node to your touch handler, which will either increase your score – or cost you a life!

One final step. You don't need the camera control anymore so change the line in `setupView()` as follows:

```
scnView.allowsCameraControl = false
```

Build and run; get ready to unleash your deadly finger of annihilation! :]

Tap on the spawned objects and make them disintegrate into thin air. Whoo-hoo! :]

Challenge

Time to up the cool factor – and what's cooler than *explosions*? I know: *nothing*, right?

That brings you to the challenge of this chapter: create another particle system and name it **Explode.scnp**. See if you can figure out what attributes to modify to make those particles explode.

The effect should look something similar to this:

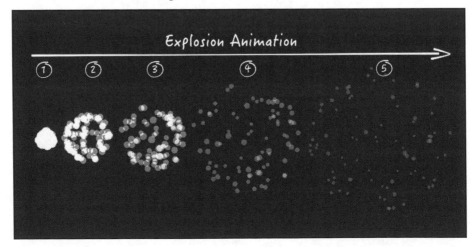

You can use the following image as a starting point for your particle system:

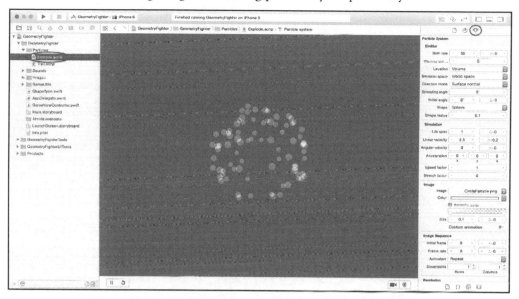

> **Note**: You can find the solution under the **/challenge/Geometry Fighter/** folder.
> Open up **Explode.scnp** under the **Particles** group to get a closer look.

Shaping particle explosions

Now that you've created the explosion particle system, you need to add some code to make those nodes explode. You're going to use some special properties to make the explosion take the same shape as whatever node you touch.

Add the following to the bottom of GameViewController, below touchesBegan(_: withEvent):

```
// 1
func createExplosion(geometry: SCNGeometry, position:
SCNVector3,
  rotation: SCNVector4) {
  // 2
  let explosion =
    SCNParticleSystem(named: "Explode.scnp", inDirectory:
  nil)!
  explosion.emitterShape = geometry
  explosion.birthLocation = .Surface
  // 3
```

```
  let rotationMatrix =
    SCNMatrix4MakeRotation(rotation.w, rotation.x,
      rotation.y, rotation.z)
  let translationMatrix =
    SCNMatrix4MakeTranslation(position.x, position.y,
      position.z)
  let transformMatrix =
    SCNMatrix4Mult(rotationMatrix, translationMatrix)
  // 4
  scnScene.addParticleSystem(explosion, withTransform:
    transformMatrix)
}
```

Here's the play-by-play of the above code:

1. `createExplosion(_: position: rotation:)` takes three parameters: `geometry` defines the shape of the particle effect, while `position` and `rotation` help place the explosion into the scene.

2. This loads **Explode.scnp** and uses it to create an emitter. The emitter uses `geometry` as `emitterShape` so that particles will emit from the surface of the shape.

3. Enter the Matrix! :] Don't be scared by these three lines; they simply provide a combined rotation and position (or *translation*) transformation matrix to `addParticleSystem(_: withTransform:)`.

4. Finally you call `addParticleSystem(_: wtihTransform)` on `scnScene` to add the explosion to the scene.

You're so close to replicating those great Hollywood explosions! Add the following line twice inside `handleTouchFor(_:)`, once to the "good" `if` block and once to the "bad" `else` block, right before you remove `node` from the parent:

```
createExplosion(node.geometry!, position:
node.presentationNode.position,
  rotation: node.presentationNode.rotation)
```

This uses the `presentationNode` property to retrieve the `position` and `rotation` parameters of `node` . You then call `createExplosion(_: position: rotation:)` with those parameters.

> **Note**: You're using `presentationNode` because the physics simulation is currently moving the node.

Build and run; tap away and make those nodes explode!

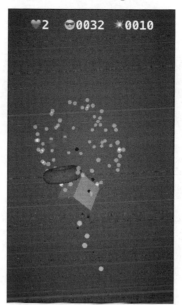

Note: You can find the project for this challenge under the **projects\challenge \GeometryFighter** folder.

Juice

Your game is not quite done yet, there's still plenty room for improvement, right? To push your game to that next level, you absolutely have to add something known as *juice*. Juice will give your game that little something special, just to make it stand out above the rest.

Here's a few ideas that will definitely juice things up:

- **Game state management**. With basic game state management you'll be able to control certain game machanics based on a game state like TapToPlay, Playing or GameOver.

- **Splash screens**. Use pretty splash screens. They provide the player with visual clues of the current game state.

- **Sound effects**. Add cool sound effects to provide the player with crucial audio feedback of good and bad interaction with the game elements.

- **Camera shakes**. Really bad explosions produce really big shockwaves. Adding a shaking camera effect just that little something extra.

> **Note**: Now for a special bonus! :] There's a ready made project waiting for you under the **projects\juiced\GeometryFighter** folder. Open it up and go try out the game. Feel free to explore the code; see how just a few lines of added code will juice up your game to that next level.

Where to go from here?

You've reached the end of the first section of this book – and you have a great Scene Kit game to boot! Feel free to do your happy dance! :]

In this chapter you've learned about the following:

- **Particle Systems**: How to add particle effects to your game using particle systems.
- **Particle System Editor**: How to navigate the built-in particle system editor and how to preview your effects.
- **Particle System Attributes**: How to work with the numerous attributes that define the workings of a particle system.
- **3D Touch Handling**: How to manage touch events in 3D and how to use `hitTest(_: options:)` to determine which nodes were touched inside your scene.

Congratulations again on completing your first Scene Kit game - now get ready to level up your skills with something completely new!

Section II: The Scene Kit Editor

Xcode include a variety of standard built-in tools, and in this section, you'll take an in-depth look at them. These tools will make building your 3D games with Scene Kit so much easier, faster and even more fun.

Throughout this section you'll be making a game called **Breaker**, which is based on *Breakout*, but it adds a nicc new 3D look and feel. Keep your paddle and ball close by, so you can go bust up some bricks! :]

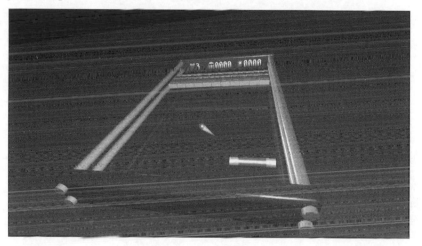

Chapter 6: Scene Editor

Chapter 7: Cameras

Chapter 8: Lights

Chapter 9: Primitives

Chapter 10: Basic Collision Detection

Chapter 6: Scene Editor

Chris Language

With the latest release of Xcode, Apple has shown the world just how important they consider game development by exerting monumental effort to help game developers. Specifically, Apple has created several new, essential tools for Scene Kit game development in Xcode.

Xcode goes much further than just editing and compiling code, especially when it comes to games. With the release of Xcode 6, Apple introduced a built-in scene editor for Sprite Kit, and now with the release of Xcode 7, Apple introduced a built-in scene editor for Scene Kit too.

Similar to how the Sprite Kit scene editor helps you design 2D Sprite Kit games visually, the Scene Kit scene editor helps you work with 3D objects and design 3D Scene Kit games. The main purpose of these editors is to provide you a what-you-see-is-what-you-get (WYSIWYG) design environment, so that you can visualize the end result without stepping foot outside Xcode or even building and running your game. How cool is that?

But wait, there's more! These scene editors take it a step further by allowing you to play the scene's animations and physics simulation, giving you an even more accurate depiction of the end result.

Although Xcode 7 is mighty and powerful, it still can't do your laundry, nor can it take the doggie for a walk – perhaps in a few years.

And you'll still need to add some code behind the scenes, but fear not, you'll learn all about that and more right here, right now.

Getting started

It's time to kick-off your next game by creating a new project for it. To do this, you'll use the same techniques as the previous section and make use of Xcode's built-in **Game Application Template**.

> **Note:** This is an optional section that shows you how to create a bare-bones project from scratch - it's a review of material you've already learned in Section I. If you'd like the review keep reading, but if you'd like to get straight to the fun new stuff, skip ahead to the next section, "Scene Kit editor". We'll have a starter project waiting for you there.
>
> Also note this chapter won't go into the same level of gory details as previous chapters, so if you're struggling with the specifics of starting a new project, be sure to refer back to Section I for more details.

Creating the Scene Kit game project

Open Xcode, and create a new project and select the **iOS\Application\Game** template. Enter **Breaker** for the project name, and make sure you're using **Swift** for Language, **SceneKit** for Game Technology, **Universal** for Devices and have both test options unchecked.

Once you finish creating the project, delete the existing **art.scnassets** folder and replace the contents of **GameViewController.swift** with the following:

```
import UIKit
import SceneKit

class GameViewController: UIViewController {

  var scnView:SCNView!

  override func viewDidLoad() {
    super.viewDidLoad()

    // 1
    setupScene()
    setupNodes()
    setupSounds()
  }

  // 2
  func setupScene() {
      scnView = self.view as! SCNView
```

```
        scnView.delegate = self
    }

    func setupNodes() {
    }

    func setupSounds() {
    }

    override func shouldAutorotate() -> Bool {
      return true
    }

    override func prefersStatusBarHidden() -> Bool {
      return true
    }
}

// 3
extension GameViewController: SCNSceneRendererDelegate {
    func renderer(renderer: SCNSceneRenderer, updateAtTime time:
NSTimeInterval) {
    }
}
```

This code snippet should look familiar to you because it's a barebones version of GameViewController you used in Section I. There are a few things to note:

1. You call a few stub methods inside viewDidLoad(). A bit later, you'll add code to these methods to set up your game.

2. The scene setup consists of casting self.view as a SCNView and storing it for convenient access, as well as setting up self to be the the render loop delegate.

3. As the delegate for the scene, GameViewController conforms to the SCNSceneRendererDelegate protocol, and there is a stub for renderer(_: updateAtTime:) that is called once for every frame update.

Adding the app icon

App icons are a player's first impression of a game, so it's important to make something very pretty, shiny and even flashy. Let's add your cool app icon for the game.

Take a look under the **/resources/AppIcon/** folder and note the variously sized app icons in there. To add these to your project, open up **Assets.xcassets** and select **AppIcon**. Now, drag and drop the icons from the resources folder to the appropriate spots.

Your AppIcon pane should look like this when you're done:

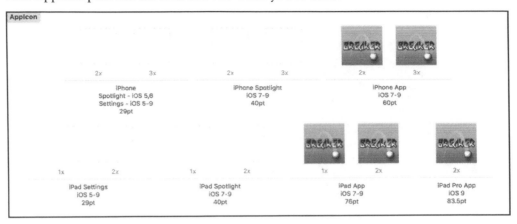

Adding the asset catalog

Next, you need to add some wow factor to your game – the graphics and sound assets. You'll find these resources inside the **/resources/Breaker.scnassets** asset catalog, so drag and drop the entire folder into your game project. Make sure that **Copy items if needed**, **Create groups**, and your **Breaker** target are selected.

Once done, the folder will be part of your project. Inside **Breaker.scnassets** there are a few sub-folders; **Sounds** and **Textures** hold all the sound and graphic assets are stored, respectively.

Adding the launch screen image

With the asset catalog in place, you can go about configuring your launch screen.

Select **Assets.xcassets** first, then drag and drop **Breaker.scnassets/Tetures/ Logo_Diffuse.png** into it.

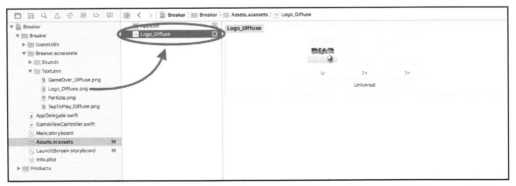

Open up your **LaunchScreen.storyboard** next, and change the view's background color to a dark blue. Next, find **Logo_Diffuse** under the **Media Library** at the bottom right and drag it onto your launch screen. Change the image's **View Mode** to **Aspect Fit**, and make sure to add constraints to the image so it looks correct on all screen sizes:

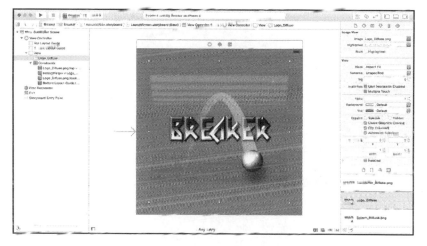

That's it, you're done setting up your launch screen! Your result should look something like this:

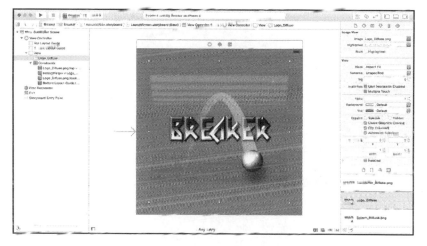

Adding the game utilities

You're going to make use of the same game utilities as before, but this time around you'll use some extra methods and extensions that will make life a little easier when dealing with 3D math.

Drag and drop the **/resources/GameUtils/** folder into your project under the **Breaker** group.

Note: This will import the entire folder into your project as a group folder called **GameUtils**. It's a good idea to take a closer look at the files inside this folder, but don't worry about racking your brain to decode all the math behind it right now, because it's more important to know how to *use* it than understand *how* it works! :]

Adding the game helper

Now that you have the game utilities inside your project, you can start taking advantage of them by adding a GameHelper to your game. It is the same helper class you used in the previous section, and its purpose is to do some of the heavy lifting, so that you can stay focused on the topics at hand.

Open up **GameViewController.swift** and add a new property to GameViewController, right below scnView:

```
var game = GameHelper.sharedInstance
```

This gets a shared instance of GameHelper and stores it in game for later. Finally, build and run.

Although the game starts up in total darkness, it does sport a flashy icon and launch screen at start up. More importantly, your game now has a solid base on which to start.

Scene Kit editor

> **Note**: If you skipped the previous section, you can find a starter project that matches the project at this point under **projects/starter/Breaker/ Breaker.xcodeproj**.

It's almost time to delve into the Scene Kit editor and explore its myriad of features.

But first, you need a new scene in your game so you have something to play with. This time, instead of creating a scene via code, you'll be making one inside a scene file.

Adding a Scene Kit scene

Right click **Breaker.scnassets**, then create a **New Folder** named **Scenes** for all your scenes.

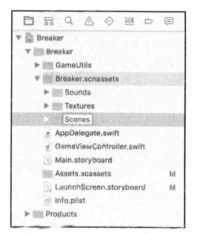

Now, with the **Breaker** group selected, create a new file and select the **iOS\Resource \SceneKit Scene File** template. Name the file **Game.scn**, and where it says **Group**, make sure to navigate to the new **Scenes** folder inside your **Breaker.scnassets** asset catalog:

> **Note**: The reason you had to select the **Breaker** group and then manually change the **Group** option is because if you created a new file with an asset catalog selected, Xcode would just create a brand new file and not bring up the file creation wizard. Try it and see for yourself!

Select **Game.scn** and you should now see the Scene Kit editor in its full glory.

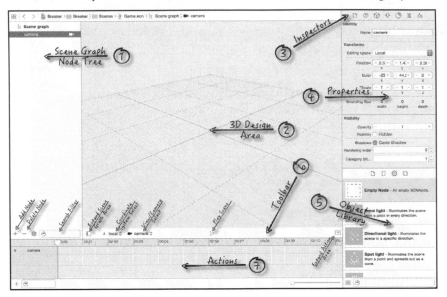

Learning your way around Scene Kit

This might look like a crazy diagram for a football play, but rest assured, there is method to this madness. :] Each numbered arrow is pointing to an important element in the interface, so take a closer look:

1. **Scene graph**: This tree structure is your scene graph. Every element you add to the scene will be visible in here. You can drag and drop elements around within the tree hierarchy in order to control the parent-child relationships.

2. **Design area**: This is the visual representation of your scene. You'll be able to pan, rotate and zoom around in this view just like a typical first person shooter. You'll also be able to drag and drop primitive nodes from the object library into the scene, where you'll be able to copy, move and rotate them.

3. **Inspectors**: These inspectors are context dependent, and their contents will change based on the active selected node in your scene graph. You should already be familiar with the File and Quick Help Inspectors, but there are five new inspectors to take note of here:

- *Node Inspector*: These properties refer to the base SCNNode object properties, so every node in your scene will have the same set of properties found in this inspector.

- *Attributes Inspector*: These properties are based on the type of node object you selected. So if you select a *Box*, for example, you'll be able to set its width and height here, or if you select a *Sphere*, you'll be able to set its radius here.

- *Material Inspector*: This is where you'll come to assign colors and textures to the nodes in your scene.

- *Physics Inspector*: This is where you'll be able to enable and configure physics behaviors for the nodes in your scene.

- *Scene Inspector*: This inspector is global to all the nodes in the scene, because it allows you to set a few of your scene's properties. However, you have to select at least one node in your scene to be able to access these properties.

4. **Properties**: This is where you'll be able to adjust the properties for the selected inspector.

5. **Object Library**: This is where you'll find all the available SCNNode objects, from primitive nodes to user-defined nodes. You can drag and drop these nodes right into the design area, where you can then further visually manipulate the objects. Also note that SCNAction objects are stored in this list.

6. **Toolbar**: This contains several elements of importance. From left to right, here's a closer look at each:

- *Add/delete node*: When a node is selected in the scene graph, you can use this to add an empty child node or delete the currently selected node.

- *Search filter*: When you're building wonderfully complex scenes, you can use this to filter the scene graph to find a specific node quickly.

- *Expand/collapse scene graph area*: This button will expand or collapse the scene graph area.

- *Coordinate system*: This allows you to choose an active coordinate system for editing your nodes in the designer area. You can choose from local, parent, world or screen.

- *View/camera select*: When your scene has more than one camera, you'll be able to select the active viewpoint from this dropdown list of cameras.

- *Play/stop scene*: This starts or stops the physics and actions simulation.

- *Expand/collapse actions*: This button expands or collapses the actions area.

7. **Actions area**: When you start adding actions to your nodes, this is where you'll be able to drag and drop actions from the object library that will affect the selected node.

Basic scene navigation

To design your scenes properly -- and the way you've envisioned them -- you'll need to know the secrets to moving around with ease while you're viewing the scene.

Put your mouse cursor inside the design area, and try out the following gestures to navigate the active view:

- **Pan**: Roll the imaginary mouse wheel in any direction on a Magic Mouse or use a two-finger gesture on a trackpad to move your view left, right, up or down. On a regular mouse, you can hold down option and drag.

- **Rotate**: Click and hold the left mouse button down while moving the mouse cursor around to rotate the view.

- **Zoom**: Hold Option while rolling the imaginary mouse wheel up or down to zoom with a Magic Mouse. On a trackpad, you can pinch-in and pinch-out to adjust the zoom.

- **Multi-selection**: Press and hold Command, and then left-click and drag the mouse cursor over multiple nodes to select them at once.

Basic node manipulation

For sake of having a subject to work with, first add a basic box node into the scene. Find the *Box* object inside the Object Library in the bottom right. Then, simply drag and drop the **Box** from the Object Library to anywhere in your scene. Make sure you've selected this new node in the scene graph, and then open the Node Inspector:

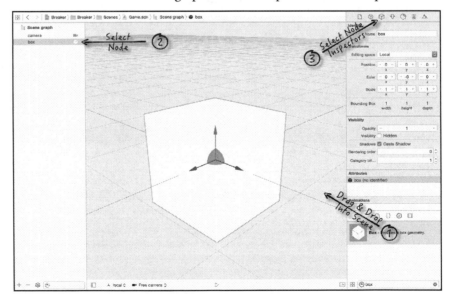

You've just added your first node to the scene graph using the Scene Kit Editor. Now for a breakdown of this node:

When you move your mouse over the colored lines, the gray sectors, or the colored arcs, you'll notice that they light up. These guides will allow you to manipulate the following node properties:

1. **Positioning**: Pull on a highlighted axis arrow and you'll be able to move the node on that specific axis without affect on the other two axis positions. By dragging the gray sectors, you'll be moving the node along the two axes the sector is touching.

2. **Rotatation**: By pulling on the highlighted axis curve, you'll be able to rotate the node around that specific axis without affect on the rotation of the other two axis rotations.

There are some additional options that you should take note of for positioning and rotating a node:

- **Position snapping**: While moving the node, press and hold Command to snap the node to the grid layout, or to a nearby surface. This allows for quick and precise node positioning.

- **Angle snapping**: While rotating the node, hold Command to snap to 45 degree angles around selected axis. This allows for quick and precise node rotation.

- **Copying**: While holding Option, you can move a node to create a shared instance of the node. This allows you to quickly copy a node. It's important to note that this creates a *shared* instance of the original node. Any changes to the node attributes will affect all shared copies. There is a button to unshare these projects inside the Attributes Inspector under the geometry sharing category should you feel the need to do that.

If you moved your box to experiment, use the Attributes Inspector to set the Position back to 0, 0, 0 before moving on.

Loading and presenting a scene file

To wrap up your learnings for this chapter, all you need to do is load up the newly created scene file and present it in your view.

Load and present the scene

To present your scene, add a new property inside `GameViewController` right below the `scnView` property:

```
var scnScene: SCNScene!
```

This property grants you convenient access to the game's scene.

Next, at the bottom of `setupScene()`, add the following code:

```
scnScene = SCNScene(named: "Breaker.scnassets/Scenes/Game.scn")
scnView.scene = scnScene
```

Conveniently, `SCNScene` has an initializer that allows you to pass in the file name of a scene file. It's important to note that you specified the path **Breaker.scnassets/Scenes/ Game.scn** because it points to the scene file. Then, once the scene is created, you set `scnScene` as the active scene for the view.

Wow, that was easy! :] Build and run at this point and you should see your scene:

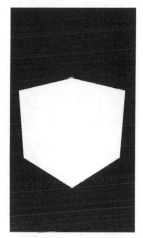

Although things are still looking dull at this point in time, it's only because there's no lighting or color in the scene.

So the answer to your question of *why* is: "We're not there yet!" :]

Cleaning up the scene

It's time to close it out and clean it up before you move on to the next chapter. Simply delete all the nodes in your scene graph – including the **camera** node.

You'll need to start from scratch in the following chapters. The nodes you added in this chapter were simply playthings used familiarize yourself with the tools.

Deleting all the nodes

In the scene graph, press Command-A to select all nodes in the scene, then press the delete key to kill them all:

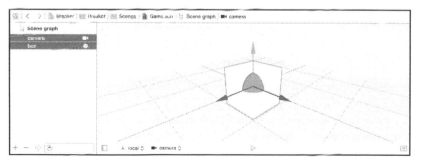

No need for a build and run at this point, because the scene is empty and it would be an unimpressive lot of emptiness. :]

Where to go from here?

You're one step closer to mastering the art of science of 3D game creation. And during this chapter, you also learned quite a few important concepts that you'll need to move forward:

- **Scene Kit editor**: You've learned how to create a new Scene Kit scene file and view it using the built-in Scene Kit editor.

- **Navigation**: You've learned how to pan, move and rotate around the scene designer area.

- **Adding nodes**: You've learned how to add nodes to your scene from the Object Library.

- **Manipulating nodes**: You've learned how to manipulate a node's position and rotation, and how to make copies of it from inside of the desiger.

Stay tuned for the next chapter, where you'll add the camera back into the game!

> **Note**: You can find the final project for this chapter under the **projects/final/ Breaker/** folder.

Chapter 7: Cameras

Chris Language

In Section I, you learned about the camera and its role in the rendering pipeline where it controls things like the visible frustum distance and area. It also sets up a specific point of view in your scene.

All that is pretty cool, but wouldn't it be nice if you could capture the action from several different angles? Well, you can! :]

Scene Kit, as you're learning, makes you rather powerful; for instance, you can actually create as many different cameras in your scene as your heart desires. Want a top-down camera to show the whole board? Do it. Want a view that shows the floor as if you were a cat? You can do that. Want to switch between cameras based on device orientation? Stay tuned – that's covered in this chapter.

But there is a drawback to all of this power, from the perspective of the director anyways. Only one camera can be selected as the active view point for your scene at any given time, meaning the user sees just one camera view at time.

However, as the game plays out, you can actively pick and choose the best camera for each part of the game.

> **Note:** This chapter begins where the previous chapter left off. If you skipped ahead from an earlier chapter, don't worry - simply open the starter project from this chapter to pick up where the previous chapter left off.

Getting started

Before you add some cameras to the scene, you need to create some visible content to show. A good place to start is by making a floor.

Adding a floor node

The **floor node** is a special node with some interesting features. It's basically a plane that stretches infinitely in all directions, so your floor can be as large as you want, which is cool. That's not its best feature though, because it *also* has the ability to act as a reflective surface.

If you let those creative juices flow for a bit, you'll realize the floor node can be so much more than just a simple floor. It could be a mirror, a dangerous quicksilver spit or even a massive body of water.

Now let's dive in and walk through adding that oh-so-important floor node to your game. Open up your project and select **Game.scn**. This should open up the scene editor. From the Object Library on the bottom-right, drag and drop a **Floor** into the scene:

 Floor - Provides an infinite plane with reflection support.

Select the newly added floor in the scene graph, and open up the **Node Inspector** in the top-right.

Change the name to **Floor**, and adjust **Position** so that **x** is **0**, **y** is **-1.5** and **z** is **2**. The steppers – the plus and minus buttons – may not offer adjustments that are precise enough, so you'll have to either manually type in the values or click and drag the value itself to change it. You should end up with something like this:

Identity		
Name	Floor	

Transforms		
Editing space	Local	
Position	0 x	-1.5 y	2 z
Euler	0 x	-0 y	0 z
Scale	1 x	1 y	1 z

Every node you add to the scene will have specific properties, so you'll want to know and understand the following settings that are inside the Node Inspector:

- **Identity**: This defines the node's handle, and giving it a proper identity is critical. When you start working on your scene from a coding perspective, you'll need to use the **Name** to identify and find the node you're looking for.

- **Position**: This defines where the node is placed within the scene, and it's relative to the parent node.

- **Euler Angles**: These allow you to control the rotation of your node relative to its parent node. Euler angles control pitch, yaw and roll, allowing you to specify a precise rotation angle around each axis.

- **Scale**: This allows you to apply overall scaling to your node's contents and children, again relative to the parent node. Changing the size of your node is one way you'd use scale.

Next, select the Attributes Inspector, which should be a tab to right of the Node Inspector. Change **Reflectivity** to **0.3** and **Falloff end** to **3**:

Floor		
Reflectivity	0.3	
Falloff start	0	
Falloff end	3	
Resolution fa...	0	

> **Note**: It's important to remember that the **Attributes Inspector** is contextual, so its contents change based on the type of node you've selected. Because you're working with a floor node, only properties that specifically apply to a floor will show.

Speaking of floor-specific properties, these are what you should see:

- **Reflectivity**: This controls the reflectiveness of the surface. A value of 1.0 would make the floor a perfect mirror and a value of 0.0 would make the floor completely matte.

- **Falloff Start/End**: These two properties adjust the reflection's gradient – specifically, where it starts and ends. When Scene Kit renders reflections off the floor, it applies an opacity gradient, which can fade parts of the reflection based on the distance between the object(s) and the floor. Close objects will render a sharper reflection, while more distant objects will have more obscure reflections.

- **Resolution Factor**: This defines how crisp a reflection's resolution should be; for example, a value of 1.0 would create a "pixel perfect" reflection, while a value of 0.1 would create a rather rough, pixelated reflection. These calculations are costly, so sacrificing some quality on the reflection can make your game run more smoothly. Needless to say, understanding this property will come in handy when you tweak your games to optimize performance.

So you've got your floor, but without color it's hard to see. So, select the Material Inspector, and under **Properties**, click on **Diffuse** to bring up the color picker. Navigate to the **Color Sliders** tab, find the drop down and select **RGB Sliders**.

You can either set each color component separately, using **0** for **Red**, **64** for **Green** and **128** for **Blue**, or you can set all three at once by setting **Hex Color #** to **004080**. Whichever approach you take, this should be the result:

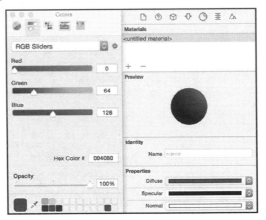

Heads Up Display (HUD)

Besides the dark floor, there's nothing in your scene to look at, so before moving on how about you give yourself something else to see? :]

Adding a HUD

As mentioned in Chapter 6, "Scene Editor", you're making use of the same game utilities you used in the last section. Here you'll use them to add a heads up display to your scene, and this HUD will give players a quick overview of their available lives and score.

Open **GameViewController.swift** and add the following line of code to 'setupNodes()':

```
scnScene.rootNode.addChildNode(game.hudNode)
```

This line of code will add the HUD from the game utitiles to your scene. `hudNode` is a plane with some images and labels that display the player's remaining lives and score.

Next, add the following to the body of `renderer(_,updateAtTime)`:

```
game.updateHUD()
```

This line updates the HUD on every frame by calling the `updateHUD()` on the game helper.

> **Note**: The HUD is somewhat special, and you have to remember that because you add it to the scene in code. Also, you won't see the HUD in the scene editor when designing your scene visually.

Camera nodes

Okay finally, we get back to the subject at hand – cameras! Scene Kit offers two types of cameras: *perspective* and *orthographic*.

Perspective camera

Perspective cameras are the commonly used cameras for 3D games like first-person shooters, because they give you depth perception; objects in the distance appear smaller than objects that are closer to the camera.

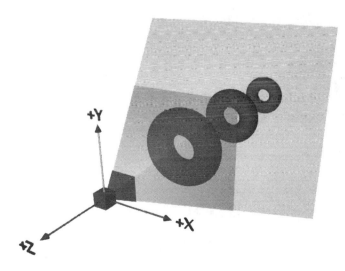

Take a moment to review the most important attributes of a perspective camera:

- **Projection**: The x and y fields of view (FOV) determine the camera's visible viewing angle. When both values are 0, then Scene Kit will default to a 60 degree vertical viewing angle and adjust the horizontal viewing angle to fit the screen's aspect ratio.

- **Z Clipping Range**: This determines the frustum depth range, which defines how close or far objects need to be to the camera in order to render. Objects closer than the **Near** distance and further than **Far** distance from the camera are clipped and not rendered.

- **Depth of Field**: This controls the aperture of your camera, allowing you to introduce blurriness to the scene by controlling the focal point and size. Blur can add a great sense of realism to your scene, but it does come with a high performance cost.

- **Category Bitmask**: This allows you to mask objects so that the camera only sees certain things.

Orthographic Camera

Orthographic cameras are becoming more popular, and you can see them in games like *Crossy Road* and *Pacman256*, where objects near and far from the camera all appear to be the same size.

Here's a closer look at some of the important attributes of an orthographic camera:

- **Projection**: This applies when working with orthogonal projections where you have to make use of the projection scale to increase or decrease the size of your view. Picture this as controlling the distance of your camera because the physical distance between the camera and object effectively has no meaning. Remember that with an orthographic camera, all objects appear to be the same size, no matter how far away they are.

- **Z Clipping Range**: This behaves the same as it does for a perspective camera and determines the frustum depth range.

- **Depth of Field**: This also behaves the same as a perspective camera and allows you control the focal point and size of the camera.

- **Category Bitmask**: Again, similar to a perspective camera, you use of this mask to only show certain objects in your camera's view.

Add a camera node

You did really well hanging in there for all the explanations, and now that you know more about cameras, you're finally going to get to add some to your scene!

Select **Game.scn** to open up the Scene Kit editor.

Start off by selecting the + button in the bottom-left of Scene Kit editor toolbar. This will create a empty node named **untitled**. Just rename it to **Cameras** and know that it will be home for your camera nodes.

> **Note**: To name a node, you can either select and rename it within the scene graph by pressing **return**, or with the node selected, you can open up the Node Inspector on the right, and then set its **Name** under the Identity section.

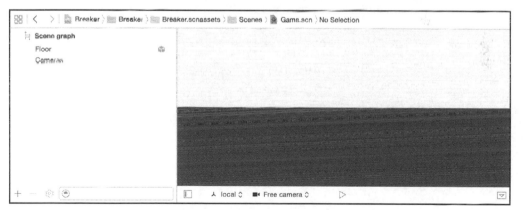

From the Object Library on the bottom-right, drag and drop two **Camera** nodes into your scene.

Camera - Provides a camera that can be used as a point of view to render the scene.

Name the one **VerticalCamera** and the other **HorizontalCamera**. You'll learn why you need to make two cameras in more detail later in this chapter; but the short answer is it gives you more fine-grained control to make your game look the way you want when it's viewed in different device orientations.

Move both the cameras so that they are children of **Cameras**:

⛓ **Scene graph**
Floor   ⬢
▼ Cameras   ▣◀
VerticalCamera   ▣◀
HorizontalCamera   ▣◀

> **Note**: Nodes all need unique names, so it's important to be purposeful and give them unique identities that you'll be able to easily remember and keep straight in your mind. You'll get a feel for this when you find the node within the scene via code.

Configuring the vertical camera

Cameras, by default, have no idea what you want them to look at, so after making the cameras you need to point them in the right direction.

X's and Y's and Eulers, oh my!

Select **VerticalCamera** inside the scene graph and open the Node Inspector. Set the **Position** so that **x** is **0**, **y** is **22** and **z** is **9**. Next, set the **Euler** angles so that **x** is **-70** and both **y** and **z** are **0**. This places the camera **22** units high, and **9** units away from the center of the scene. It then tilts the camera **70°** downwards to give the player a spectacular bird's eye view of the scene.

You should have something like this:

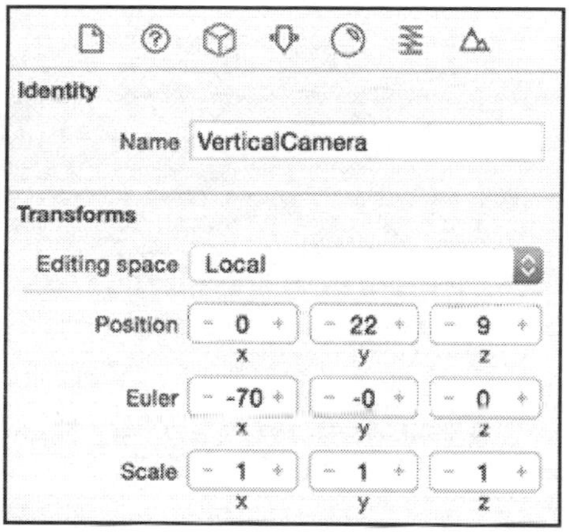

Configuring the horizontal camera

Select **HorizontalCamera** in the scene graph and bring up the Node Inspector. Set the **Position** so that **x** is **0**, **y** is **8.5** and **z** is **15**. Next, set the **Euler** angles so that **x** is **-40** and both **y** and **z** are **0**. This places the camera **8.5** units high, and **15** units away from the center of the scene. It then tilts the camera **40°** downwards to give the player a nice wide angle view of the scene.

You should have something like this:

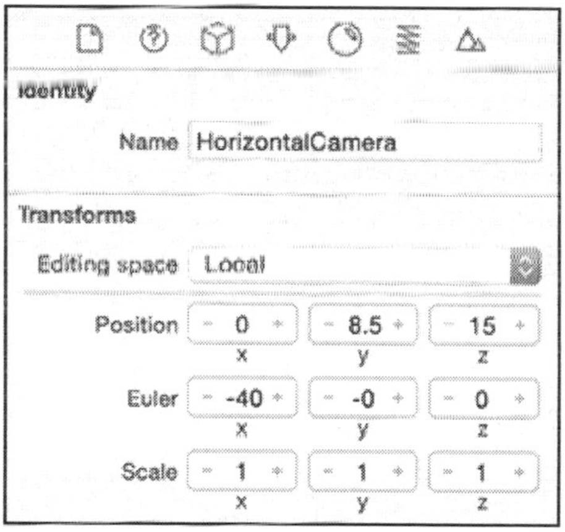

When comparing the two cameras, you'll notice that the horizontal camera is closer and at a lower angle than the vertical camera.

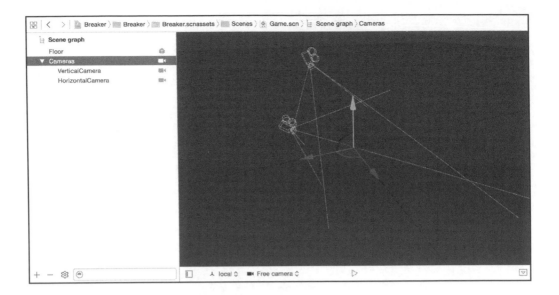

Node binding

Just because you've added cameras doesn't mean that they actually do anything. You need to bind your code to them so that you can actually see your scene through them.

Binding to the cameras

Add the following properties to `GameViewController` inside **GameViewController.swift**:

```
var horizontalCameraNode: SCNNode!
var verticalCameraNode: SCNNode!
```

This defines two camera nodes that you'll use to keep track of your two cameras in the scene. Note that the nodes use a similar name to the cameras themselves.

Add the following to the beginning of `setupNodes()`:

```
horizontalCameraNode =
scnScene.rootNode.childNodeWithName("HorizontalCamera",
recursively: true)!
verticalCameraNode =
scnScene.rootNode.childNodeWithName("VerticalCamera",
recursively: true)!
```

Remember that the scene file is already loaded, so your mission here is to bind properties via code to the camera nodes inside of your scene. To do this, you need to go and find them inside of your `scnScene.rootNode`, and you use `childNodeWithName(_:recursively:)` to look. Every node has this functionality to allow you to find a specific child node by its identity.

By setting the `recursively` parameter to `true`, you tell the method to drill down into the children node's entire subtree in order to find the requested child. It's important that when you use this functionality, you name your nodes uniquely.

Names. Unique. Always.

Device Orientation

You're probably wondering why in the heck you need two cameras. Well wonder no more, because you'll now learn a neat trick to overcome a common problem that your game might face when dealing with multiple device orientations.

As the device changes orientation, the screen's real estate changes too. Instead of trying to make a single camera with a sweet spot to cater to both orientations, you created two separate cameras that will make the best use of the available screen real estate for the active screen orientation.

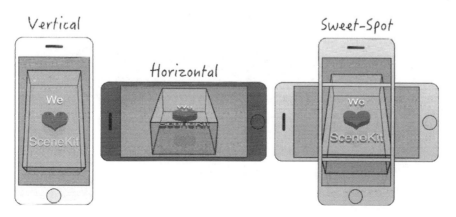

> **Note**: The camera angle changes to accomodate the device orientation, thus utilizing the available screen real estate much better. With the single camera view, the sweet-spot approach might utilize all the screen real estate in both orientations, but at the cost of not always having the entire scene visible in view.

Tracking device orientation

Each orientation change triggers an event, and you need the game to actively switch between your two cameras to fit the new orientation during these events.

To achieve that, override `viewWillTransitionToSize(_:withTransitionCoordinator:)` inside `GameViewController` with the following:

```
// 1
override func viewWillTransitionToSize(size: CGSize,
withTransitionCoordinator coordinator:
UIViewControllerTransitionCoordinator) {
  // 2
  let deviceOrientation = UIDevice.currentDevice().orientation
  switch(deviceOrientation) {
  case .Portrait:
    scnView.pointOfView = verticalCameraNode
  default:
    scnView.pointOfView = horizontalCameraNode
  }
}
```

Let's take a look at this code:

1. By overriding `viewWillTransitionToSize(_:withTransitionCoordinator:)`, you tell your game to run code every time the device changes size. Inside this method, you need to inspect device's orientation to see which orientation is coming next.

2. Here, you `switch` based on the `deviceOrientation`, which you get from `UIDevice.currentDevice().orientation`, so if the orientation is about to change to `.Portrait`, you set the view's point of view to be `verticalCameraNode`. Otherwise, you set the point of view to be `horizontalCameraNode`.

You're done! Build and run and reap the rewards:

You should now see a reflective floor with a HUD hanging in mid-air. Be sure try out different screen orientations and take note of how the point of view changes.

> **Note**: Instead of having the traditional HUD overlay; this time around the HUD is placed at position (x: 0 , y: -0.3, z: -9.9) within the game scene. The HUD appears somewhat distant, and slightly above the reflective floor in relation to the bird's eye view of the camera. The effect might appear misleading at first, but will become more apparent as you build the rest of the scene in the next chapter.

Where to go from here?

Stellar performance! You've reached the end of this chapter, which means you're now one step closer to completing your game.

Here's what you touched on in this chapter:

- **Cameras**: You learned about the two types of cameras available in Scene Kit: perspective and orthographic. You even know the differences between them!

- **Node Inspector**: You learned about the Node Inspector and how it's used to position, rotate and scale any node. You used it to position both the cameras and the floor nodes.

- **Floor Node**: As an added bonus, you learned about the floor node and its super powers of reflectivity and perpetuity.

- **Attributes Inspector**: You also now know that the Attributes Inspector is contextual, and it changes depending on the type of node you're working with. If you're working with a camera, you'll see camera-related properties, or if you're working with a floor, you guessed it, you'll see floor-related properties.

- **View Points**: Last but not least, you learned a nifty little trick to switch between different camera view points based on the device orientation.

Stay tuned for the next chapter, where you'll add some light to the scene!

> **Note**: You can find the final project for this chapter under the **projects/final/ Breaker/** folder.

Chapter 8: Lights

Chris Language

Lighting is the spice of life and is often the secret sauce of design. Ask any photographer what's most important in capturing a good shot, and she'll tell you it's all about the lighting.

The same is true of any game. Sure, you could just illuminate the entire scene like a vintage console game and play would still go on. However, as you observed in Chapter 7, "Cameras", lighting literally changes the look and feel of a game.

Without any lighting your objects appear flat and dull; you'll also struggle to see the finer details of objects in the scene.

Before you start playing with lights, you need to first understand how they work in a 3D rendering engine. When you add a light source to the scene, the rendering engine kicks in to determine how light should reflect off the scene's objects. It factors in:

- Color
- Direction
- Position

All calculations are based on each object's **surface normal**.

Feeling a bit lost? Let's shine some *light* on the subject! :]

> **Note:** You can find the starter project for this chapter under the **projects/starter/Breaker/** folder. It continues where the previous chapter left off.

Getting Started

Before you begin, it's imporant to understand the concept of a **surface normal**.

You can think of a surface normal as an imaginary vector that's perpendicular to the surface of a polygon, or in game design terms, a node.

In the 3D world, it's a rather crucial vector that is used not only for lighting purposes, but also to determine whether a polygon is facing the camera view. Perhaps this is a good time to share a diagram:

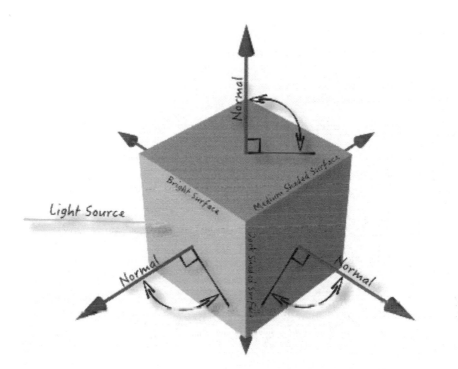

There are a couple of points to note:

- **Normal vectors**: See those red vectors? Those are the imaginary surface normals. Note how each one forms a perfect 90-degree angle to the surface of the cube.

- **Light source vector**: That's the yellow ray of light coming in from the left side.

- **Surface shading**: See how each surface has different shading? Take note of the angle between the light source vector and each surface normal. Smaller angles yield a brighter surface, while larger angles yield a darker and shadier surface. The rendering engine performs that calculation to determine how bright or dark a surface should be.

- **View source vector**: The camera is the view source because it is the point of view into the scene. When you see this term, think of a vector that points from the camera into the scene. In the diagram above, the view source vector would directly beam right off the page towards your eyes.

- **Surface culling**: Notice how only the surfaces that have a part of their surface normal pointing towards the view source – your eyes in this case – are visible. That's exactly how the rendering engine determines which surfaces to cull (not draw) to save precious drawing time.

Sphere nodes

Your game needs some balls – well, right now it just needs one, and its real name is sphere node. Aside from being essential to game play, adding the ball will also give your scene some content to light up.

Adding a sphere node

Open up your project and select **Game.scn**. Under the Object Library, drag and drop a **Sphere** into your scene:

Make sure the sphere node is selected in the scene graph, then select the Node Inspector. Enter **Ball** for **Name**, and zero out the position so that the ball sits smack bang in the middle of the scene:

Next, open the Attributes Inspector. You want to shrink the ball down to size, because by default a radius of **1.0**, produces a massive sphere, that's just too big for what you need for the game. Change **Radius** to **0.25**, **Segment count** to **17**:

Note: Both the sphere and geosphere are essentially the same thing, the only difference is the state of the geodesic checkbox.

Sphere nodes have the following specific attributes:

- **Radius**: As you might have guessed, when you change the radius, you change the sphere's size.

- **Segment count**: Scene Kit approximates curved surfaces by using many small, flat polygons joined together in a mesh. In effect, a sphere actually comprises many smaller polygons. Segment count controls the number of segments to use when generating the sphere's geometry. The more segments, the smoother the sphere and the higher the polygon count. The higher the polygon count, the more processing time it takes to render. Try to keep this setting low.

- **Geodesic**: You'll notice that Scene Kit provides two different types of sphere nodes, the difference being how the polygon mesh is generated. By default, the surface of the sphere is simply a grid of rectangles, but a geodesic sphere uses equally sized *triangles* to generate its mesh. This setting affects how you use **Segment Count** to break down the sphere into smaller polygons.

Next, select the Material Inspector. Change **Diffuse** to a dark gray by setting the **Hex Color #** to 7F7F7F in the **RGB Sliders**. Next, change **Specular** to **White** by using the dropdown. You should have something like this:

> **Note**: Specular controls how shiny and reflective your material is, with white being very reflective and shiny and black being dull and matte. For now, you'll just work with it a little, but later chapters will cover it in more detail.

Further down in the Material Inspector, find the **Settings** section and change **Shininess** to **0.3**:

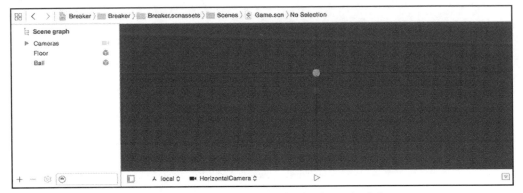

Once you're done, select **HorizontalCamera** as your active viewpoint by selecting it in the toolbar at the bottom of the scene editor, and your scene should look something like this:

But something isn't quite right; the ball is completely devoid of shine.

This is because no lights have been added to the scene. Don't worry, you'll take care of that soon!

Bind to the ball

Before you add the lights, you first need to quickly add some code to bind the ball in the scene to a property in your view controller, so that you'll be able to access it via code later on when you're modifying the game.

Open **GameViewController.swift** and add the following property to `GameViewController`:

```
var ballNode: SCNNode!
```

Then to actually bind this property to the ball in the scene, add the following line of code to the end of setupNodes():

```
ballNode = scnScene.rootNode.childNodeWithName("Ball",
  recursively: true)!
```

The childNodeWithName() method does a recursive search for a node named *Ball* in the root node of the scene. Once found, you bind it to ballNode so that you'll be able to access it later on.

Light nodes

Congrats! You've made it to the part where you finally learn about lights. Scene Kit has four different types of light sources: omni, directional, spot and ambient.

Whoa, with so many, how do you pick? :]

Omni light - Illuminates the scene from a point in every direction.

Directional light - Illuminates the scene in a specific direction.

Spot light - Illuminates the scene from a point and spreads out as a cone.

Ambient light - Illuminates the scene equally in every directions.

Although the built-in descriptions are pretty good already, let's elaborate a little bit more on each type to give you that ninja edge:

- **Omni light**: That bright ball of light in the daytime sky – the Sun – is basically an omni light, meaning it emits light in all possible directions from a single point in space. However, when trying to mimic sun in a 3D game, an omni light is generally not the best type to use. It's a nice effect that's well-suited for things like a burning candle or a lightbulb hanging from the ceiling.

- **Directional light**: This type emits parallel rays of light in a specific direction. It's highly recommended to make use of this type of light when you want to mimic sunlight in your 3D game.

- **Spot light**: This type of light is also directional, but the light emits from a single point in space and spreads out in a cone shape. Use it for a more focused light source, like in a crazy nightime car chase scene where a police helicopter is tracking fleeing robbers in a car.

- **Ambient light**: The ambient light is a source that controls the overall brightness of your scene. Another way to think of it is using ambient light as a way to control the darkness level of the shadows in your scene.

Three point lighting

One of the secrets to making 3D graphics more realistic is to make use of real-life lighting techniques.

In traditional photography, a very popular and higly effective lighting technique is the three point system. As its name suggests, there are three points of light. Sometimes there are two lights on either side and another illuminating the subject head on, and then some configurations call for backlighting. Regardless of setup, three lights will fully illuminate the subject and minimize shadowing.

Here's an example of what a three point lighting setup looks like:

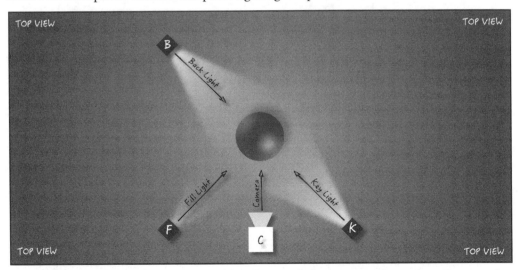

It's good to remember that you can add and control shadows on objects by adjusting the angles of the lights.

Let's take a closer look at each light source:

- **Key light**: This is the main light source that will light up your subject from the front.

- **Back light**: This sits behind the subject, directly on the opposite side of your key light. The main purpose of this light is to produce a rim light effect that highlights the edges of your subject.

- **Fill light**: This light source is placed perpendicular to your key light. The main purpose of this light is to control the darkness level of the shadows on the subject.

Adding light nodes

It's finally time to add some lights to your scene, so let there be light! :]

First open up **Game.scn** and create an empty node under the scene graph by clicking the + button. Then, rename this new node to **Lights**. This will act as a group container for all the lights in your scene:

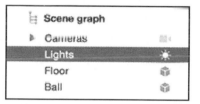

From the Object Library, drag and drop an **Omni light** into your scene. Make sure to move the light under the lights group node:

Omni light Illuminates the scene from a point in every direction.

With the light node still selected, open the Node Inspector and rename the node to **Back**. Adjust **Position** so that **x** is **-15**, **y** is **-2** and **z** is **-15**. This represents the back light, so you are positioning it behind the ball. You should have something like this:

Select the Attributes Inspector to see the different attributes you can adjust for an omni light source:

You can leave the default settings as is for this exercise, but you'll want to learn about what they do:

- **Mode**: You can choose from either **Dynamic** or **Baked**. For light sources that move around or apply their effects to nodes that move, you should use a dynamic light. For static lighting, you can use baked lighting where you create a light map texture in an external 3D authoring tool, and then the lighting effects are applied to the textures of the objects in the scene.

- **Color**: This allows you to specify the light's color.

- **Attenuation**: This controls the intensity of the light source over a distance. When a node is closer than the start distance, the light applies its full intensity, whereas a node that is further than the end distance is not affected by the light at all. By default, the value is 0, meaning that attenuation will not apply. Sitting between the start and the end is the falloff, which is an exponetial factor that controls how quickly the intensity diminishes.

Add another light source by dragging and dropping another **Omni light** from the Object Library into your scene. Make sure you move it under the **Lights** group node as well.

Name this new node **Front** and set the **Position** so that **x** is **6**, **y** is **10** and **z** is **15**. This represents the front light, so you are placing it in front of the ball:

You're almost done, but the scene still needs an ambient light. To add it – you guessed it – drag and drop an **Ambient light** from the Object Library:

Ambient light - Illuminates the scene equally in every directions.

Again, make sure you move this new node into the **Lights** group node. Name it **Ambient**, and simply zero out the **Position** since position for this kind of light source has no effect on the result:

Now take a look at the Attributes Inspector for the ambient light:

You can leave the settings as the defaults, but take note that only thing you can configure on an ambient light is its color.

Finally! ;]

After adding all those lights to your scene, the final result should resemble something like this:

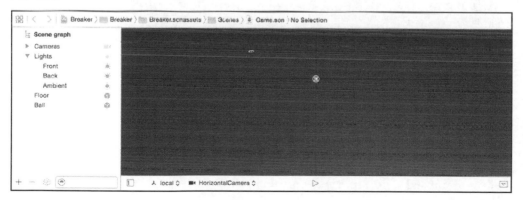

Take particular note of the scene graph structure, where all the lights are grouped under the **Lights** group node.

Conclusion

Not only are you empowered with the knowledge to implement the three point lighting technique, but you also added plenty of lighting to your scene.

To understand what you've just done a bit better, take a look at the following:

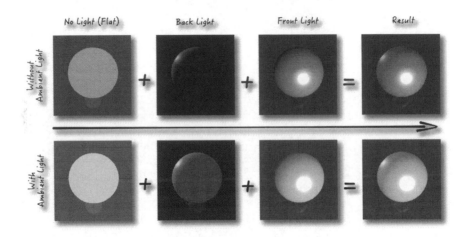

You can see the effect that each individual light has on the ball, as well as the combined effect in the last column. Note that the first row is without an ambient light, while the second row has an ambient light. Let's take a closer look at each step:

- **No light**: When you started off, the ball was flat and dull because the scene had no light source. Scene Kit uses a constant light in the absence of added light sources, hence, you get a very flat looking ball.

- **Back light**: As soon as you add a light to the scene, everything that's not in the light darkens. Scene Kit stops applying a constant light to the whole scene, and starts using the added light sources to apply lighting and shading effects. This particular light is currently acting as your backlight, creating a very subtle rim light effect around the edge of the ball.

- **Front light**: This lights up the ball even more, acting as the key light on the ball. Note that the key light and backlight are across from each other.

- **Ambient Light**: This acts as the fill light in your scene by filling the whole scene with light, especially filling those dark shadowed areas with some light.

Build and run and see the fruits of your labor. :]

Well done, just look at how nice and shiny that ball is! Things are certainly starting to shape up.

Where to go from here?

You just finished yet another chapter. Good job! Clearly there's no stopping you. :]

You've learned quite a mouthful; let's take a moment to recap:

- **Surface normal**: You now know how the surface normal plays its part in light calculations.

- **Sphere node**: You know more about spheres in Scene Kit, and how you can adjust the size of a sphere by adjusting its radius.

- **Lights**: You've learned about all the different types of light sources Scene Kit has to offer. You've also now seen omni lights and ambient lights in action by adding them to you scene.

- **Three point lighting**: As an added bonus, you've also learned about a very cool lighting technique that makes your 3D scenes look more realistic.

> **Note**: You can find the final project for this chapter under the **projects/final/Breaker/** folder.

Chapter 9: Primitives

Chris Language

Your game is making great progress so far. There's a very shiny floor with cameras, lights and even a ball. However, there's still plenty of components missing before it comes close to resembling *Breakout*.

Rest assured, by the end of this chapter you'll have a game because the main focus will be adding walls, bricks and a paddle to the game. But you're not going to take the quick and easy way out here; no, you'll create each component from scratch by using primitive shapes, right in the awesome Scene Kit scene editor.

> **Note**: You can find the starter project for this chapter under the **projects/starter/ Breaker/** folder.

Getting started

As you know by now, Scene Kit comes with a whole bunch of primitive shapes out of the box. Here's a nice little grid of all the shapes you'll find under the Object Library:

Plane - Provides a plane geometry.

Box - Provides a box geometry.

Sphere - Provides a sphere geometry.

Geosphere - Provides a geodesic sphere geometry.

Capsule - Provides a capsule geometry.

Torus - Provides a torus geometry.

Floor - Provides an infinite plane with reflection support.

3D Text - Provides 3D Text with extrusion and chamfer support.

Pyramid - Provides a pyramid geometry.

Cylinder - Provides a cylinder geometry.

Cone - Provides a cone geometry.

Tube - Provides a tube geometry.

You've encountered a few of these shapes already, and probably found that they're pretty easy to use. Additionally, those pretty little Xcode icons also do a nice job of visually representing them.

The main thing you need to remember is that once you've dragged one of these primitive shapes into your scene, you need to adjust the shape node's properties in the Attributes Inspector.

Stop for just a second and let your imagination run wild and free. Think of all the marvelous creatures you'll be able to create with these basic shapes.

Believe it or not, this little guy comprises only spheres and cones, and was created right inside of Xcode using the Scene Kit designer:

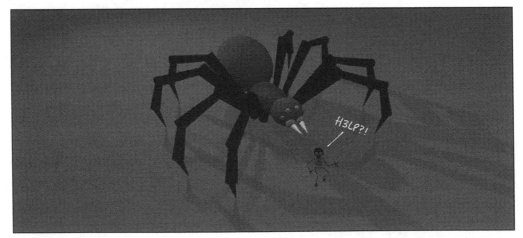

> **Note**: If you're brave enough, go take a closer look at this spider under the **projects/resources/Spider/** folder. Double click the **Spider.scn** file to open it up in **Preview** or **Xcode**.

Just look at the handsome little primitive spider with its shiny, little, beady-red eyes staring right at you. Don't you just love these harmless looking little critters? :]

For your game, you'll make use of the box shape to create the top and bottom barriers as well as the bricks that will be smashed to bits. The cylinder shape will be what you use to make side barriers and the paddle.

Build barriers

In real life, too many barriers can be a bad thing, but in a game, you need plenty of them to make gameplay fun and fair. For instance, think about what would happen in your game, once the ball starts moving.

Right now, there's nothing to stop it – not even resistance – so you could gently tap the ball and send it flying off the screen into a parallel universe; it's an outcome that's exciting for the purposes of discussing theoretical physics, but it sure makes for some lame gameplay.

To stop it from flying off into Neverland, you need barriers! :]

Create a barriers group

You'll make the top and bottom barriers from box nodes.

The first thing you need to do is open up your project and select **Game.scn**. In the Scene Kit editor, use the + button on the toolbar create an empty node, and then rename it to **Barriers**.

This will be your group node that contains all the barriers you'll add:

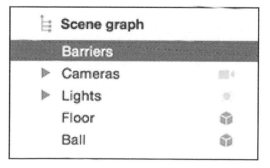

Add the top barrier

From the Object Library, drag and drop a **Box** into your scene:

Box - Provides a box geometry.

Under the scene graph, drag the new box node into your **Barriers** group node. Next, open the Node Inspector, name this node **Top**, and then set its position to (x:0, y:0, z:-10.5):

Open the Attributes Inspector and set **Size** to (width:13, height:2, length:1), and then adjust the **Chamfer radius** to 0.3:

While the width, height and length attributes determine the size of the box, the *Chamfer radius* controls edge and corner rounding on the box.

Next, change the color of the barrier so it isn't just a white box. Bring up the Material Inspector, change the **Diffuse** to a dark gray color by setting the **Hex Color #** to **333333**, and change the **Specular** color to **White**.

You should have something like this:

Copy the bottom barrier

The next part involves some trickery, because rather than create another barrier from scratch for the bottom barrier, you'll simply make a copy of the top barrier.

It's a good trick of the trade, so it's worth your time to learn it.

To copy nodes in the Scene Kit editor, you simply drag from the node you want to copy while pressing the Option key.

So, create a copy of **Top** and select it in the editor. While pressing the Option key, click and drag the blue-axis downwards:

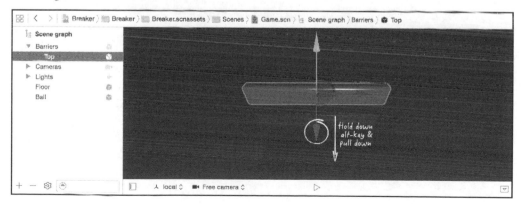

Excellent, now you hace a new copy of the **Top** barrier. Fix it up by renaming the copied node to **Bottom** and drag it under the **Barriers** group:

Reposition that bottom barrier so it's in the right place. Open the Node Inspector and change **Position** to (x:0, y:0, z:10.5):

The final result should look like this:

Most importantly, take note of the final scene graph tree structure and how the Barriers group contains both the top and bottom barriers.

Create a left barrier group

Now that you have a top and bottom barrier, you need barriers for the left and right sides of the game. You're going to construct each side barrier with two long cylinders stacked atop one another, and the cylinders for each barrier will be grouped together so that you end up with a **Barriers/Left** group and a **Barriers/Right** group.

You're going to start off with the left barrier first, so highlight your **Barriers** group node and press the **+** button on the toolbar. Rename this new node to **Left**:

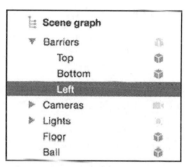

Next, you're going to change the position of this group node. The reason is that because all nodes are positioned relative to their parents. By adjusting the position of the left group node, any child nodes you're adding to the group will get an offset applied to their positions.

With the **Barriers/Left** node still selected, select the Node Inspector and change the **Position** to (x:-6, y:0, z:0):

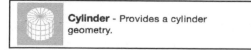

Add the left side top barrier

Here's where you actually get to create the side barrier. Drag and drop a **Cylinder** from the Object Library into your scene:

Cylinder - Provides a cylinder geometry.

Rename this node to **Top** and fix its position in the scene graph by dragging it under the **Barriers/Left** group node:

```
      Scene graph
   ▼  Barriers
         Top
         Bottom
      ▼  Left
            Top
   ▶  Cameras
   ▶  Lights
      Floor
      Ball
```

> **Note**: Because a node's position, rotation and scale are relative to its parent, rearranging the scene graph means the Scene Kit editor will automatically recalculate the node's properties to maintain the editor's visuals. This can be both a blessing and a curse, so just be aware of this feature.

Place the node in the right location by going to the Node Inspector and setting its **Position** to (`x:0, y:0.5, z:0`) and **Euler** to (`x:90, y:0, z:0`):

```
Identity
          Name  Top

Transforms
  Editing space  Local

       Position  –  0  +    –  0.5  +    –  0  +
                     x            y           z

          Euler  –  90  +    –  -0  +    –  0  +
                     x            y           z

          Scale  –  1  +     –  1  +     –  1  +
                     x            y           z
```

> **Note**: The cylinder node is positioned to the left because it is relative to its parent group node, which has a position of (`x:-6, y:0, z:0`).

Stretch the cylinder to the correct length and thickness by opening up the Attributes Inspector and setting its **Radius** to **0.3** and **Height** to **22.5**:

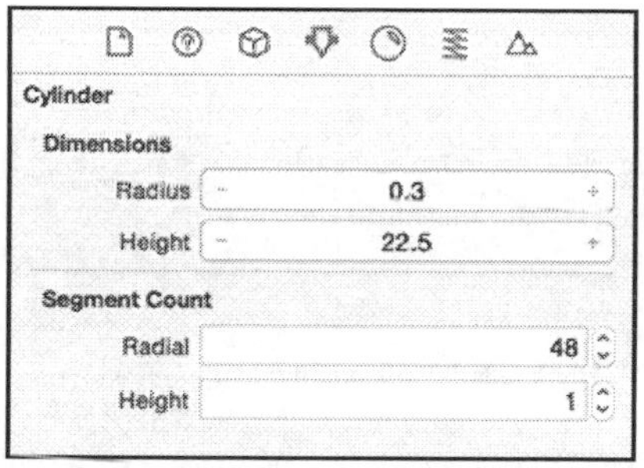

Finally, give the node some color by going to the Material Inspector. Change the **Diffuse** to use a **Hex Color #** of **B3B3B3** which corresponds to a light gray color, and the **Specular** to **White**:

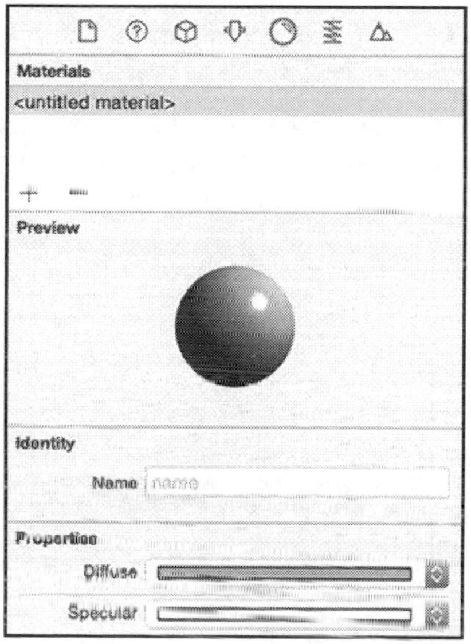

Add the left side bottom barrier

Now that you've got the top left bar of the barrier sorted out, the easiest way to create the bottom bar is to make a copy of it.

Select the **Barrier/Left/Top** node and you should see a little 3D axis on it:

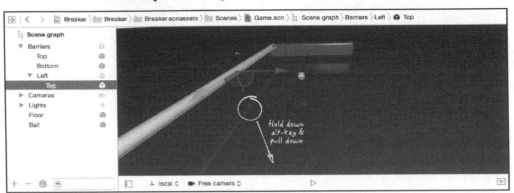

Press and hold the Option key, and then click-drag the blue axis downwards. Once you're done, just let go to create a copy of the bar.

This new copy should be located at the bottom of the scene graph, but that's not where you want it. Move it under the **Barriers/Left** group. Remember to rename it to **Bottom** as well:

Go into the Node Inspector and adjust **Position** to (x:0, y:-0.5, z:0):

Your final result should look something like this:

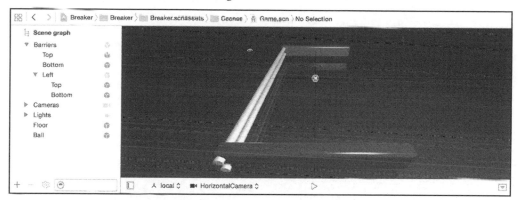

Again, take note of the scene graph and the node tree structure.

Add right side barrier

Look at that left side barrier in its completed state. Looks pretty nice, right? You did quite a bit of work, and it would be a shame to trudge through all that agin.

Good thing you have the ability to copy it all – you've got better things to do than repeat all those steps, like finishing this chapter and having a beer.

What's a little different about copying things this time is that you want to copy the entire group rather than just a single node. So, make sure you select the **Barriers/Left** group in the scene graph:

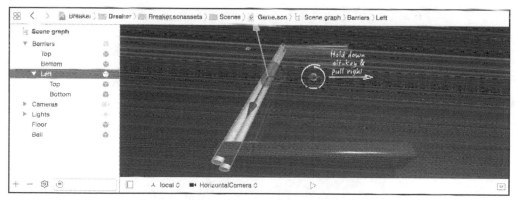

This time, try and do a snap to move and copy, which you do by pressing the Command and Option keys then click-dragging the red axis right. As you drag it to the right, you'll notice how the position snaps to the grid layout.

See if you can place it at position (x:6, y:0, z:0), and with that, you just created a new copy of the left barrier.

> **Note**: When holding down the Command key while dragging, Scene Kit not only snaps the node to the grid, it also snaps to nearby nodes. This useful feature speeds up level design, and it quite possibly makes life in general easier.

Now, rename the group to **Right** and rearrange the scene graph so that the node is a child of the **Barriers** group:

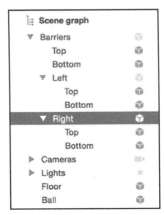

Just to double-check the position, select the Node Inspector, and make sure **Position** is set to (x:6, y:0 z:0):

You should end up with the following result:

Great job, you're like real-life Bob the Builder! :]

Now is the perfect time to do a quick build and run to see those awesome barriers. Your game should look like this:

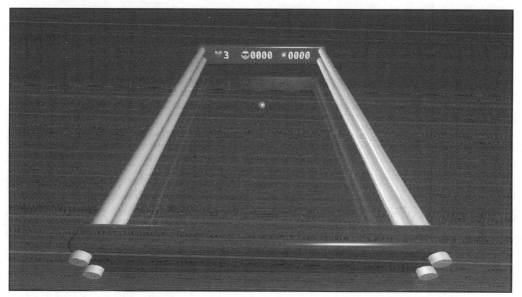

Oh, so pretty and shiny! :]

To top it off, you created all of that by using built-in primitive shapes. However, you're not there just yet. You're missing the bricks you'll bust up and the paddle that controls the ball.

Build the paddle

This game is no fun without some means of destruction. Although the paddle is only one part of the "weaponry", it's essential, and at this point, missing entirely.

Time to change that.

Create the paddle group

Once again, you'll use cylinder shapes – no surprise there, I hope. The first thing you need to do is create an empty node called **Paddle**, which will be your group node for all the paddle's components.

Use the **+** button in the toolbar and rename the node accordingly:

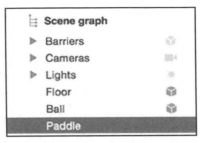

Now set the paddle group's position, so that all of its children are placed relative to that group's location. Open the Node Inspector and set **Position** to (x:0, y:0, z:8):

Create the center of the paddle

It's time to build the actual paddle. Start by creating the center part by dragging and dropping a cylinder shape into your scene.

Cylinder - Provides a cylinder geometry.

First, rename it to **Center** and sort out its position under the scene graph by dragging it under the **Paddle** group node:

Next, select the Node Inspector and zero out the **x**, **y** and **z** components of the **Position**. Change **Euler** so that it is set to (x:0, y:0, z:90), which will rotate it 90 degrees on the z-axis:

Fix up the size by going to the Attributes Inspector and changing **Radius** to **0.25** and **Height** to **1.5**:

Finally, select the Material Inspector and give this cylinder some color by setting **Diffuse** to a **Hex Color #** of **333333** and **Specular** to **White**:

Create the left edge of the paddle

To create the left edge of the paddle, drag and drop a new cylinder shape into your scene. You know the drill by now; name this new node **Left** and drag it under the **Paddle** group node:

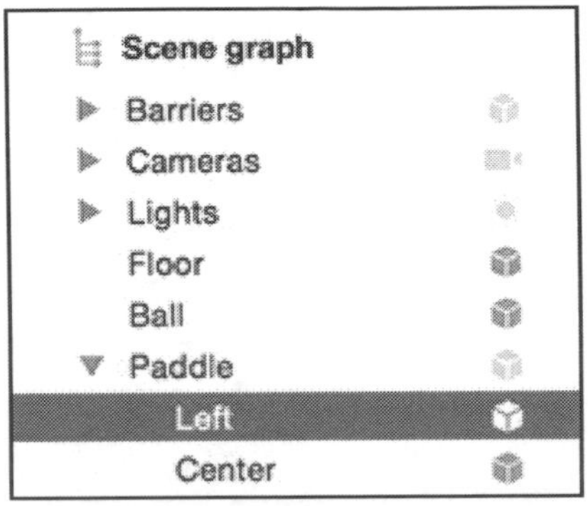

Adjust **Position** to (x:-1, y:0, z:0) and **Euler** to (x:0, y:0, z:90) to rotate it 90 degrees on the z-axis:

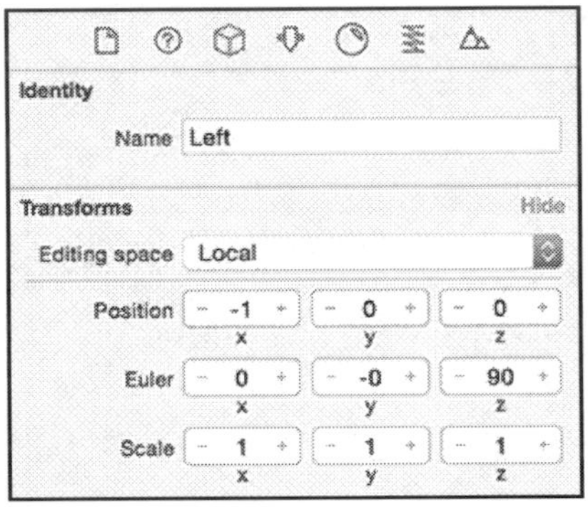

Open the Attributes Inspector and set **Radius** to **0.25** and **Height** to **0.5**:

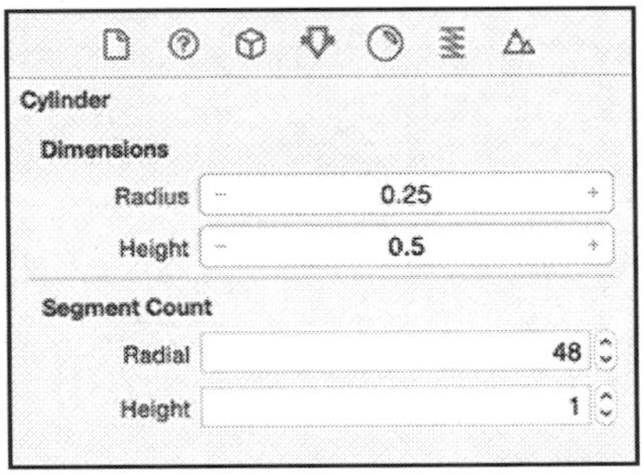

Finally, select the Material Inspector give it a **Diffuse** color using **666666** as the **Hex Color #** and a **Specular** color of **White**:

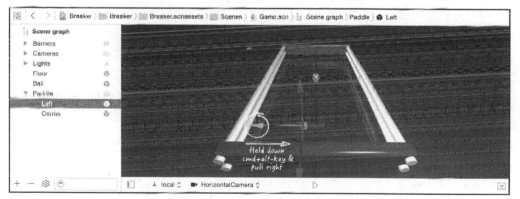

Copy the right edge of the paddle

To create the right edge you can simply copy the left edge of the paddle. Just like before, highlight the **Paddle/Left** node, hold down the Command and Option keys, and drag the green-axis to the right:

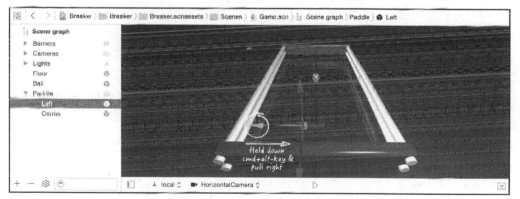

As you move it take note of how the paddle piece snaps to different parts of the center node. See if you can place it at position (x:1, y:0, z:8). If not, you can always go adjust it in the Node Inspector.

Excellent, now that you have a copy the **Left** paddle edge, rename this node to **Right** and rearrange it in the scene graph (which will update its position to be relative to its parent; i.e. (x:1, y:0, z:0)).

You should now have the following:

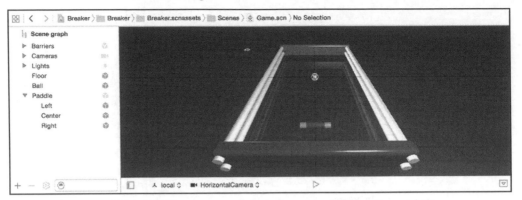

Again, take note of the **Paddle** group and the structure of the nodes within.

Bind to the paddle

So you have a paddle but no way of moving it. That's going to make for some pretty atrocious game play.

The next step is to add some code that will bind to the paddle so you'll be able to control it later on.

Open **GameViewController.swift** and add the following property to GameViewController class:

```
var paddleNode: SCNNode!
```

Then bind the paddle in the scene to this property by adding the following line of code to the end of setupNodes():

```
paddleNode =
  scnScene.rootNode.childNodeWithName("Paddle", recursively:
true)!
```

This will bind paddleNode to the actual paddle group node in Game.scn.

> **Note**: You can find the final project, including this most recent section, under the **projects/final/Breaker/** folder.

Challenge

Let's take a look at the checklist for your game so far:

* Barriers ✓

* Paddle ✓

* Ball ✓

* Bricks ✗

Of course, to complete your game, you still need something to destroy! :]

This time around, it's going to be a little challenge for you. With all the experience and knowledge you've gained so far – such as how to create groups, shapes and how to set their respective properties – see if you can build the bricks for your game without detailed instructions.

Here are some pointers.

* First create a group node called **Bricks**, and place all your bricks under this group.

* Position the **Bricks** group at position (x:0, y:0, z:-3.0).

* For each brick, use a **Box** with a size of (width:1, height:0.5, length: 0.5) and a **Chamfer Radius** of 0.05.

* Start off by creating a single column of all the various colored bricks using white (#FFFFFF), red (#FF0000), yellow (#FFFF00), blue (#0000FF), purple (#8000FF), and green (#00FF80).

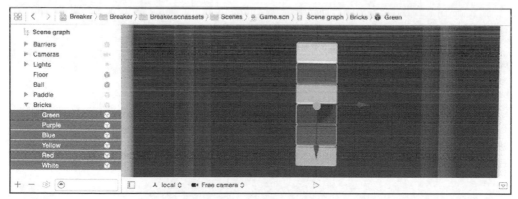

* To help you with positioning, I'll tell you that the white brick should be at position (x:0, y:0, z:-2.5), while the green brick should be at position (x:0, y:0, z: 0).

* Name the bricks according to their color.

- Use the copy techniques learned. (Press the Option key to copy and the Command key to snap.)

- When making copies, remember to use the **Unshare** button when you make color changes to the copied versions under the Material Inspector, so that you don't end up changing the color of the original.

- Once you have one column, use the copy technique to fill up the area from the left to right barrier.

The final result should look like this:

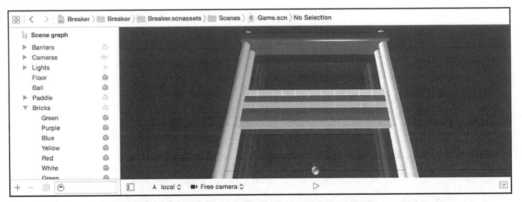

Build and run and see the entire scene all done:

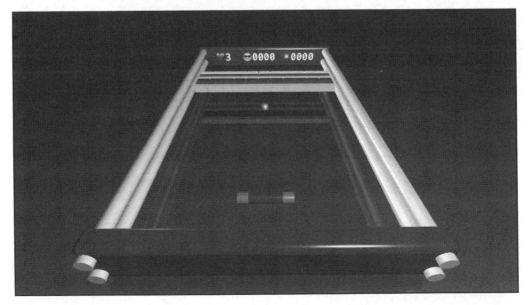

Where to go from here?

Fantastic, you just took your game from barely done to mostly ready.

More importantly, you're a whole lot smarter. Let's recap what you've learned so far:

- **Primitive shapes**: You built an entire scene out of primitive shapes.

- **Practical experience**: You gained valuable practical experience. You built and maintained the scene graph tree structure while keeping all the nodes neat and organized. You learned how to save yourself countless hours by copying nodes. You've also worked with lots of objects together in one scene, and you survived the ordeal! :]

> **Note**: You can find the complete project for this chapter, including the challenge section, under the **projects/challenge/Breaker/** folder.

Chapter 10: Basic Collision Detection

Chris Language

Your game is not quite done yet; there are still a few things standing between you and being a legend in the gaming world:

1. **Physics**: Without any physics for basic collision detection, the ball has no concept of barriers, bricks and paddles. Adding physics to the mix lets that ball detect and collide objects in its path as it bounces about.

2. **A way to move the paddle around**: Without control, you've got no game! You'll add a simple touch control to solve this and learn how to make the camera track the paddle as it moves around, giving the game a very cool 3D feel. :]

By the time you've found the end of this chapter, most loose ends will be neatly tied and you'll be the proud designer of another playable, fun game.

> **Note**: You'll find the starter project for this chapter under the **projects/starter/ Breaker/** folder, it continues with the previous chapter's challenge completed.

Add physics

The first step is to add physics for basic collision detection with the game: for the ball, barriers, bricks, and paddle. Let's start with the ball.

Add physics for the ball

A ball without bounce is like a kitten without attitude, so you need to add some physics so the ball behaves as you'd expect. Open up **Game.scn** and select the **Ball**. This time, open up the **Physics Inspector**, which is denoted by the little spring icon and located to the right of the Material Inspector.

By default, any nodes you add to the scene will be devoid of physics, but adjusting the **Type** of the **Physics Body** to **Dynamic** will bring up a list of settings:

Let's go through each category's properties and how you should set them up:

- **Physics Body**: determines the type of body. Set the ball's **Type** to a **Dynamic** body, which means that the Scene Kit physics engine will take full control over the ball's movement.

- **Settings**: allows you to fine tune the behavior of the physics body. For the ball, set both **Mass** and **Restitution** to **1**. Zero out all the other physics settings, and uncheck both **Affected by gravity** and **Allows resting**. This will set the ball to bounce freely without constraint from gravity.

- **Velocity**: affects the speed and direction of the physics body. Give the ball a **Linear velocity** of (x:5, y:0, z:5). This will give the ball an initial force once the scene starts running. Set the **Linear factor** to (x:1, y:0, z:1) which will zero out any physics forces that might be applied to the ball in the y-axis, thus keeping the ball fixed on in the same y position no matter what.

- **Bit Masks**: used to set up collisions later. Set the **Category mask** to **1**. This assigns a bitmask value of 1 to the ball. This mask is used to create collision groups and uniquely identify certain nodes. The physics engine then uses this information to then apply collision calculations based on these masks to determine which objects collides and which ones don't.

- **Physics Shape**: defines the actual shape of the physics body that will be used during collision detections. Set the **Shape** to **Sphere**.

Note: At the time of writing this chapter, there appear to be a few bugs in the Scene Kit Editor relating to physics. Sometimes, when you re-position a node with attached physics, the physics wireframe gets left behind due to some refresh issue. If you run into this problem, the best way around it is to make sure that all your work is saved, then restart Xcode.

Add physics for the barriers

Your barriers are already there and functional, but they're rather static, stiff and antiquated. They'll look out of place once the ball and paddle are finished.

To configure the physics properties for the barriers, you're going to make use of a very cool feature of the Scene Kit editor. Instead of setting up each object individually, you can select multiple nodes and configure them all in one fell swoop.

To select all four parts of the barrier at once, there are two different techniques:

1. Hold down the Command key while clicking each node individually in the scene graph, allowing you to select the desired nodes, one by one.

2. Select a range of nodes in the scene graph at once. Select the **Top** node first, press and hold the Shift key, and then click the **Right** group node; it will also highlight everything between the two nodes you select.

Whichever method you choose, your goal is to select every part of the barrier:

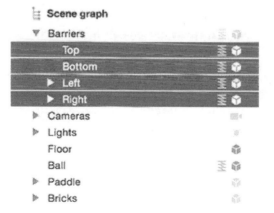

Now, with all the parts still highlighted, open the Physics Inspector. Under the **Physics Body** section, change the **Type** to **Static**, and then this list of settings will show up:

It's broken out into lists, and here's what to do with each part and why you're choosing each setting:

- **Physics Body**: For the **Type**, set it as a **Static** body so the barriers will not move, nor will you move them around with any actions.

- **Settings**: Zero out all the settings and set **Restitution** to **1**, making it so that no energy is lost when collisions happen. Uncheck both checkboxes so the barriers aren't influenced by gravity either.

- **Bit masks**: Set **Category mask** to **2** and **Collision mask** to **1**. This gives the barriers a category bitmask of 2 and sets them to collide with objects that have a category bitmask of 1 – the same category bitmask you gave to the ball.

- **Physics Shape**: Set **Shape** to **Default shape**, and **Type** to **Bounding Box**. Because the two side barriers are nodes with children, this option is more fitting because a bounding box creates a boundary around all the child nodes within the group. If you look at the scene editor, you'll find that there's a red wireframe that shows you how the physics body will look when you run the game.

Do something fun here and press the little play button on the toolbar:

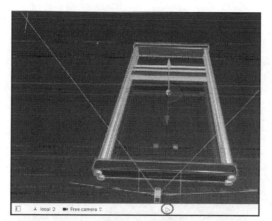

You should see the ball bounce like crazy off all four barriers. Sweet! :]

Here you have a quick simulation of your game's physics. Talk about a handy tool! You're testing out your physics without the hassle of building and running. Stop the animation by pressing the stop button on the toolbar.

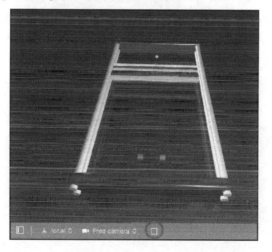

> **Note:** While you could have selected the **Barriers** group itself and applied physics to the entire group, it wouldn't have been the most logical approach. See, it's not the group that has a physics body, rather, it's the fact that you want to apply physics to each section of the barrier.

Add physics for the bricks

Right now each brick is just another boring brick in a wall. If you don't give them some physics, how can you have any collisions?

To configure the physics properties for the bricks, select all the bricks under the scene graph tree.

Use the Shift key technique to select a range by pressing and holding the key, clicking the first brick then selecting the last brick. It sure beats having to click on every single brick node like you would if you used the Command key technique!

This is how it should look when you've selected all the bricks:

Select the Physics Inspector and change the bricks to be a **Static** body:

Set the following settings for the bricks:

- **Physics Body**: The bricks are not going to move around and you won't move them with actions, so set the **Type** to **Static**.

- **Settings**: Like you did with the barriers, zero out all the settings and set **Restitution** to **1**. Again, make sure to uncheck the two checkboxes.

- **Bit masks**: This time, set the **Category mask** to **4** and the **Collision mask** to **1**. This gives the bricks a category bitmask of 4, and makes it so they will collide with objects that have a category mask of 1 – critical because the ball needs to be able to smash bricks.

- **Physics Shape**: Set **Shape** to **Default shape**, and **Type** to **Bounding Box**.

Add physics for the paddle

Now for the last piece of the physics puzzle: the paddle. To configure, start by selecting all the child nodes under the **Paddle** group. You'll configure all three nodes together:

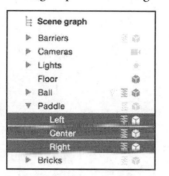

Open the Physics Inspector and adjust the **Type** to **Kinematic**. Oooh, look! Another list of properties to set:

Let's step through the properties you'll need to set for the paddle:

- **Physics Body**: Since the paddle must move around, you set the **Type** to **Kinematic**. This lets the physics engine know that you'll take control of the object's movement, but still allows these nodes to participate in collisions.

- **Settings**: Once again, zero out all the settings, but this time also set **Restitution** to **1**. Make sure to uncheck the checkboxes.

- **Bit masks**: Set the **Category mask** to **8** and the **Collision mask** to **1**. This gives the paddle a category bitmask of 8 and sets it to collide with the ball, which by now you know has a category bitmask of 1.
- **Physics Shape**: Set **Shape** to **Default shape**, and **Type** to **Bounding Box**.

At this point, build and run. You outta be pretty happy with the result:

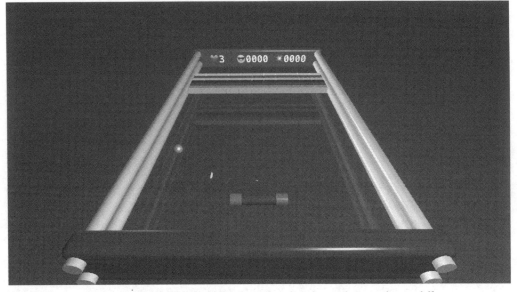

The ball should bounce like crazy off the barriers, bricks and even the paddle.

> **Note**: If performance is slow on the simulator, be sure to run on a physical device instead. Scene Kit apps will often run far slower on the simulator than how it will run on an actual physical device.

Handling collision detection

You're getting closer to applying gameplay logic, but you can't tap into the moments when collisions happen until you've gone through the steps to set up the physics.

So how exactly does one tap into these so-called moments? Meet the **SCNPhysicsContactDelegate** protocol! This protocol defines the following methods that you can override to respond to collision events:

- **physicsWorld(_:didBeginContact:)**: This method gets called once two physics bodies come into contact with each other.

- **physicsWorld(_:didUpdateContact:)**: This method gets triggered after contact has begun and provides additional information about an ongoing collision between two bodies.

- **physicsWorld(_:didEndContact:)**: This method gets called once contact between bodies comes to an end.

> **Note**: Each one of these methods will be passed a SCNPhysicsContact object that contains the two nodes that are in contact with one another.

Implementing the protocol methods

Before you start implementing the methods in SCNPhysicsContactDelegate, you need to set up a helper property to use a bit later.

Open **GameViewController.swift** and add this new property to GameViewController:

```
var lastContactNode: SCNNode!
```

You'll use this property to keep track of the last node with which the ball made contact. It's important because there's a little side effect you need to overcome. See, the physics engine will continuously report a collision with the same node if two nodes slide against each other.

Another reason for the property is that although they are still colliding, in *Breaker*, the ball cannot make contact with the same node until it hits another node, so you need it to make sure that you only handle the collision once.

Now that you have this helper set up, it's time to implement the protocol so that you can add gameplay logic for collisions.

Add the following extension to the bottom of **GameViewController.swift**:

```
// 1
extension GameViewController: SCNPhysicsContactDelegate {
  // 2
  func physicsWorld(world: SCNPhysicsWorld,
    didBeginContact contact: SCNPhysicsContact) {
    // 3
    var contactNode: SCNNode!
    if contact.nodeA.name == "Ball" {
      contactNode = contact.nodeB
    } else {
      contactNode = contact.nodeA
    }
    // 4
    if lastContactNode != nil &&
```

```
        lastContactNode == contactNode {
      return
    }
    lastContactNode = contactNode
  }
}
```

Let's take a closer look at this chunk of code:

1. This extends `GameViewController` to implement `SCNPhysicsContactDelegate`.
   Pro tip: Using extensions to add protocol conformance is a good way to organize
   your code.

2. The method you're implementing inside the protocol is
   `physicsWorld(_:didBeginContact:)`, and it's called when two physics bodies
   you're interested in start making contact with each other. By default, collisions don't
   trigger this method, so you'll opt in to it shortly.

3. When this method is called, a `SCNPhysicsContact` is passed to you as a parameter,
   so you can determine the two nodes that are making contact by accessing
   `contact.nodeA` and `contact.nodeB`. With Breaker, you know that one of them
   will be the ball and the other will be a barrier, brick or paddle. This bit of code
   applies a nifty little trick to filter out which node is which, and once done,
   `contactNode` end up being the one the ball made contact with.

4. This last bit will also prevent the ball from making contact with the same node more
   than once per interaction by using `lastContactNode`, which you set up earlier.

Detecting contact with bitmasks

Earlier when you set up the physics properties for the different elements for your game,
you put in various numbers for the **Category bitmask**. The values you used were
actually numbers chosen to represent a certain value in binary representation.

Take a look at the categories you used for *Breaker* and you should notice a pattern:

```
Ball:       1 (Decimal) = 00000001 (Binary)

Barrier:    2 (Decimal) = 00000010 (Binary)

Brick:      4 (Decimal) = 00000100 (Binary)

Paddle:     8 (Decimal) = 00001000 (Binary)
```

The position of the bits in binary representation is used to store a **1** or **0** when dealing
with bitmasks.

First define a new **enum** for the above list, add the following code to the top of

GameViewController, just after the imports section, but before the class definition:

```
enum ColliderType: Int {
   case Ball = 0b1
   case Barrier = 0b10
   case Brick = 0b100
   case Paddle = 0b1000
}
```

Now instead of remembering numbers, you can use ColliderType.Ball.rawValue as bit mask value for the ball.

To see this in action when dealing with collisions, add the following line of code to the end of setupNodes():

```
ballNode.physicsBody?.contactTestBitMask =
ColliderType.Barrier.rawValue |
   ColliderType.Brick.rawValue | ColliderType.Paddle.rawValue
```

As mentioned previously, the physics engine doesn't call physicsWorld(_:didBeginContact:) for every collision by default. To start getting these calls, you need to set the contactTestBitMask of a physics body to tell the physics engine that you're interested in notification when collisions happen.

In the line above, you let the physics engine know that you want to call the protocol method whenever the ball collides with nodes that have a category bitmask of either 2, 4, or 8 – respectively, these represent a barrier, brick or paddle.

> **Note**: You can also define more complex scenarios, by making a body part of multiple categories.

Now that you have defined when the protocol method gets called, it's time to jazz things up with more functionality based on the nodes with which your ball will collide.

Add the following lines of code to the bottom of physicsWorld(_:didBeginContact:):

```
// 1
if contactNode.physicsBody?.categoryBitMask ==
ColliderType.Barrier.rawValue {
   if contactNode.name == "Bottom" {
     game.lives -= 1
     if game.lives == 0 {
       game.saveState()
       game.reset()
     }
   }
}
```

```
  }
  // 2
  if contactNode.physicsBody?.categoryBitMask ==
CollderType.Brick.rawValue {
    game.score += 1
    contactNode.hidden = true
    contactNode.runAction(
      SCNAction.waitForDurationThenRunBlock(120) {
        (node:SCNNode!) -> Void in
        node.hidden = false
      })
  }
  // 3
  if contactNode.physicsBody?.categoryBitMask ==
CollderType.Paddle.rawValue {
    if contactNode.name == "Left" {
      ballNode.physicsBody!.velocity.xzAngle -=
(convertToRadians(20))
    }
    if contactNode.name == "Right" {
      ballNode.physicsBody!.velocity.xzAngle +=
(convertToRadians(20))
    }
  }
  // 4
  ballNode.physicsBody?.velocity.length = 5.0
```

Let's take a closer look at the code:

1. Earlier in the method, you added a way to the node the ball makes contact with into a `contactNode`. This section checks whether the ball is making contact with a barrier by looking at the `categoryBitMask` of `contactNode`. Then, you check the name of the node to find out which barrier was hit – remember, you named all your nodes when creating them earlier in the Scene Kit editor. With the barrier now being a known factor, you can tell when the ball hits the bottom. It matters because there's a penalty involved: you reduce the number of lives and if there are zero lives left, you save the high score and reset the game. Game over!

2. This checks whether the ball is making contact with a brick using the same technique as above. The rest of the code lets the brick disappear for 120 seconds then it reappears from the dead like a zombie. Yeah! This basically simplifies the game and makes it endless in nature. Oh yes, contact with the brick increases the score as well.

3. The last type of node to check is the paddle, so this checks which part of the paddle the ball hits. If it hits the left or right side, it adjusts the velocity of the ball by 20 degrees. You do this by first using a helper function from Game Utils to convert the angle from degrees to radians, and then you use this value to adjust the `xzAngle` of the ball's velocity. This added functionality gives the player a little variation in the ball's movement to keep things interesting.

4. Once all checks are performed, this last step brings some control over the physics behavior, forcing the ball to a constant speed of five. Remember that you're dealing with physics simulation, which is somewhat unpredictable, so bringing in adjustments like these puts the player in control of the game.

Setting up the delegate

Now that you have all the pieces ready, the last thing you need to do is hook up the delegate.

Add the following line of code to bottom of `setupScene()`:

```
scnScene.physicsWorld.contactDelegate = self
```

In order to be notified of contact events, you need to tell the physics engine that your class will now take responsibility for handling the protocol methods. You do that by setting the physics world's `contactDelegate` to `self`.

Build and run, and you should see the ball bounce around the screen, destroying bricks along the way!

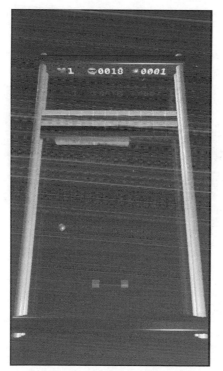

Add touch controls

What fun is a game without any controls? Not much! In this section, you're going to add some simple touch controls so the player can slide the paddle to and fro.

Start by adding the following properties to `GameViewController`:

```
var touchX: CGFloat = 0
var paddleX: Float = 0
```

These properties simply store the touch's initial x-position and the paddle's x-position.

Next, add the following method to `GameViewController`:

```
override func touchesBegan(touches: Set<UITouch>, withEvent
event: UIEvent?) {
  for touch in touches {
    let location = touch.locationInView(scnView)
    touchX = location.x
    paddleX = paddleNode.position.x
  }
}
```

Here you override `touchesBegan(_:withEvent:)` which gets called every time the user touches the screen. As soon as a touch starts, this code simply stores the touch and paddle's x-position.

Now, you can finally get the paddle moving by adding the following method to `GameViewController`:

```
override func touchesMoved(touches: Set<UITouch>, withEvent
event: UIEvent?) {
  for touch in touches {
    // 1
    let location = touch.locationInView(scnView)
    paddleNode.position.x = paddleX + (Float(location.x -
touchX) * 0.1)

    // 2
    if paddleNode.position.x > 4.5 {
      paddleNode.position.x = 4.5
    } else if paddleNode.position.x < -4.5 {
      paddleNode.position.x = -4.5
    }
  }
}
```

Similar to before, you override `touchesMoved(_:withEvent:)` to detect when the user moves their finger around the screen. Here's a closer look at the code:

1. As the touch location moves, this updates the paddle's position relative to the initial touch location stored in touchX. It's a technique that allows the paddle to be moved left and right as if you were using the screen as a touchpad.

2. This simply limits the paddle's movement and confines it between the barrier's limits.

Build and run, and you can now drag to move the paddle across the screen:

Camera tracking

You're thinking in 3D, but the game's cameras are still living in 2D. A really simple, yet effective way to demonstrate the 3D nature of your game would be to let the cameras track the paddle around as it moves across the screen.

Woo-hoo! Let's introduce some larger than life (and possibly motion sickness inducing) effects! :]

Add camera tracking

To add some basic tracking, add the following lines of code to the bottom of touchesMoved():

```
verticalCameraNode.position.x = paddleNode.position.x
horizontalCameraNode.position.x = paddleNode.position.x
```

This updates both cameras' x-position to be the same as the paddle, allowing the cameras to track the paddle's every move. It gives a really cool effect. Build and run to try it out for yourself!

Add camera constraints

You're making progress, but there's problem with the tracking at the moment: The cameras scroll too far to the right and left, leaving the player without a view of the play area.

It's easy to solve this by pointing the cameras to the center of the play area where the floor node is positioned. You'll add constraints to the camera to accomplish this.

Add a new property to store the floor node in `GameViewController`:

```
var floorNode: SCNNode!
```

This will be where you store the floor node once you've found it in the scene.

Next, add the following to the bottom of `setupNodes()`:

```
floorNode =
  scnScene.rootNode.childNodeWithName("Floor", recursively:
true)!
verticalCameraNode.constraints =
  [SCNLookAtConstraint(target: floorNode)]
horizontalCameraNode.constraints =
  [SCNLookAtConstraint(target: floorNode)]
```

This bit of code first finds the node named **Floor** and binds it to `floorNode`. Then, it adds a `SCNLookAtConstraint` to both cameras in the scene, which will force the camera to point towards the targeted node.

Remember that the floor is positioned undeneath the center of the play area. So now, no matter where you move the cameras, they're always looking toward the center of the play area.

It's time to try all these awesome new features out, so build and run your game:

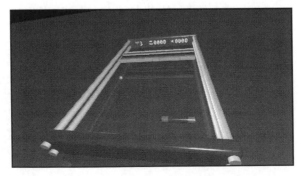

Excellent! Slide your finger left and right across the screen, and experience the sheer joy of sliding the paddle across the screen. What's even cooler is how the camera tracks the paddle wherever it goes, but it always keeps on its eye on the center of the scene.

Add a trailing effect

You've probably see the trailing effect in other *Breakout* style games, where the ball leaves a streak in its wake. With a particle system, you can add this effect with relative ease.

Add a particle system to the ball

You're going to use the Scene Kit editor to add a particle system to the ball this time around. It sounds rather futuristic, doesn't it?

Start off by selecting your game scene again under **Breaker.scnassets/Scenes/Game.scn**.

Drag and drop a **Particle System** from the Object Library to your scene:

Name this node **Trail** and reorganize the scene graph so that the particle system is a child of **Ball**:

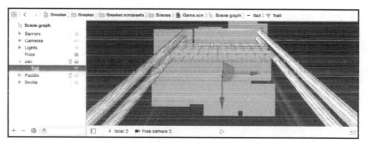

What you're doing is allowing the particle system to be positioned relative to its parent, the ball. So now, when the ball bounces around, the particle system will move along with it.

As soon as you drop the particle system into your scene, it emits big, ugly squares. Don't be alarmed; you've done nothing wrong. :] The reason why it looks like a hot mess is because you still need to give the particle system a proper image to use for each particle it emits.

This is your next bit to fix up, so first make sure your particle system is positioned correctly by opening the Node Inspector:

Zero out its position to (x:0, y:0, z:0). Great, now the particle system should start emitting particles smack bang from the center of the ball. Getting better already.

Next, select the Attributes Inspector to configure the properties of the particle system:

You need to configure the particles so that they fade away and are emitted right from the center of the system. Because the particle system moves with the ball, you'll create the effect of a trail behind the ball.

Let's go through the properties that you'll change from the defaults:

- **Birth rate** to **5**: This controls how often particles spawn. An increase here makes the particles more dense.

- **Location** to **Vertex**: This controls the particles' spawn point.

- **Direction mode** to **Constant**: This controls how to launch the emitted particles from the emitter. **Constant** applies a constant vector to each particle.

- **Direction** to (x:0, y:0, z:0): This zeros out the constant directional vector that gets applied to the particles once they spawn so they stay in place.

- **Life span** to **0.5**: This controls the particles' life span; go ahead and play with this setting to lengthen or shorten the trail.

- **Linear velocity** to **0**: The particles will not move after being spawned.

- **Image** to **Particle.png**: You can find this image under **Breaker.scnassets/Textures**. All particles spawned from this system will use this image as their texture.

- **Color** to **White**: This sets the overall tint color over the particles' texture.

- **Animate color**: Enables the checkbox, and once you enable this, a bar appears to allow you to specify how to animate the tint color over the particle's life span. It's where you create a fade effect! So, create two markers and place them on the beginning and end of the timeline. Set the color for each so that it animates from **White** at 50 percent **Opacity** to **White** at 0 percent **Opacity**. Note that to remove markers, just drag them off the track until an X appears, then release.

- **Size** to **0.3**: This scales the particle down to 30 percent of its original size as determined by the image.

- **Blending** to **Screen**: This controls how the particles are drawn, as well as where multiply mode darkens and screen mode lightens.

- **Emission duration** to **0**. This will control how long the particle system emits particles. Since you really want it to emit perpetually, set it to **0**.

All done! Click the play button at the bottom of the editor to see the resulting effect:

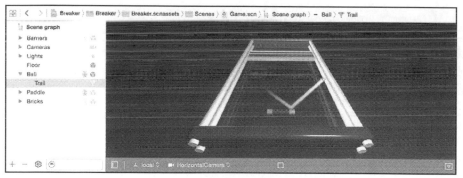

Just look at that pretty tail, it's just like Halley's Comet! :]

Time to build, run and play! :]

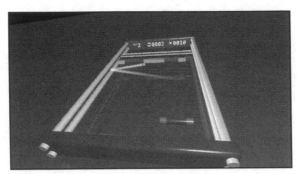

Look at all of those little details that you've added to the game: the trailing effect, the camera movement and the gameplay-oriented camera that always keeps its eye on the prize.

Note: You can find the completed project up to this point under the **projects/ final/Breaker/** folder.

Challenge

Well-done, your core game is done, but the hardest part is still left: adding juice! A quick juice infusion would be to add some sound effects.

Add the following lines of code to `setupSounds()`:

```
game.loadSound("Paddle",
  fileNamed: "Breaker.scnassets/Sounds/Paddle.wav")
game.loadSound("Block0",
  fileNamed: "Breaker.scnassets/Sounds/Block0.wav")
game.loadSound("Block1",
  fileNamed: "Breaker.scnassets/Sounds/Block1.wav")
game.loadSound("Block2",
  fileNamed: "Breaker.scnassets/Sounds/Block2.wav")
game.loadSound("Barrier",
  fileNamed: "Breaker.scnassets/Sounds/Barrier.wav")
```

This will use a helper method to load a whole bunch of sounds into memory from **Breaker.scnassets/Sounds**. You'll find them stored into a dictionary with named keys for simple access later on.

Now see if you can play the right sound at the precise moment of contact. Here are some hints:

- Use `game.playSound(scnScene.rootNode, name: "SoundToPlay")` to trigger one of the named sound effects that you loaded beforehand.

- Give the **Block** sound effect some randomness by using `random() % 3` to generate a random number from 0 to 2.

Good luck! :]

> **Note:** You can find the completed challenge project for this chapter under the **projects/challenge/Breaker/** folder.

Where to go from here?

You just finished yet another game and had another stellar performance! Are you sure you're not a machine? I think you might just have some machine-like qualities, so well done, T-1000! :]

You've come a long way, and you really have a lot more smarts now when it comes to 3D games, too. In this chapter you've learned a lot of different topics:

- **Physics Inspector**: You learned how to enable and configure physics bodies for all the nodes in your game right inside of the Scene Kit editor.

- **Basic Collision Detection**: You learned how to use the `SCNPhysicsContactDelegate` protocol to listen to collision events in your game and responded by adding game logic in code.

- **Juice!**: You've just scratched the surface of adding "juice" to your game by adding a particle system to display a trail effect on the ball and you had the added challenge of getting sounds to play at the right moments.

With that said, there is always room for improvement and more juice. Here are some ways you could take it up a notch:

- The game still needs some basic state management, which would allow you to transition between different states for your game, for instance, `WaitForTap`, `Playing` and `GameOver` states.

- The physics still needs a bit more tweaking so you can make sure the ball does not fall into an eternal bounce between the side barriers.

- The game definitely needs more juice too! :]

Section III: Intermediate SceneKit

In this section you will create stunning a make belief world, with a shiny wooden relic awaits brave warriors with exceptional balancing skills to guide it through a maze high up in the sky. The game is called **Marble Maze**, and is somewhat based on the *Labyrinth* styled games with a twist.

Chapter 11: Materials

Chapter 12: Reference Nodes

Chapter 13: Shadows

Chapter 14: Intermediate Collision Detection

Chapter 15: Motion Control

Chapter 11: Materials

Chris Language

Take a moment and look around. Pick up something close by and examine it. Aside from its geometrical shape, what makes the object look the way it does? What do you see or feel?

Consider the shiny football below - or for our American friends, the shiny soccer ball:

It looks quite realistic; wouldn't you agree? Believe or not, that's all generated in real time within Scene Kit.

Getting started

Let's see if you picked up on the following qualities of the ball:

- See how each patch bulges out? You can even notice the stitching between the patches.

- Do you see the bumpiness of the leather texture as the light bounces off?

- How about the shiny polished parts that contrast with the matte RW logo on the black patches?

- Do you notice the three rectangular lights from the ceiling reflecting off the ball?

- What about the dark floor reflecting off the bottom of the ball?

- Can you see how light struggles to reach the deep ridges between the patches?

You're probably thinking that all that added detail puts the polygon count off the charts! Well, think again. It's all just eye trickery, because what you're seeing is just a basic primitive sphere wrapped with different types of special materials. Surprised?

The following sections show the details of each material and how it helps contribute to the overall effect.

Lighting models

Scene Kit supports four different lighting models, which define mathematical equations that combine the properties of different materials with the lights in the scene to produce the exact final color of every rendered pixel.

Here's a representation of the different models available in Scene Kit:

Here's each model in detail:

- **Constant**: Uses a flat lighting model that only incorporates the ambient lighting into the equation when calculating the color of a rendered pixel.

- **Lambert**: Incorporates ambient lighting and diffuse information when calculating the color of a rendered pixel.

- **Blinn**: Incorporates ambient, diffuse and specular lighting information, where the specular highlights are calculated using the Blinn-Phong formula.

- **Phong**. Incorporates ambient, diffuse, and specular lighting information, where the specular highlights are calculated using the Phong formula.

> **Note**: You'll use the Phong model in this chapter so you can see all available effects.

Materials

Materials are more commonly known as **textures**; they let you introduce more detail and realism into your scenes without the need for more geometry.

Textures are essentially flat 2D images wrapped around your 3D geometry that use special **texture coordinates** stored within the geometry. All Scene Kit primitive shapes already contain this information out of the box, so all you need to do is provide them with some pretty textures to make them pop.

All the effects on the ball above were created through different types of texture maps: one to give the ball its base color, another to make certain parts bumpy, another to make certain parts shiny or matte, and so forth.

To see how each texture works, you'll see how we created that shiny ball from scratch. Get ready for some material mathematics! :]

> **Note**: Just for fun, there's a little starter project under the **projects/starter/ SoccerBall/** folder. Start off with **ball.scnassets/00_Start.scn** scene. Select the **Ball** node, then select the **Material** inspector. See if you can follow the steps below to re-create the final effect yourself. Alternatively, just use the provided solution step to have a more hands-on experience of the resulting effect.

Diffuse map

The diffuse map gives your geometry a base coloring texture. This texture typically defines what your object is, regardless of lights and special effects:

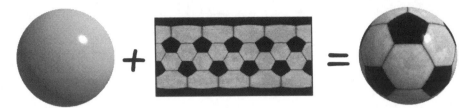

Adding the diffuse map clearly defines the sphere as a football. Looks like one of those cheap $2 plastic balls that wouldn't even last five minutes with your dog, doesn't it? :]

> **Note:** Select the **01_Diffuse.scn** scene to see this effect in action.

Normal map

The normal map feels like sorcery from another planet. Recall the discussion from Chapter 8, "Lights", about how lights use the normal vector to shade and light up a surface. Now combine that single surface normal vector with a whole bunch of detailed normal vectors that define exactly how each pixel on your surface will bend the light, and you've got your normal map.

Think of the normal map as a texture that defines the *bumpiness* of your geometry; you can use it to simulate rough surfaces such as the craters on the surface of the moon, engravings on an ancient stone tablet, or perhaps even the bulging patches and leather pattern on a shiny football:

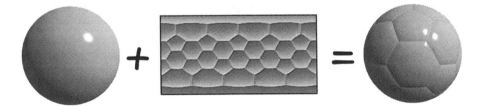

Applying the normal map delivers one heck of a graphics punch; it's taken a basic, dull-looking sphere to a detailed football bulging with awesomeness! :]

> **Note:** Select the **02_Normal.scn** scene to see this effect in action.

Now see what happens when you add the normal effect to the existing diffuse effect:

That certainly makes the ball pop out – no pun intended! Suddenly, your $2 ball becomes a $20 ball. Awesome! But don't celebrate just yet; you can make it look even better.

> **Note**. If you want to generate your own normal maps, there's an awesome tool called *CrazyBump*. You can find it at **crazybump.com**. Hurry, while it's still in beta for Mac owners.

Reflective map

Before diving into reflective maps, you first need to understand the concept of **cube mapping**. You know that a cube consists of six sides. Similarly, a cube map consists of six equally sized textures, all contained within one large map used to texture all sides of a cube.

Scene Kit uses the following pattern to define a cube map, where each tile represents a specific side of the cube:

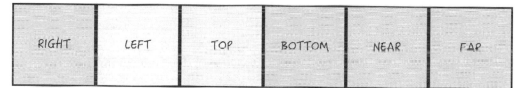

> **Note**: Make a mental note of cube mapping and how Scene Kit uses it, because you'll see it uses again for a different effect.

A reflective map, as the name might suggest, defines reflection. The beauty of using a cube map is that you can define details on your object; the reflectiveness of your object determines how much of this reflection will be visible. For instance, a mirror finish would make your object highly reflective and produce a chrome effect.

Let's create a little light room for the ball:

The light room has three ceiling lights and a dark floor. Note that the reflectiveness has been toned down quite a bit; the ball is shiny and reflective, but it's not a mirror ball either.

> **Note:** Select the **03_Reflective.scn** scene to see this effect in action.

See what happens when you combine the results of this effect with the previous effects:

This effect makes the ball even shinier than before. Although subtle, it's still an effective way to provide realism to your objects.

Occlusion map

The occlusion map, also known as the **ambient occlusion map**, is only effective when ambient light exists in your scene. This black-and-white texture map defines how much ambient light reaches certain parts of your geometry; black parts block out ambient light entirely, while white allows all ambient light to shine through.

When it's done well, the occlusion effect lends a lot of realism to a scene. For complex geometrical forms, portions of the geometry will block ambient light from other spots of the geometry, such as the deep ridges around the patches of the ball:

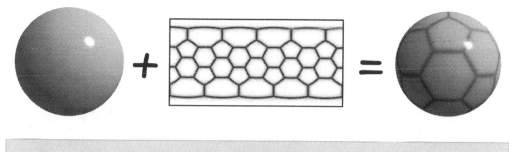

> **Note**: Select the **04_Occlusion.scn** scene to see this effect in action.

Here's what the effect looks like combined with the previous effects:

It's a subtle effect, but it still shows how occlusion mimics the natural properties of light.

Specular map

The **specular map** controls the *shininess* of your geometry. Black sections of the map define matte portions, while white sections indicate a glossy effect:

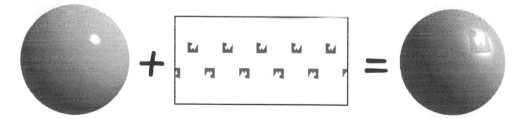

See how the RW logo appears as matte and blocks out all light from the reflective map and the shiny specular light reflection?

> **Note**: Select the **05_Specular.scn** scene to see this effect in action.

You'll get the following effect when you add the specular map to the existing effects in your scene:

Again, it's very subtle, but this effect adds more depth and realism to your scene, bringing you to the final result of a very shiny $50 football! :]

Emission map

In the absence of light, the ball wouldn't be visible at all. But if you slapped some phosphorous paint on it, you could make it glow in the dark!

The **emission map** overrides all lighting and shading information to create a light-emitting effect, which is even more pronounced when you add some blur effects to the map. This is a colorized texture where the brighter colors emit most strongly, darker colors emit less and absolute black emits nothing at all:

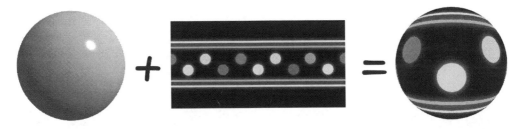

Note: Unlike many 3D authoring tools, the emission map doesn't generate light in Scene Kit; it merely simulates the emission effect. Select the **06_Emission.scn** scene to see this effect in action.

When you dim the lights a bit and apply the emission effect to the ball, you'll see it light right up:

You don't have to worry about lights anymore; this puppy glows in the dark! :]

Multiply map

The **multiply map** is applied after all other effects; it can be used to colorize, brighten or darken the final result:

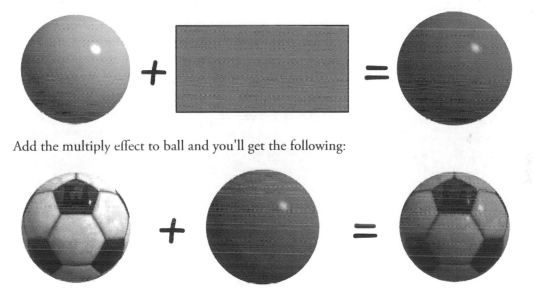

Add the multiply effect to ball and you'll get the following:

Transparency map

Transparency maps make parts of your geometry transparent, or even completely invisible. Black sections define opaque sections, while white parts end up as transparent:

If you enable double-sided mode, you'll be able to see right through the object.

> **Note:** Select the **07_Transparency.scn** scene to see this effect in action.

If you add the transparency effect to your ball, you'll end up with a ball that defies the laws of physics:

It's like an alien football from a different dimension!

> **Note:** To see the final result select **08_Final.scn**. Also have a look at steps 09, 10 and 11 to see the Multiply, Emission and Transperancy maps in action.

Creating the game project

The good news is that you're all done with materials theory, but the bad news is that you haven't yet begun to build your stunning game! Time to take care of that.

Creating a Scene Kit game project

To keep things easy, you'll start with the built-in Scene Kit Game template. Here's the super-short version of the setup:

1. Open up Xcode, create a new Scene Kit Game project for **iOS** and name it **MarbleMaze**.

2. Delete the **art.scnassets** folder.

3. Drag and drop the new **art.scnassets** folder from the **projects/resources** folder into the project.

4. You'll only play the game in portrait mode, so uncheck **Landscape Left** and **Landscape Right** to disable the other orientations:

Now you can replace the contents of **GameViewController.swift** with the following lines of code:

```
import UIKit
import SceneKit

class GameViewController: UIViewController {

  var scnView:SCNView!

  override func viewDidLoad() {
    super.viewDidLoad()
```

```
    // 1
    setupScene()
    setupNodes()
    setupSounds()
  }

  // 2
  func setupScene() {
      scnView = self.view as! SCNView
      scnView.delegate = self
      scnView.allowsCameraControl = true
      scnView.showsStatistics = true
  }

  func setupNodes() {
  }

  func setupSounds() {
  }

  override func shouldAutorotate() -> Bool {
    return false
  }

  override func prefersStatusBarHidden() -> Bool {
    return true
  }
}

// 3
extension GameViewController: SCNSceneRendererDelegate {
  func renderer(renderer: SCNSceneRenderer, updateAtTime time:
NSTimeInterval) {
  }
}
```

This code snippet should look familiar; it's the same bare-bones **GameViewController**
class you used in the previous sections.

Here's a closer look at the commented sections:

1. These stub methods are called from `viewDidLoad()`; you'll add code to these
   methods to set up your game.

2. This simply casts **self.view** as an **SCNView** and stores it for convenience. It also sets
   the render loop **delegate** to **self**.

3. The class now conforms to the **SCNSceneRendererDelegate** render loop protocol
   and contains a stub that is called on every frame update.

Note: For a more detailed version of these instructions, you can refer to the previous chapters of this book; for the rocket-fuelled approach, simply load up the starter project from the **projects/starter/MarbleMaze/** folder. :]

Creating a skybox

No, it's not the VIP seats at the stadium; rather, a **skybox** is a massive box around your scene that gives the impression of a real backdrop or scenery. Most 3D games today use this clever little trick to create an environment that resembles distant skies and hills for example.

All Scene Kit scene camera nodes have a **background** property. You *could* simply set it to a specific color if that's all you wanted, but it has a hidden superpower: you can set the background to a cube map instead. Scene Kit will detect the cube map and automatically create a massive skybox for you, with your cube map texture applied.

Note: As a reminder, a cube map is constructed of six equally sized images, all combined into one single large image. Scene Kit uses the pattern (right, left, top, bottom, near, and far) for cube maps.

Create a skybox

Inside **art.scnassets** you'll find an empty Scene Kit scene named **game.scn**. Open it and select the default **camera node**, then select **Scene Inspector** on the top right:

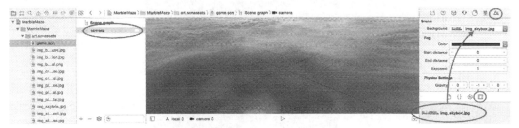

Find **img_skybox.jpg** from the Media Library at the bottom right and drag and drop it into the Background property of the scene.

Load and present the scene

All that's left to do is load and present the scene.

Add the following property to your **GameViewController** class:

```
var scnScene:SCNScene!
```

scnScene provides convenient access to the **SCNScene.scene** property.

Add the following lines code to setupScene():

```
// 1
scnScene = SCNScene(named: "art.scnassets/game.scn")
// 2
scnView.scene = scnScene
```

Taking a closer look at the code:

1. This creates an instance of **SCNScene** using your new scene. Note the specified path **art.scnassets/game.scn** to the scene file.

2. This sets your new scene as the active scene for the view.

Build and run; take a look at the heavenly universe for your game:

Breathtaking, don't you think?

Where to go from here?

You can find the final project for this chapter under the **projects/final/MarbleMaze/** folder.

To recap some highlights from this chapter:

- **Lighting Models**: Scene Kit supports several different lighting models, along with mathematical definitions of how different textures can be combined to determine the color of every rendered pixel.

- **Materials**: Various types of textures used together can create all sorts of special effects and details in your 3D models.

- **Skyboxes**: Cube map textures can create stunning skyboxes in Scene Kit.

In the next chapter you'll get your hands dirty, build game assets from scratch and give them textures to make them look absolutely stunning.

Chapter 12: Reference Nodes

Chris Language

Image for a moment you've created an epic monster, but you can't quite decide what color its eyes should be. Bloodshot red? Werewolf green? Zombie haze? To top it off, you've just spent hours scattering the monster all over your level, so when you *do* finally decide on the color, you'll have to go back and re-color all their eyes with the color you chose!

Fear not — **reference nodes** are here to save you from this scary scenario. :]

Reference nodes let you build your monster in its own little scene; when you're building your level, you can simply pull in a *reference* to that scene that contains the original monster. If you need to modify something on your monster, simply make the change in the original and the change will propagate to all referenced versions.

Using reference nodes saves hours of hard labor, and lets you make those difficult last-minute decisions without driving your graphics artists insane with change requests. In this chapter, you'll learn how to use them in your own games.

> **Note:** You can continue with your project where you left off in the previous chapter, or alternatively you can begin with the starter project for this chapter found in **projects/starter/MarbleMaze/MarbleMaze.xcodeproj.**

Getting started

The most important component of your game is your main character. For Marble Maze, this will be marble - specifically a shiny wooden relic. In the following steps you'll create a primitive sphere inside its own little scene and apply a few different types of textures to make the relic look quite realistic.

You'll create an empty scene that will hold only the geometry of the main character. Later, you'll reference this scene from another scene so that it becomes a reference node.

Start by dragging and dropping a empty Scene Kit scene file into your project:

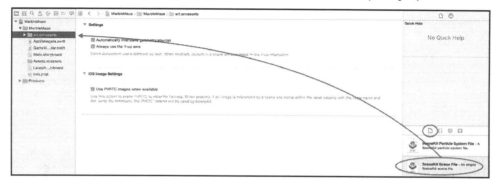

When prompted, select **art.scnassets** as the destination folder for the new scene and name the file **obj_ball.scn**.

Select **art.scnassets/obj_ball.scn**, expand the scene graph, then select the default camera node. All new empty scenes contain this default camera node, which is a real pain when you work with reference nodes. It's best that you get rid of it right away, before you continue. Select the default camera in your scene, then delete it like so:

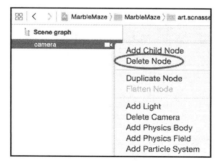

Your wooden relic will start off life as a sphere. Drag a sphere from the Object Library into the scene:

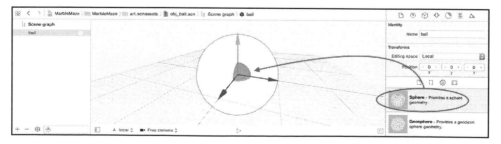

With the sphere still selected, select the Node Inspector. Name your new shape **ball** and place it at position **(x:0, y:0, z:0)** using the inspector:

The sphere is much too big at the moment, plus it needs some more detailed geometry.

Select the Attributes Inspector. Change the radius to **0.45** and bump up the segment count to **36**:

Changing the radius of the ball to 0.45 shrinks it to a size where it would easily fall through a 1x1 gap. Setting the segment count to **36** smooths out the sphere's geometry so that close up views of the sphere will appear more, well, spherical. .]

Materials

Now on to the fun part: adding materials! :]

Select the **Material Inspector** on the top right, and change the Diffuse, Normal, Reflective, and Emission settings as shown in the sub-sections below.

Diffuse

- **Diffuse**: Instead of a solid color, select **img_ball_diffuse** from the dropdown as the diffuse map. Note you must click to the far right of the dropdown where the up/down arrows are for this to work.

- **Intensity**: Leave this set to **1.0**. This controls the brightness level of your base diffuse material; **0.0** would make it completely black.

- **Mip Filter**: Set this to **Linear**, which enables mip mapping for the diffuse texture.

> **Note**: Wondering what *mip* means? This will be discussed along with its brethren *min*, *mag*, *wrapT* and *wrapS* in the next section, so hold tight for a moment — there's need to scream and pull your hair out just yet. :]

Normal

- **Normal**: Select **img_ball_normal** for the normal map.
- **Intensity**: Set this to **0.8** to make the effect just a little less prominent.
- **Mip Filter**: Set this to **Linear**.

> **Note**: If you want to use a different texture, as mentioned in Chapter 11, "Materials", you can use the tool *CrazyBump* to generate a normal map from the diffuse texture.

Specular

- **Specular**: Change the specular color to pure white, which gives the ball a nice glossy effect.

Reflective

- **Reflective**: Select **img_skybox** for the reflective map. This reflects the environment onto the ball and makes it reflective like a mirror.

- **Intensity**: Set the intensity to **0.3** so it isn't perfectly reflective.

- **Mip Filter**: Set this to **Linear**.

Emission

Emission	img_ball_emis
Path	/Users/rwenderlich/ Desktop/MarbleMaze/ MarbleMaze/ art.scnassets/ img_ball_emission.jpg
Relative Path	img_ball_emission.jpg
Intensity	0.2
Min filter	Linear
Mag filter	Linear
Mip filter	Linear
WrapS	Clamp
WrapT	Clamp
UV Channel	0
Offset	0 0
Scale	1 1
Rotation	0

- **Emission**: Select **img_ball_emission** for the emission map.

- **Intensity**: Set this to **0.2** for now; you'll animate the intensity later and change the emission map dynamically.

- **Mip Filter**: Set this to **Linear**.

The images below show the cumulative effect of adding each material type:

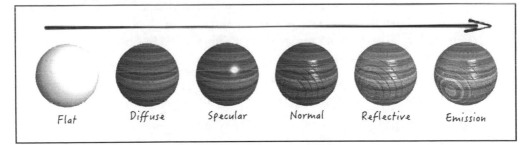

Flat   Diffuse   Specular   Normal   Reflective   Emission

Note: You won't experience the exact same result as above while working in the scene editor. This is due to the lack of lights in your scene.

You've added some great detail to your sphere, but high-resolution textures can come at a serious performance cost. If you're viewing your objects from a distance, isn't it wasteful to use high-resolution textures on objects where the effect is only visible when you're viewing the object up close?

Yes, it can be wasteful, but you can use a technique known as **mip map filtering** to render your objects efficiently.

Texture filtering

3D rendering engines use the mip map filtering technique to speed up the rendering performance of textured objects at a distance; basically, you use smaller pre-generated versions of the original texture.

Scene Kit indeed supports mip mapping; all you need to do is enable it (which it is by default) and decide which technique to use when generating smaller sized textures.

The results of mip mapping can be subtle; you might need a magnifying glass to spot the differences in the following images! :]

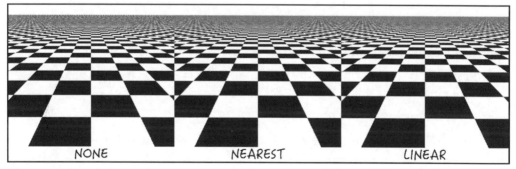

The image above shows three versions of the same scene of a patterned floor stretching to the horizon, each using a different mip mapping technique. Look closely at the appearance of the check pattern as it approaches the horizon:

- **None**: This has no mip mapping enabled; note how the pattern generates all sorts of interesting visual artifacts and Moiré patterns near the horizon.

- **Nearest**: This samples pixels from the nearest level mip map when it textures a object.

- **Linear**: This samples pixels from the two nearest-level mip maps and interpolates the result between those two maps when it renders a object. This is the default option that is selected when you choose a texture.

> **Note**: The minification and magnification filters use the exact same techniques when dealing with textures at smaller or larger sizes than the original.

Adding the ball as reference node

Now that you have your relic set up, it's time to pull it into the main game scene.

First select the **art.scnassets/game.scn** scene, then drag and drop the **art.scnassets/obj_ball.scn** into the scene. Set your relic's position to **(x:0, y:0, z:0)** and name it **ball**:

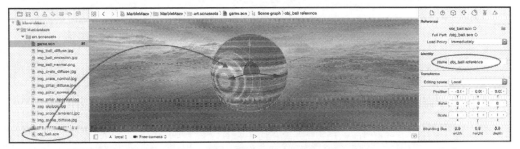

You'll see the wooden relic in your scene, but notice that its identity shows it's been added as a **reference**. Well done – you just mastered the dark art of reference nodes. :]

Build and run your game, and take stock of your scene:

Like magic, the wooden relic defies gravity and hangs in mid-air. Pan around and enjoy the view – but wait a minute. What happened to all those cool texture effects?

That's because there aren't any lights in the scene! Texture effects need light to be visible. You'll need to wait until the next chapter to add some light sources; for now, you'll focus on building the game level with reference nodes. Patience is a virtue. :]

> **Note**: At the time of writing this chapter, there appear to be a few bugs in the Scene Kit Editor relating to reference nodes. When making changes to the origin node, the scene with the referenced version does not always get refreshed properly. If you run into this problem, simply make sure all your work is saved, then restart Xcode.

Challenge

Time for a fun little challenge! Simply read the following hints and apply the skills you've learned so far to create the objects below from scratch:

1. Create each object in its own little empty scene.

2. Delete that pesky default camera node from each empty scene; otherwise it will show up when you create a new reference to your object.

Okay – now try to create the following objects:

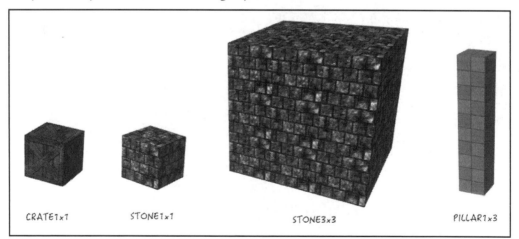

CRATE1x1   STONE1x1   STONE3x3   PILLAR1x3

- **obj_crate1x1**: Name it **crate** and set its size to **(x:1, y:1, z:1)**. Use the **img_crate_diffuse** texture as diffuse, and **img_crate_normal** as normal. Add a mid-grey specular color; if you make this pure white the crates will look like plastic.

- **obj_stone1x1**: Name it **stone** and set its size to **(x:1, y:1, z:1)**. Use the **img_stone_diffuse** and **img_stone_normal** maps, but lower the normals intensity to

0.5. Give it a nice **white** specular color.

- **obj_stone3x3**: Name this one **stone** as well, but set its size to **(x:3, y:3, z:3)**. This one will be a bit trickier, as you will have to use the texture scale settings and wrapT and wrapS to make it work. Use the same textures as you did for **obj_stone1x1**, and again use a **white** specular color.

- **obj_pillar1x3**: Name it **pillar** and set its size to **(x:1, y:3, z:1)**. Use the **img_pillar_** textures; this one has a specular texture as well, so make use of that. You'll also have to play with the scale and wrap settings a bit.

> **Note**: Don't freak out — you got this! Refer back to the previous section if you get stuck, or take a peek at the finished project located in the **projects/challenge/ MarbleMaze** folder. The section below walks you through the creation of the 3x3 stone block in particular.

Scaling and wrapping textures

Here's a little more detail on how to solve the challenge of the 3x3 block:

First off, adjust its size to **(x:3, y:3, z:3)** using the **Attributes Inspector**:

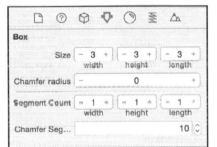

This is where things get interesting. Using the Materials Inspector, change each setting as described below:

- **Diffuse**: Select the diffuse map; the pattern tries to fill the whole block. Since it's such a large block, you need to scale it the texture down to fit the perspective of the smaller stone block.

- **Scale**: Adjust the scaling factor to **(x:3, y:3, z:3)**, which scales down the texture – but to one corner only. To let it fill the block, you have to tell the pattern to repeat.

- **WrapS**: Set wrapS to **repeat**, which enables horizontal texture wrapping; suddenly the texture pattern repeats horizontally.

- **WrapT**: Set wrapT to **repeat**, which enables vertical texture wrapping; the texture pattern repeats vertically and fills the entire block.

Here's how your Materials Inspector will look when you're done:

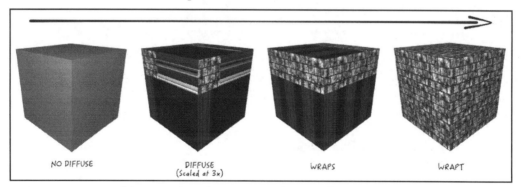

Here's the end result of each step in succession:

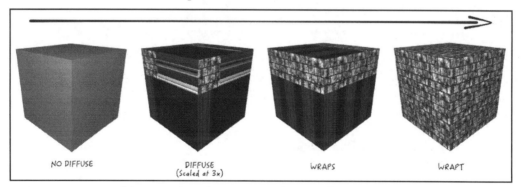

You can use some of these same techniques to solve the 1x3 pillar as well.

Where to go from here?

This brings you to the end of this chapter. Your game is coming along nicely – great job!

Here's a quick recap of what you've learned in this chapter:

- **Reference Nodes**: A reference node is basically a scene all on its own with its own set of objects. The reference part comes in when you've re-used that scene within another scene. Any changes made to the original referenced scene will automatically change all the referenced nodes.

- **Mip Map Filtering**: Mip mapping can make your game look better *and* perform better too.

- **Texture Scaling & Wrapping**: Textures can be scaled, wrapped and repeated to fill in large areas.

In the next chapter, you'll use the objects you created in this chapter to build little mini sets, which you will ultimately reference when you build your main game scene.

Chapter 13: Shadows

Chris Language

If you suffer from Sciophobia, then this chapter's going to be a bit of a challenge for you – but if not, you've got this one in the bag. This chapter deals with a very dark subject matter shadows! .]

One thing comic books have taught us all is that evil cannot exist without good. One villain in particular pointed this fact out in the movie *Unbreakable*; Mr. Glass knew that an arch-villain can only exist if there's a hero. Well the same goes for shadows – they can only exist in the presence of light.

You've already learned about all the different types of light sources available in Scene Kit. Unfortunately, not all lights are capable of casting shadows; only the **spot** and the **directional** lights have this *dark* ability.

Getting started

In order to demonstrate how lights and shadows work, we had to fabricate a sample scenario, leading you to this very important question: ♫ Do You Want to Build a Snowman? ♫ :]

The neighborhood kids built this little guy on your front lawn, and now he's casting a shadow thanks to the directional light that's simulating sunlight. How sweet; now go grab a shovel and show Olaf's distant cousin what you think about little kids' art projects on your property! :]

Directional shadows

You know how a laser shines a thin beam of light into the distance? You can think of a directional light as a million little laser lights, streaming light in parallel in a given direction.

Unlike a spot light shadow, the size of the shadow cast by the directional light won't change as the distance to the light source changes. However, the length of the shadow is affected by the angle at which the light hits the 3D object, just as your shadow grows longer towards sunset.

Directional lights are somewhat strange when it comes to casting shadows, because the node's scale property plays a big part in determining the area of the shadow it creates. Scene Kit creates a 2D shadow map from the light nodes point of view. Directional lights ignores position information because the light has a constant direction. Directional lights requires an orthographic projection. That's why the scale property controls the visible extents of the orthographic projection.

If you're using a directional light in your scene and you don't see a shadow, you probably need to adjust the node's scale. This can be done by either tweaking the node scale, or the light shadow attributes scale:

The image below demonstrates the effect that adjusting the directional light's node scale has on the resulting shadow:

![The effect of adjusting directional light's node scale on snowman shadows: SCALE = (x:1, y:1, z:1), SCALE = (x:2, y:2, z:2), SCALE = (x:5, y:5, z:5)]

At a scale of 1, you can clearly see a square shadow that's clipped in both the x and y directions. As you increase the scaling to 2, you start to notice the shadow of the rounded body, but still no hands, nose or head. Finally by increasing the scale to 5, you're able to see all the body parts, even the pointy nose.

> **Note**: For a more hands-on experience, have a look under the **projects/resources/Snowman** folder. Double click the **Snowman_Directional.scn** scene file to open it up in Xcode. Select the **directional** light under the scene graph, then press ⌥⌘4 (Option+Command+4) to open up the attributes inspector.

Take a closer look at the directional light's Attributes Inspector; you'll notice there's a **shadow** section at the bottom:

Iterating through all the available shadow properties:

- **Behaviour**: Determines whether the light will cast a shadow.

- **Color**: Determines the color of the shadow cast. You can modify the color and transparency level; this lets other colors show through the shadow.

- **Sample radius**: Scene Kit can produce soft shadows by rendering a silhouette of your 3D object onto a 2D shadow map; this radius is used to generate several sample shadow maps. A lower radius will result in a sharper shadow, while larger radii will produce softer shadows.

- **Near/Far clipping**: Any object outside the range of these values from the light source will not produce a shadow, thus clipping its own shadow. This property can be tweaked when performance starts to become an issue.

- **Scale**: Determines the resolution of the generated shadow maps. A scale of 1 will produce the highest resolution, while higher values produce lower-resolution shadow maps.

- **Sample count**: This property works hand-in-hand with the sample radius property. Specifying higher numbers of shadow samples produces softer shadows.

- **Bias**: Sometimes rendered shadows might not render onto all pixels as expected, causing an effect known as *shadow acne*. You can use this property to fix those types of artifacts.

The image below shows the effect of adjusting the shadow sample count on a spot light shadow with a fairly large sample radius:

With a sample count of 2, you can see two distinct shadows produced. Pushing the sample count higher produces more shadow samples, and eventually ends with a soft shadow on the far right.

The next image shows the impact of shadow scale and reducing the generated shadow map resolution:

With a resolution of 1, you can see a nice crisp shadow edge. Pushing the shadow map resolution lower produces blockier and blockier shadows.

> **Note:** Finding the sweet spot between the shadow Scale and Sample Count plays an important part in tweaking the performance of your games. Crisper shadows are less processor-hungry than soft, smooth shadows. Keep that in mind when you're trying to manage performance issues in your game.

Spot shadows

Arkham City is in trouble; mass riots have broken out, pushing the police force to the breaking point. Arkham has only one hope left – signal the Batman! :]

The Batman signal is a good example of a spot light that casts a shadow. The closer the object is to the light source, the bigger the shadow it casts due to the cone structure of the spot light.

Let's return to Olaf's distant cousin for a moment. Night has fallen upon Winter Wonderland, and a nearby street light now shines its light onto the little snowman, casting a shadow in front of it.

> **Note:** For a more hands-on experience, have a look under the **/projects/resources/Snowman** folder. Double click the **Snowman_Spot.scn** scene file to open it up in Xcode. Select the **spot** light under the scene graph, then press ⌥⌘4 (Option+Command+4) to open up the attributes inspector.

Take a look at the spot light's Attributes Inspector; you'll notice a **shadow** section at the bottom:

The options for spot lights are similar to the options for directional lights:

- **Behavior**: Determines whether the light will cast a shadow.

- **Color**: The color of the shadow cast. You can choose both color and transparency level, this will allow the shadow to allow other colors through.

- **Sample radius**. Scene Kit can produce soft shadows by rendering a silhouette of your 3D object onto a 2D shadow map, this radius is then used to generate several sample shadow maps. A lower radius will result in a sharper shadow, where larger radiuses will produce softer shadows.

- **Near/Far clipping**. Any object not within the range of these values from the light source will not produce a shadow, thus clipping their shadows. This property can be tweaked when performance starts to become an issue.

- **Sample count**. This property works hand in hand with the sample radius property. Specifying how many shadow samples to generate when generating the shadow map. Higher numbers should produce softer shadows.

- **Bias**. Sometimes rendered shadows might not render onto all pixels as expected, causing an effect known as shadow acne. You can use this property to fix those types of artefacts.

The image below shows the effect of adjusting the sample count of the spot light shadow with a fairly large sample radius:

A sample count of 1 creates a crisp, clean and sharp shadow. With a sample count of 2, you can clearly see two distinct shadows, as if the shadows were produced from two light sources that are close in proximity. Pushing the sample count up to 5 produces a softer, smoother shadow.

OK that's it for your snowman - time to add some shadows to Marble Maze using what you've learned so far!

> **Note**: Before you continue, load up the starter project under the **projects/starter/ MarbleMaze** folder. It continues where you left off with the previous chapter.

Organizing the scene

At this point, you need to do some basic housekeeping on the main game scene.

Select the **art.scnassets/game.scn** scene. You should already have a ball and a camera node in the scene. You're going to organize the scene graph so it looks like the following:

You'll deal with the scene graph first.

Create an empty node named **follow_camera**:

Zero out its position and set its rotation angle to (x:-45, y:0, z:0).

Make the **camera** node a child of **follow_camera**:

Set the **camera** position to (x:0, y:0, z:5).

> **Note**: By making the **camera** a child node of the **follow_camera** node and placing it at a z-position of 5 units, you have essentially placed it on an imaginary selfie stick. If you move the parent node position, the **camera** will simply follow. If you rotate the parent node, the **camera** will swing around, but it will always face the parent position – it's a neat little trick. Selfie time! :]

Create another empty node named **follow_light**:

Zero out its position as well. You'll add a spot light to this node that always shines light on its subject. Set the node's rotation to (x:-25, y:-45, z:0). Spin the scene around and you'll notice the background source of light comes from that precise direction.

Add the following empty nodes and zero out their positions; they're simply placeholders for later:

• **pearls**: You'll add collectable pearls under this group.

• **section1**, **section2**, **section3**, **section4**: These groups will hold different sections of the level. This will also help you hide certain sections to simplify level editing.

Create a final empty node and name it **static_lights**:

Set its position to (x:-25, y:25, z:25); you'll use this node to group additional lights.

You're all organized and ready to carry on.

Adding lights

You're going to add some static lights to the scene; these are lights that don't move around. You'll also add a spot light to the scene which will move around, following the relic as it rolls through the maze. This spot light will also cast the shadows in your scene.

Add static lights

First you'll add the static lights to the scene. The purpose of these lights is to give the scene some basic lighting, break up the darkness a little and help those normal maps pop.

Drag and drop an omni and an ambient light into the scene and place them under the **static_lights** group node:

Select the omni light, then select its Node Inspector:

Name the light **omni** and zero out its position and angle; this will place the light right in the middle of its parent node.

Select the Attributes Inspector next:

Give the omni light a dark grey color, so that it's not too bright but still has a visible effect.

Select the ambient light next, then select its node inspector.

Zero out its position and angle information, which places it right on top of the **omni** light, inside the **static light** group node parent

Select its Attributes Inspector:

It might seem odd, but give the ambient light a dark grey color as well to lift those dark shadows up a bit.

The final result should resemble the following scene, if you zoom in a bit closer to the ball:

You should be able to see the normal map, and the dark side of the relic shouldn't be black, but softly shaded.

Now to add the light that will follow the relic as it rolls around the scene.

Add the follow light

Drag and drop a spot light into the scene, and place it under the **follow_light** group node:

```
▼ follow_light
      spot
```

Select the spot light and then select its Node Inspector:

Identity

Name spot

Transforms

Editing space Local

Position   – 0 +   – 0 +   – 10 +
              x   y   z

Euler   – 0 +   – -0 +   – 0 +
           x   y   z

Scale   – 1 +   – 1 +   – 1 +
           x   y   z

Name the light **spot** and set its position to (x:0, y:0, z:10). This light is a child of the **follow_light** group node, which is at (x:0, y:0, z:0) with a angle of (x:-25, y:-45, z:0); therefore the spot light will shine directly on the relic.

> **Note**: This is the selfie stick trick in action, making your life *so* much easier. To keep the light shining on the rolling relic, you simply need to make sure the position of the **follow_light** node matches that of the relic.

Now to add some light and shadow magic. Select the spot light, then select its Attributes Inspector:

First, set the color of the light to a nice bright golden yellow. This will breathe some warmth into the light and mimic the environmental sunlight shining on the relic.

For a hard-edged shadow, enable **Behavior** so that the light casts shadows. Set **Sample Radius** to 0 to get a crisp shadow. You can leave Near and Far Clipping as they are. Set **Sample Count** to 1 so that you sample the shadow at least once, and leave **Bias** at 1.

Your scene should now resemble the following:

Behold the glorious golden sun shining warmth onto the relic! :]

Building re-usable sets

Building small little re-usable sets will make your life easier. This way you don't have to manually repeat common patterns and structures, you simply re-use the set where you need it in the level.

In this section, you'll create a resting point for the relic. It will consist of a nice big 3x3 stone, with 4 pillars stacked on top of it.

Drag an empty **Scene Kit** scene file, from the **File Template** library into the root of your project. Name it **set_restpoint.scn**, then select the group as **art.scnassets** before you hit the **Create** button.

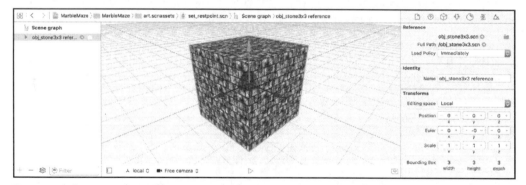

Drag and drop an **obj_stone3x3.scn** reference node into your new empty scene. Make sure to position it at (x: 0, y: 0, z:0).

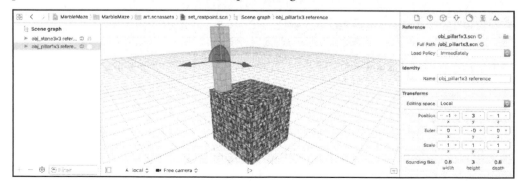

Drag and drop an **obj_pillar1x3.scn** reference node on top of the big stone. Set the position to (x: -1, y: 3, z: 1), so place it right in the corner.

With one pillar down, you still need to create 3 more. Use the ⌥⌘ (Option +Command) key combination to drag copies and place them precisely at the following locations:

- **Top-Left**. Positioned at (x: −1, y: 3, z: −1).
- **Top-Right**. Positioned at (x: 1, y: 3, z: −1).
- **Bottom-Right**. Positioned at (x: 1, y: 3, z: 1).

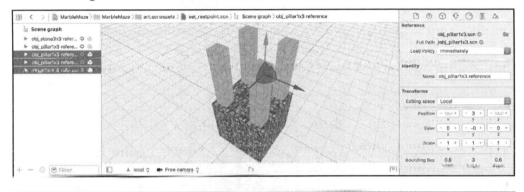

Note: Don't forget to delete that default camera node out of the reference scene before you save it.

Select your **game.scn**, then drag and drop that freshly built **set_restpoint.scn** below the relic. Make sure to position it at (x: 0, y: 2, z: 0)

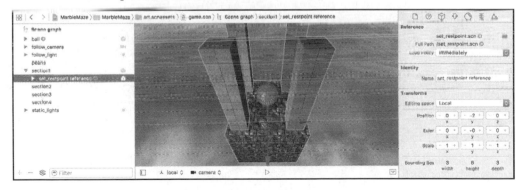

Finally, you can do a build and run, to admire those pretty shadows. :]

Behold the glorious golden sun with a soft cool shadow casted over the relic! :]

> **Note**: You can find a project containing all the work done up to this point under the **projects/final/MarbleMaze** folder.

Challenge

Surprise challenge! You didn't see that one coming, did you? :]

Now that you've mastered the skill of using reference nodes and building small scenes and sets, you'll need to build some more basic sets, which will be referenced in the main game scene.

Build the following sets for the game, making use of the following samples:

The **straight_bridge**:

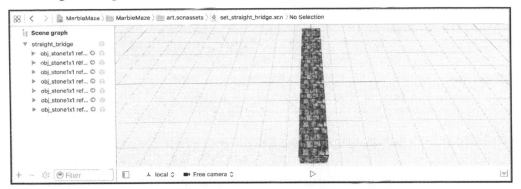

This set consists of seven small **stone1x1** blocks, all neatly packed next to each other.

The **zigzag_bridge**:

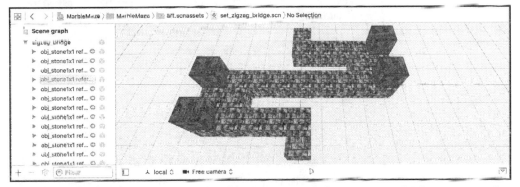

This set might be a bit trickier, but nothing's too tough for you now! :] It's constructed of **stone1x1** blocks and **crate1x1** blocks. It's 9 blocks wide and 7 blocks deep. Make sure to place those crates right on the corner edges.

> **Note:** Each set starts with a blank scene, then uses reference nodes to build up the set. Remember to remove all lights and cameras from these sets as they'll be referenced in your main game scene.

Once you've created all those little sets, see if you can build the first section of the main game scene.

Here's a sample of what the final result should look like:

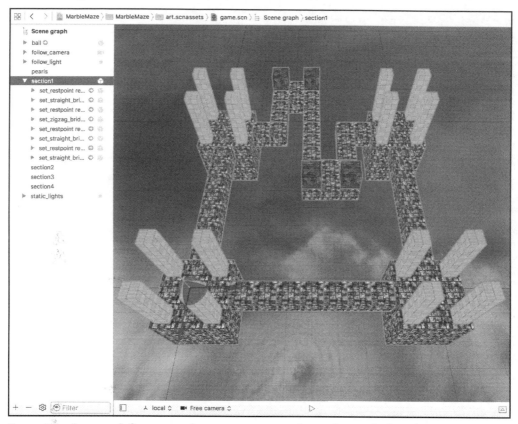

Start at the bottom left corner, place a **restpoint** right underneath the relic positioned at (x:0, y:0, z:0), then pull in the rest of the reference sets to complete the entire scene.

Make sure you place all the sets under the **section1** group node. This is a neat little trick you can apply when you start building large scenes: simply segment the set into sections, then use the **visible** flag to show or hide the set as required. This will definitely speed up the editing process.

> **Note**: Fear not, if this challenge pushed you out of your comfort zone, you can download the final project under the **projects/challenge/MarbleMaze** folder.

Finishing up

To see the stunning result first-hand on a device, build and run and pan the camera around the scene. If you prefer, you can just press the **play** button under the scene:

Did your jaw bone just dislodge itself? :] It's an absolutely stunning view.

Before you continue, see if you can spin the view around so that you have the sun light shining in your eyes, like so:

Lights placed at strategic locations in your scene, along with your environmental map, make for some impressive realism. You almost want to squint your eyes, even though your screen can't go any brighter than white. It's all just an illusion – thanks to those stunning silhouetted pillars caused by the shadows.

Where to go from here?

You've reached the end of this chapter; your game is in good shape. In this chapter, you covered the following concepts:

- **Lights**: Shadows needs lights, specifically a spot light or a directional light when dealing with Scene Kit.

- **Soft and hard shadows**: The shadow's Sample Radius and Sample Count settings have a definite effect on the hardness of the shadow edge.

The next chapter will make your game come alive and let your player take control of the relic, rolling it through your maze in the sky!

Chapter 14: Intermediate Collision Detection

Chris Language

In this chapter, you'll enable physics within your game and add collision detection. For the most part, the player will roll the ball around the maze, bumping into stone blocks and crates, while trying to keep the ball from falling off the maze. Although rolling around on a sky maze is pretty cool, it's still lacking that *fun* factor – something that will force the player to take on the maze as fast as possible.

If nothing pushed the player to roll through the maze, then the player could simply park the ball in a corner and take a nap until they felt like tackling the next part of the maze. That's just not acceptable! :]

Therefore, the ball will have to consume pearls of life in order to survive. You'll use the rings of light on the ball as a visual indicator of how much life the player has left; the brighter the rings of light shine, the more life that's left in the ball. The player's life reduces over time, which forces the player to scout for more pearls of life scattered all over the sky maze.

> **Note:** This chapter continues where the previous one left off; you can find the starter project for this chapter under the **projects/starter/MarbleMaze/** folder.

Getting started

Drag an empty Scene Kit file into your project:

Name it **obj_pearl.scn** and save it to the **art.scnassets** folder. Remember to delete the default camera node; you don't want extra lights and cameras in reference nodes.

Next, drag and drop a sphere node from the Object Library into your new scene:

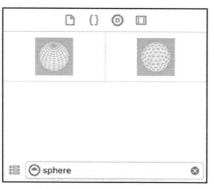

Use the Node Inspector to name the node **"pearl"** and zero out its position and angles:

Use the Attributes Inspector to set the radius to `0.2` and reduce the segment count down to 16:

Sphere	
Dimensions	
Radius	0.2
Segment count	16
Geodesic	geodesic

This shrinks the pearl down to a consumable size. :] There's going to be plenty of pearls in the game, so keeping the polygon count low is important.

Your next task is to make the pearl shiny. Use the Materials Inspector to set the diffuse color to black, with a white specular. Pearls are very reflective, so use **img_skybox.jpg** as a reflective map, but drop the intensity down to `0.75`:

Properties	
Diffuse	
Specular	
Normal	
Reflective	img_skybox.jpg
Intensity	0.75
Min filter	Linear
Mag filter	Linear
Mip filter	None
WrapS	Clamp
WrapT	Clamp
UV channel	0
Offset	0 0
Scale	1 1
Rotation	0

You'll end up with something that resembles this little golden nugget. Just look how shiny it is! :]

Adding game utilities

To keep you focused on collision detection, we've provided a bunch of game utils for you matters outside the focus of this chapter, like some math utility functions, Sprite Kit integration, and so on. All you need to do is add them to the project.

Drag and drop the **GameUtils** folder into your project from the **projects/resources/ GameUtils** folder:

Select **Finish** to complete the process.

Now you'll need to handle the collisions between the ball and the pearls of life. Before you dive into that, you need to understand how bit masks work. The next section covers just that.

Working with bit masks

Bits are those 1's and 0's computers use to represent numbers that looks like this: 00101011. A collection of 1's and 0's is known as a **binary** number. Each bit represents a specific numerical value and reads in reverse, from the lowest-significant bit to the highest-significant bit. If the bit is 1, it's considered ON, while 0 means it's OFF.

Below is crude example of an 8-bit binary value, counting up from zero to seven:

BIT	7	6	5	4	3	2	1	0	INTEGER
VALUE	128	64	32	16	8	4	2	1	VALUE
1.	0	0	0	0	0	0	0	1	0+0+0+0+0+0+0+1 = 1
2.	0	0	0	0	0	0	1	0	0+0+0+0+0+0+2+0 = 2
3.	0	0	0	0	0	0	1	1	0+0+0+0+0+0+2+1 = 3
4.	0	0	0	0	0	1	0	0	0+0+0+0+0+4+0+0 = 4
5.	0	0	0	0	0	1	0	1	0+0+0+0+0+4+0+1 = 5
6.	0	0	0	0	0	1	1	0	0+0+0+0+0+4+2+0 = 6
7.	0	0	0	0	0	1	1	1	0+0+0+0+0+4+2+1 = 7

The first row represents the bits 7 to 0 and counts in reverse starting on the right. The next row shows the value each bit represents. The last column adds all the represented values together of the bits that are ON. The binary value 01010101, where bits 0, 2, 4 and 6 are all ON and the rest are all OFF, represents the following calculation: 64 + 16 + 4 + 1 = 85. So 01010101 is the binary representation of 85. Easy!

Bit masks are basically binary numbers in disguise. Bit masking is a clever way of giving all objects in a physics simulation a low-level identity. You can then perform bitwise operations on your objects to quickly filter out which objects can collide with each other. This technique reduces the amount of objects involved when performing collision detection, hence speeding up the collision checking process by quite a bit.

Category masks

The category mask gives an object a unique ID for collision detection. Besides giving an object a unique ID, you can also group objects together.

Consider *Pac-Man* as an example. There are lots of things Pac-Man can collide with; some good, and some bad. So you could create two groups, one for good things to collide with, and one for bad things – like ghosts!

Here's a few category bit mask examples you might see in a typical *Pac-Man* game:

BIT	7	6	5	4	3	2	1	0	INTEGER
VALUE	128	64	32	16	8	4	2	1	VALUE
Good	0	1	0	0	0	0	0	0	0 + 1 + 0 + 0 + 0 + 0 + 0 + 0 = 64
Bad	1	0	0	0	0	0	0	0	1 + 0 + 0 + 0 + 0 + 0 + 0 + 0 = 128
Blinky	1	0	0	0	0	0	0	1	1 + 0 + 0 + 0 + 0 + 0 + 0 + 1 = 129
Pinky	1	0	0	0	0	0	1	0	1 + 0 + 0 + 0 + 0 + 0 + 2 + 0 = 130
Inky	1	0	0	0	0	1	0	0	1 + 0 + 0 + 0 + 0 + 4 + 0 + 0 = 132
Clyde	1	0	0	0	1	0	0	0	1 + 0 + 0 + 0 + 8 + 0 + 0 + 0 = 136
Blue	0	1	0	0	0	0	0	1	0 + 1 + 0 + 0 + 0 + 0 + 0 + 1 = 65

Here, the 8th bit is set to 1 to indicate membership in the **Bad** group, and since all the ghosts (Blinky, Pinky, Inky and Clyde) have the 8th bit set, they can be tested for "Badness" in a bitwise check.

For example, you could have a collision test to determine what exactly should happen to Pac-Man when he collides with an object, like the following:

```
// 1
let good = 64
let bad = 128
let blinky = 129
let pinky = 130
let inky = 132
let clyde = 136
let Blue = 65

func testCollision(contactNode:Int) {
  // 2
  if contactNode & bad == bad {
    // Bad things happens to Pacman
  } else if contactNode & good == good {
    // Good things happens to Pacman
  }
}
```

Taking a closer look:

1. This defines all the category masks as depicted in the table above.

2. This uses the bitwise & operator against the contactNode to filter out all the other bits. If the result matches **bad**, it means that the **bad** bit was set, which means **contactNode** is a bad guy, and Pac-Man has to die. :[Since the contactNode for each of the ghosts in *Pac-Man* has the 8th bit set, it will always match the **bad** category mask in a bitwise & test.

Defining category masks

Marble Maze is a bit simpler than *Pac-Man*; it will use the following set of category masks:

CATEGORY MASK									
BIT	7	6	5	4	3	2	1	0	OBJECT
VALUE	128	64	32	16	8	4	2	1	VALUE
AIR	0	0	0	0	0	0	0	0	0
BALL	0	0	0	0	0	0	0	1	1
STONE	0	0	0	0	0	0	1	0	2
PILLAR	0	0	0	0	0	1	0	0	4
CRATE	0	0	0	0	1	0	0	0	8
PEARL	0	0	0	1	0	0	0	0	16

All the objects have been defined with their own unique ID, so there's no need to worry about groups in this case. Your next task is to define these category masks somewhere.

Open **GameViewController.swift** and add the following collision categories to the top of the class:

```
let CollisionCategoryBall = 1
let CollisionCategoryStone = 2
let CollisionCategoryPillar = 4
let CollisionCategoryCrate = 8
let CollisionCategoryPearl = 16
```

Collision masks

You use collision masks to tell the physics engine that some objects are allowed to collide with each other; the physics engine will then prevent these objects from simply passing through each other and trigger an effect within the dynamics of the physics engine. To define a collision mask, you'll need to add together all the category masks of objects that collide with your object.

For Marble Maze, you want the ball to collide with everything *except* for the pearls – you don't want the ball to push the pearls out of the way! Conversely, you'll also need to set everything, except for the pearls, to collide with the ball.

You can use the following collision mask table to keep track of things:

COLLISION MASK									
BIT	7	6	5	4	3	2	1	0	MASK
VALUE	128	64	32	16	8	4	2	1	VALUE
AIR	0	0	0	0	0	0	0	0	0
BALL	0	0	0	0	1	1	1	0	14
STONE	0	0	0	0	0	0	0	1	1
PILLAR	0	0	0	0	0	0	0	1	1
CRATE	0	0	0	0	0	0	0	1	1
PEARL	0	0	0	0	0	0	0	1	1

Refer back to the category masks; you'll see the Stone, Pillar, Crate and Pearl collision masks are set to 1, which means they'll collide with the ball. To work out what the ball collision mask should be, you'll have to add all the other categories together to form the following calculation:

CollisionMask = Stone + Pillar + Crate = 2 + 4 + 8 = 14

Aha – that's why the ball collision mask is set to **14**.

Contact masks

Contact masks tell the physics engine which objects will generate contact events that you'll respond to. These won't automatically have any effect on the physics engine dynamics; they're triggers to which you'll respond programatically. You set up contact masks in exactly the same as you do collision masks.

For Marble Maze, you want the pearl to generate a contact event, but you also want the pillars and crates to generate an event so you can play a "bump" sound when the ball hits them.

You can use the following contact mask table for that:

CONTACT MASK									
BIT	**7**	**6**	**5**	**4**	**3**	**2**	**1**	**0**	**MASK**
VALUE	128	64	32	16	8	4	2	1	**VALUE**
AIR	0	0	0	0	0	0	0	0	0
BALL	0	0	0	1	1	1	0	0	28
STONE	0	0	0	0	0	0	0	0	0
PILLAR	0	0	0	0	0	0	0	0	0
CRATE	0	0	0	0	0	0	0	0	0
PEARL	0	0	0	0	0	0	0	0	0

You're only interested in contact between the ball and pearls, pillars and crates. This gives you the following calculation:

```
ContactMask = Pearl + Pillar + Crate = 16 + 8 + 4 = 28
```

Now you can configure the contact mask for the ball in code.

Still in **GameViewController.swift**, add the following property to the top of the class:

```
var ballNode:SCNNode!
```

Now add the following code to setupNodes():

```
ballNode = scnScene.rootNode.childNodeWithName("ball",
recursively: true)!
ballNode.physicsBody?.contactTestBitMask =
CollisionCategoryPillar | CollisionCategoryCrate |
CollisionCategoryPearl
```

The first line attaches ballNode to the actual **ball** node in the scene. The next line sets up the actual contactTestBitMask by performing a bitwise OR on all category masks.

> **Note:** You can set the category mask and collision mask in the Scene Editor, but at the time of writing this chapter you can only set the contactTestBitMask in code, hence why you are doing it here. Another benefit of setting it in code is it's easier to work with OR'ing constant values than having to remember what 28 represents in binary!

Now that you've figured out all the bit mask properties for all the game objects, you can enable the physics properties of those objects.

Enabling physics

The ball will be a *dynamic* physics body; this means the physics engine will take full control over the movement of the ball and move it based on its physics properties.

Select the **obj_ball.scn** scene under the **art.scnassets** folder, then select the **ball** node. Use the Physics Inspector to set the **Physics Body** type to **Dynamic**:

Ensure that **Gravity** is **enabled**; otherwise, the ball would float in space:

Now you can set up the bit masks. Set the **Category mask** to 1 and the **Collision mask** to 14:

You're going to leave the **Shape** at **Default shape**, and **Type** at **Convex**:

Since this is a spherical object, Scene Kit sets it up as a perfect sphere instead of generating a mesh to represent the shape of the object.

Save the scene changes before you move on.

Return to your main game scene – **game.scn** under **art.scnassets**. Press the **play** button for the scene, and...the ball falls through the stone floor! Don't worry – this is because you haven't set up any of the other physics bodies yet.

Enable static physics objects

The rest of the objects in the game will be *static* objects, which means they can't be moved.

You'll need to repeat the following steps for all of these objects:

- obj_stone1x1.scn
- obj_stone3x3.scn
- obj_pillar1x3.scn
- obj_crate1x1.scn
- obj_pearl.scn

First, select the scene under the **art.scnassets** folder, then make sure the object node itself is selected. Use the Physics Inspector of each object to set their respective **Physics Type** to **Static**:

Now for the bit masks. Set the **obj_stone1x1.scn Category mask** to 2, and the **Collision mask** to 1:

Configure the rest of the objects as follows:

- **obj_stone3x3.scn**: **Category mask** to 2, and **Collision mask** to 1.
- **obj_pillar1x3.scn**: **Category mask** to 4, and **Collision mask** to 1.
- **obj_crate1x1.scn**: **Category mask** to 8, and **Collision mask** to 1.
- **obj_pearl.scn**: **Category mask** to 16, and **Collision mask** to –1.

> **Note:** The pearl is special, and will not cause an actual collision with the ball. That's why it's set to –1.

You're almost done – the only thing left is to configure the physics shapes. The pearl uses a Physics shape of **Default shape**, with a Type of **Convex**:

Since the pearl is a sphere, Scene Kit will generate the physics shape as a perfect sphere.

The rest of the objects should be configured as follows, with **Default shape** and **Bounding Box**:

Physics shape	
Shape	Default shape ⬦
Type	Bounding Box ⬦

This creates a perfect box around the edges of the object. Since all these bodies are square by nature, the bounding box will fit them perfectly.

> **Note**: The sphere is the most efficient physics shape you can use. The second-most efficient? The bounding box type.

Adding collision detection code

To complete the collision detection, you need to add the code that will handle the actual collision events.

Add the following code to the bottom of **GameViewController.swift**:

```
extension GameViewController : SCNPhysicsContactDelegate {
  func physicsWorld(world: SCNPhysicsWorld, didBeginContact
contact: SCNPhysicsContact) {
    // 1
    var contactNode:SCNNode!
    if contact.nodeA.name == "ball" {
      contactNode = contact.nodeB
    } else {
      contactNode = contact.nodeA
    }

    // 2
    if contactNode.physicsBody?.categoryBitMask ==
CollisionCategoryPearl {
      contactNode.hidden = true

contactNode.runAction(SCNAction.waitForDurationThenRunBlock(30)
{ (node:SCNNode!) -> Void in
      node.hidden = false
      })
    }

    // 3
    if contactNode.physicsBody?.categoryBitMask ==
CollisionCategoryPillar ||
contactNode.physicsBody?.categoryBitMask ==
```

```
CollisionCategoryCrate {
      }
   }
}
```

This extends the `GameViewController` class with the `SCNPhysicsContactDelegate` protocol. Here's what goes on inside:

1. This is the nifty little trick you learned previously that lets you quickly determine the actual contact node. The `if` block sets `contactNode` to the node that collided with the ball.

2. This section tests to see if the `categoryBitMask` of `contactNode` matches that of `CollisionCategoryPearl`. If so, make the pearl invisible to make it look like the ball "consumed" the pearl. You'll spawn the pearl again after 30 seconds; this is just long enough for the ball to die if the player decides to stick around and wait for the pearl to re-spawn.

3. This section checks whether the ball bounced off of a pillar or off of a crate. This would make a great place to play a "bump" sound later on.

Your final step for this chapter is to ensure that the scene's physics world contact delegate knows that the `GameViewController` class is now responsible for handling these contact events.

Add the following to the bottom of `setupScene()`:

```
scnScene.physicsWorld.contactDelegate = self
```

Make the ball fall from the sky

There's one little thing you need to change, just to add some drama to your game.

Position the ball high up in the air, so that when the game starts, the ball will fall from the sky.

Select the **obj_ball.scn** scene, then adjust the set the y position to 10.

Build and run your game to make sure that everything is still well:

As the game starts up, you'll see the ball fall from above and come to rest on the stone platform below. Hey – it's not falling through the floor any more! Apart from that though, everything still looks pretty much the same as before.

Add a pearl of life

Now to add something special to test out the collisions.

Select the game scene, then drag and drop a **obj_pearl.scn** reference node into the scene. Position it at (x: 0, y: 0, z: 0). Also make sure to move the pearl under the **pearls** group node.

Make sure everything is saved, then do another build and run:

If you take a closer look, you should see the great relic falling from the sky, then gobbles up the pearl. Awesome! :]

> **Note:** You can find the project up to this point under the **projects/final/ MarbleMaze/** folder.

Challenge

Time for another fun little challenge; see if you can scatter a few more pearls for the player all over the level. You can use the following image as a reference:

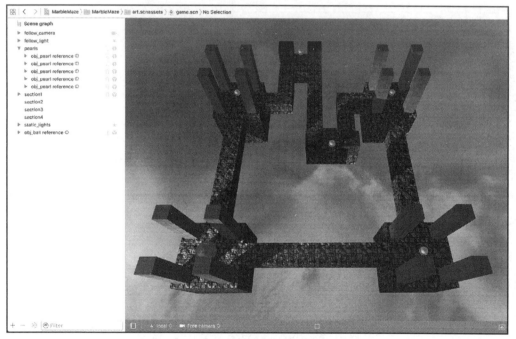

Place a pearl ontop of all the rest points, and between all the crates. Make sure to place the pearls on a y position of **0** – the same plane as the relic. Also make sure you move all the pearls to the **pearls** group node to keep things nice and organized.

> **Note:** You can find the solution for this challenge under the **projects/challenge/ MarbleMaze/** folder.

Where to go from here?

You've covered some complex topics in this chapter. To recap:

- **Collectables**: You've added a new element to your game to make it more interesting – the pearl of life. Without it, the ball would simply die a pathetic, lonely death. This also gives the player purpose to navigate the sky maze in search of more pearls.

- **Bit Masks**: You now know all about bit masks; what they look like, how they operate, and most importantly, how to use them in Scene Kit.

- **Category masks**: You've learned that this mask simply gives the object an ID and that you could employ complex grouping strategies should you need to.

- **Collision masks**: You've learned that this mask defines a list of objects that can collide with your object, and physically block them from passing through each other.

- **Contact masks**: You've learned that this mask defines a list of objects that will trigger contact events when they make contact with your object.

In the following and final chapter, you'll add the ability to move the ball. What are you waiting for? It's time to get the ball rolling! :]

Chapter 15: Motion Control

Chris Language

Up to this point, you've focused mostly on the visual aspects of your game – and a fine looking game it is! This chapter will make a detour from the aesthetics and take you through the code of the game mechanics.

First, you'll add a simple control mechanism to let the player move the ball by tilting the device. You'll then add some logic to the camera and lights to follow the ball wherever it wanders - even if it falls into the abyss! :] Finally, you'll add some basic state management, a HUD for the score, and finally finish it off with some awesome sound effects.

So what are you waiting for? Time to get cracking! :|

Getting started

To start, either load the project where you left it off last time, or laod the starter project under the **projects/starter/MarbleMaze** folder.

In the previous chapter, you added the **GameUtils** folder from the project resources. Now you need to declare a few variables so you can use of those utilities.

Add the following properties to the top of the `GameViewController` class:

```
var game = GameHelper.sharedInstance
var motion = CoreMotionHelper()
var motionForce = SCNVector3(x:0 , y:0, z:0)
```

Here's what these helpers do in detail:

- **game**: A reference to the shared instance of the `GameHelper` class. It provides some simple game state management and a HUD for your game, along with some convenience functions to load and play sound effects.

- **motion**: This creates an instance of the `CoreMotionHelper` class. It gives you a simple way to poll the Core Motion engine for motion data at set intervals.

- **motionForce**: This property will contain a motion vector; you'll use this later as a force vector to put the ball into motion.

Adding sound effects

There's a set of awesome sound effects under the **resources** folder that will bring the game to life. Drag and drop the **Sounds** folder into your project from the **projects/resources** folder:

Select **Finish** to complete the import.

Next add the following lines to `setupSounds()`:

```
game.loadSound("GameOver", fileNamed: "GameOver.wav")
game.loadSound("Powerup", fileNamed: "Powerup.wav")
game.loadSound("Reset", fileNamed: "Reset.wav")
game.loadSound("Bump", fileNamed: "Bump.wav")
```

This code is fairly straightforward: it loads the sound files into memory. You'll trigger these sound effects later in this chapter.

Attaching properties to nodes

In this section, you're going to make the camera and lights follow the ball wherever it rolls; this is a common technique in 3rd-person games where the camera trails behind the hero as she runs around the level.

But first, you'll need to attach local properties to the nodes in your game scene.

Attaching to the camera node

Your first task is to make the camera focus continuously on the ball. The camera position won't change, but the camera rotation instead will adjust to follow the ball. To demonstrate this to yourself, hold your head still and roll your eyes around looking at random objects in the room. Are you rolling your eyes at me?! :]

Add the following property to the top of `GameViewController` class:

```
var cameraNode:SCNNode!
```

This will hold your cameraNode once you've attached to it in the game scene.

Next add the following lines to the bottom of `setupNodes()` after the point where you've attached to the `ballNode`:

```
// 1
cameraNode = scnScene.rootNode.childNodeWithName("camera",
recursively: true)!
// 2
let constraint = SCNLookAtConstraint(target: ballNode)
cameraNode.constraints = [constraint]
```

Here's what's going on above:

1. Here you attach **cameraNode** to the actual **camera** in the game scene.

2. This sets up a `SCNLookAtConstraint` to look at the `ballNode` and adds the

constraint to the actual camera's constraints.

Gimbal locking

When the camera has `SCNLookAtConstraint` applied, Scene Kit will do whatever it takes to rotate the camera towards the ball as it rolls around. This "whatever it takes" approach can produce unwanted rotations where the camera might tilt to the left or right.

This wouldn't be a problem if you were controlling a light, but because you're controlling a camera this behavior could cause some odd viewing angles for the player. Instead, you want the camera to stay horizontal at all times.

Scene Kit has you covered, saving you from hours of research and a serious math-related headache. :] Enabling the `gimbalLockEnabled` property on the actual constraint tells Scene Kit to keep the camera aligned horizontally as it follows its target.

Add the following line to the bottom of `setupNodes()`:

```
constraint.gimbalLockEnabled = true
```

This will enable gimbal lock for your camera constraint – and also prevent your viewer from getting motion sick. :]

Attaching to the camera and light follow nodes

Add the following property to the `GameViewController` class:

```
var cameraFollowNode:SCNNode!
var lightFollowNode:SCNNode!
```

This will hold the `cameraFollowNode` and `lightFollowNode` once attached.

Next, add the following to the bottom of `setupNodes()`:

```
// 1
cameraFollowNode =
scnScene.rootNode.childNodeWithName("follow_camera",
recursively: true)!
// 2
cameraNode.addChildNode(game.hudNode)
// 3
lightFollowNode =
scnScene.rootNode.childNodeWithName("follow_light", recursively:
true)!
```

Taking a closer look at the code segment:

1. This attaches `followCameraNode` to the **follow_camera** node in the game scene.

2. This adds the HUD to the camera as a child node so that it remains in view of the camera no matter what direciton it faces.

3. This attaches `followLightNode` to the **follow_light** node in the game scene.

Game state management

Now that you've attached to all the important nodes in the game scene, you need to sort out some basic game states.

You'll be using three states to manage gameplay:

- **WaitForTap**: This is the moment in-between games when the player has not yet started controlling the ball. In this state, you'll let the camera spin around the ball and display a message indicating the game is waiting for input.

- **Playing**: This state triggers when the user taps the screen to start the game. The player can control the ball in this state.

- **GameOver**: This state triggers when the player fails to collect another pearl of life in time or drops into the abyss. This state will automatically move to the **WaitForTap** state after a few seconds.

Next for a few useful functions to help you manage these states. Add the following to the `GameViewController` class:

```
// 1
func playGame() {
  game.state = GameStateType.Playing
  cameraFollowNode.eulerAngles.y = 0
  cameraFollowNode.position = SCNVector3Zero
}
// 2
func resetGame() {
  game.state = GameStateType.TapToPlay
  game.playSound(ballNode, name: "Reset")
  ballNode.physicsBody!.velocity = SCNVector3Zero
  ballNode.position = SCNVector3(x:0, y:10, z:0)
  cameraFollowNode.position = ballNode.position
  lightFollowNode.position = ballNode.position
  scnView.playing = true
  game.reset()
}
// 3
func testForGameOver() {
```

```
    if ballNode.presentationNode.position.y < -5 {
      game.state = GameStateType.GameOver
      game.playSound(ballNode, name: "GameOver")
      ballNode.runAction(SCNAction.waitForDurationThenRunBlock(5)
{ (node:SCNNode!) -> Void in
        self.resetGame()
      })
    }
  }
```

Here's the purpose of each function:

1. **playGame()**: A call to this function switches the game into the .Playing state, which starts the game. It also performs some basic cleanup and resets the **cameraFollow** node's angle and position.

2. **resetGame()**: A call to this function puts the game into the .WaitForTap state. It also plays a "Reset" sound effect, then does some basic cleanup by resetting the ball's position and velocity. It also resets the cameraFollowNode and lightFollowNode positions. Note that the ballNode position is set to a high y-value; this creates the effect of the ball dropping out of thin air into the sky maze.

3. **testForGameOver()**: A call to this function checks if the ball's y-position has dropped lower than -5 units. If so, the ball has fallen off the edge into the abyss. Whoops! :] It then switches to the .GameOver state and plays the "GameOver" sound effect. After five seconds, it automatically triggers a call to resetGame(), placing the game back into the .WaitForTap state.

> **Note**: During the .WaitForTap state, there are no active animations or physics updates, so the renderer stops updating every frame. Later on in this chapter, you will be spinning the camera around the ball during this game state; therefore, the renderer will continue to update every frame. This is why resetGame() sets the view's playing property to true: this forces the renderer to update every frame.

With the basic game state functions in place, you need to set the game's initial state by calling resetGame(). Add the following function call to the bottom of viewDidLoad():

```
  resetGame()
```

Once everything has been set up, this will set the game into the initial state of .WaitForTap.

To start the game, the player simply has to tap on the display. Add the following lines of code to the GameViewController class:

```
override func touchesBegan(touches: Set<UITouch>, withEvent
event: UIEvent?) {
  if game.state == GameStateType.TapToPlay {
    playGame()
  }
}
```

This adds a `touchesBegan()` event handler to the `GameViewController` class; if the game is in the `.TapToPlay` state, this will start the game by calling `playGame()`.

Add motion control

Now that you've attached to all the important nodes and have the game states ready, you can set the ball rolling, so to speak! Can you hear the crowd chanting? "Move That Ball! Move That Ball!"" :]

First, add the following to the `GameViewController` class.

```
func updateMotionControl() {
  // 1
  if game.state == GameStateType.Playing {
    motion.getAccelerometerData(0.1) { (x,y,z) in
      self.motionForce = SCNVector3(x: Float(x) * 0.05, y:0, z:
Float(y+0.8) * -0.05)
    }
    // 2
    ballNode.physicsBody!.velocity += motionForce
  }
}
```

Taking a closer look:

1. First, the function updates the `motionForce` vector with the current motion data.

2. Then it adds the `motionForce` vector to the ball's **velocity**.

There's thing left to do: call `updateMotionControl()` from the `SCNSceneRenderDelegate`. Add the following call to `renderer(_, updateAtTime)`:

```
updateMotionControl()
```

This will perform a motion update call 60 times a second, although the actual motion sensor is polled at a much lower pace to preserve energy.

> **Note**: To play, hold the device in a comfortable position, tilted backwards at a 45° angle, just as you would normally look at your phone.

Build and run the game on your device:

The ball spawns out of mid-air and drops down onto the sky maze. This is resetGame() at work. You'll also hear a loud thundering sound – hopefully you didn't drop your phone when it went off? :]

Touching the display starts the game. Lo and behold, you can control the ball simply by tilting the device left, right, forward and back. Smooth! :]

Try to collect a pearl – careful, don't fall! :]

Adding the health indicator

Recall that the glowing effect you added to the ball was to serve as a health indicator; the ball's health will diminish over time until the emission intensity runs out at `0.0`. If the player collects pearls of life along the way, the health – and emission intensity – will be restored to `1.0`.

You'll need a function to replenish the health bar. To do that, add the following to the `GameViewController` class:

```
func replenishLife() {
  // 1
  let material = ballNode.geometry!.firstMaterial!
  // 2
  SCNTransaction.begin()
  SCNTransaction.setAnimationDuration(1.0)
  // 3
  material.emission.intensity = 1.0
  // 4
  SCNTransaction.commit()
  // 5
  game.score += 1
  game.playSound(ballNode, name: "Powerup")
}
```

Taking a closer look at exactly what the above code does:

1. To access the emission map, you need to get the first and only material for the `ballNode`.

2. This starts a Scene Kit animation transaction sequence by specifying **SCNTransaction.begin()**. At this point, you can set target values for all the animatable Scene Kit properties you want to animate; in this case, the emission intensity. `setAnimationDuration(1.0)` sets the duration of the animation sequence.

3. Here you set the material's emission intensity to `1.0`. This doesn't set the actual value, but sets the value you *want* it to be once the animation completes.

4. This commits the animation transaction. Once committed, Scene Kit will start animating the emission value from its current value to the requested value of `1.0`.

5. The rest of the code increases the score and plays a nice "Powerup" sound effect.

The first spot where you'll need to replenish the health is when you enter the `.Playing` state. Add the following line to the end of `playGame()`:

```
replenishLife()
```

Build and run, and now you'll now hear a cool sound effect and will notice that the indicator on the ball now starts nice and bright:

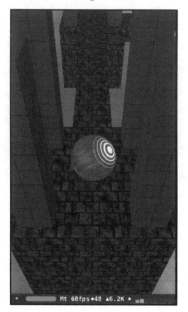

Diminishing life

You have a function that will replenish life, but what about the reverse? Health diminishes over time, so you'll need a function to call for every frame update.

Add the following to the `GameViewController` class:

```
func diminishLife() {
  // 1
  let material = ballNode.geometry!.firstMaterial!
  // 2
  if material.emission.intensity > 0 {
    material.emission.intensity -= 0.001
  } else {
    resetGame()
  }
}
```

Taking each numbered comment in turn:

1. Again, you're accessing the emission map of the ball's first and only material.

2. If the emission intensity is still above `0`, slowly decrease its value by `0.001` units. Once the emission intensity drops below `0`, life has run out for the ball so you trigger the `resetGame()` function.

You'll add a call to `diminishLife()` later in this chapter when you look at checking for the `.GameOver` state.

Other than that, there's still a few obvious problems that needs to be addressed:

• The camera is simply tracking the ball, not following it as you intended.

• The light isn't following the ball.

• There's no HUD, leaving the player wondering what the heck is going on.

• If the ball drops into the abyss, the game gets stuck and you have to restart it in order to play again.

You're so close – time to fix these issues and give your game that final polish!

Updating the camera and lights

`cameraFollowNode` is a special node that acts as a selfie stick for the camera node. But just like a real selfie stick, something needs to "hold" the other end of the stick.

You can't just make the **cameraFollow** node a child node of the ball, because the camera would spin like crazy as the ball rolls around! (Talk about game-induced motion sickness!) Instead, you created the **followCamera** node in the **rootNode**, so you can simply place it at the same position as the ball. Therefore, you need to update the `cameraFollow` position to match that of the ball as it rolls around.

Add the following function to the `GameViewController` class:

```
func updateCameraAndLights() {
  // 1
  let lerpX = (ballNode.presentationNode.position.x -
cameraFollowNode.position.x) * 0.01
  let lerpY = (ballNode.presentationNode.position.y -
cameraFollowNode.position.y) * 0.01
  let lerpZ = (ballNode.presentationNode.position.z -
cameraFollowNode.position.z) * 0.01
  cameraFollowNode.position.x += lerpX
  cameraFollowNode.position.y += lerpY
  cameraFollowNode.position.z += lerpZ
  // 2
```

```
    lightFollowNode.position = cameraFollowNode.position
    // 3
    if game.state == GameStateType.TapToPlay {
        cameraFollowNode.eulerAngles.y += 0.005
    }
}
```

Taking the above function step-by-step:

1. This is a cool set of calculations; instead of simply setting the `cameraFollowNode`
    position to that of `ballNode`, you calcualate a linearly-interpolated position to
    slowly move the camera in the direction of ball. This creates a spectacular lazy camera
    effect.

2. This sets **lightFollowNode** to the exact position as the camera so that whatever is in
    front of the camera is well lit.

3. Finally, this simply rotates the camera on its y-axis if the game is in a `.TapToPlay`
    state. This shows off the cool 3D graphics during the short intermission between
    games.

To call this function, add the following to the bottom of `renderer(_, updateAtTime)`:

```
    updateCameraAndLights()
```

This ensures that you update the camera and lights with every single frame.

Build and run your game again to see the effect of your changes:

The ball drops out of the sky into the maze and the camera starts spinning around. This is what the camera will do while the game is in a .WaitForTap state. Cool! :]

Tap on the display to start the game:

Hey! Now you can control the ball properly, and the camera and light follows it as it rolls around the maze. Wow – that was even easier than you thought?

Updating the HUD

Time to give the player something to tell them what the heck is going on! The heads-up display is sufficient for this.

Add the following function to GameViewController class:

```
func updateHUD() {
  switch game.state {
  case .Playing:
    game.updateHUD()
  case .GameOver:
    game.updateHUD("-GAME OVER-")
  case .TapToPlay:
    game.updateHUD("-TAP TO PLAY-")
  }
}
```

The HUD updates according to the current game state. When the game is in the .Playing state, the HUD will display the current score. When in the .GameOver state, it will display "-GAME OVER-"; finally, when the game is in the .TapToPlay state you'll show "-TAP TO PLAY-".

To make sure you update the HUD accordingly, add the following call to the bottom of renderer():

```
updateHUD()
```

This ensures that the HUD updates with every frame.

Build and run your game; you'll notice the HUD appears and gives the player a little more information than before:

Adding the finishing touches

Marble Maze is *so* close to being done; you just need to add a few final touches.

Testing for the game-over condition

At the moment, the ball is immortal – unless it takes a nose-dive into the abyss, at which point the game gets stuck as the camera continues to track the ball's descent.

To fix that, add the following code to the bottom of renderer():

```
if game.state == GameStateType.Playing {
  testForGameOver()
  diminishLife()
}
```

The game will only test for the game over condition while in the .Playing state; you also make a call to diminishLife() make the ball's health deteriorate.

Build and run your game; you should be able to transition the game through all available game states without issue. The ball is no longer immortal, and should die after a few seconds. Hm. That's not much fun.

Looks like it's time to add a mechanism to replenish your health!

Replenishing life

At the moment, collecting a pearl of life makes the pearl disappear, but your score doesn't increase, nor does the ball's health. To fix that, simply add a call to replenishLife() in physicsWorld(_, didBeginContact), inside the block that handles contact with pearls:

```
replenishLife()
```

Build and run your game; when you collect a pearl, the ball's health is replenished and your score increases by one. Excellent! :]

Adding bump noises

When the ball bumps against the pillars and crates, it would nice to give the player some sort of "bump" noise.

To do that, add the following bit of code to physicsWorld(_, didBeginContact), inside the block that handles contact with pillars and crates:

```
game.playSound(ballNode, name: "Bump")
```

Build and run your game, bonk that ball into a pillar or crate and you'll hear something go bump in the night! :]

Removing debug information

You can now remove the debug information, since you're done building your game. Find the following two lines of code inside setupScene() and comment them out like so:

```
//scnView.allowsCameraControl = true
//scnView.showsStatistics = true
```

This will remove the bottom debug information bar from your game and will also remove the ability to rotate the camera freely.

Congratulations! You've completed Marble Maze; build and run and enjoy the fruits of your labor. Just don't get too close to the edge! :]

Where to go from here?

A very famous astronaut once said: "One small step for (a) man, one giant leap for mankind!". Well you just took a massive leap into a bright future of 3D game development with Scene Kit. Well done! :]

Here's a recap of what you covered in this chapter:

- **3D Motion Control**: You've learned how to add basic motion control to your game by using the motion data as a force vector added to the ball velocity.

- **Gimbal locking**: You had a quick introduction to gimbal locking, and how to overcome the issue of camera rotation by enabling a simple property.

- **Animating properties**: You now know how to use SCNTransaction to animate properties.

- **Lerping Camera**: You've learned how to do a basic linear interpolation calculation to create a lazy camera effect, which adds a professional feel to the game.

Here are some other ideas you can add to make the game even better:

- **More game elements**: Think about adding bad guys that patrol certain sections of the maze. Maybe add some icy blocks that reduce friction and make the ball slip and slide?

- **More sets and levels**: You can let your imagination go wild here and create some weird and twisted sets, making the game more challenging for the player as they complete each level.

- **More juice**: More sound effects! Camera shaking! Particle effects! What else can you think to add to make the game exciting (and slightly unpredictable) for your player?

Okay, now go and play with your game some more – you know you want to! :]

> **Note**: As always, you can find the final project under the **projects/final/ MarbleMaze** folder.

Section IV: Advanced Scene Kit

"The Scene Kit Force is quite strong within you, young apprentice. (Read in a deep, heavy, asthmatic breathing voice. :])

In this section, you'll learn few more advanced techniques, as well as apply all the skills you've learned up to this point, to creating an awesome little voxel style game. By the end of this section you'll know enough to take on the big *Hipster Whales* out there with your very own game: Mr. Pig.

This is a *Crossy Road* style game with stunning voxel graphics, a catchy tune and some cool sound effects.

The premise: Mr. Pig is out and about scouting for lost coins in a nearby park while waiting for his late afternoon tea to heat up on the stove. Unfortunately, some big bad wolf decided to build a massive mall nearby, resulting in a very busy highway straight through his lovely park.

Mr. Pig better watch his step, or he'll end up as pulled pork in the road. :] Our hero can carry quite a few coins with him, but to score, he has to deposit them at his little house.

So what are you waiting for? Get *crackling*! :]

Chapter 16: Transitions

Chapter 17: Advanced Reference Nodes

Chapter 18: Actions

Chapter 19: Advanced Collision Detection

Chapter 20: Audio

Chapter 16: Transitions

Chris Language

In this chapter you'll start off by creating your game project, but in a slightly different way from what you've done in previous sections. Specifically, rather than using the Game template, you'll use the single view application template.

You'll also create the first two main scenes for Mr. Pig; one that will be your main game scene, and one to be your splash scene. Later, you'll also cover how to transition from one scene to the other.

Thankfully, you no longer have to deal with primitive shapes and geometry. This game will use graphics made in the extremely popular voxel style, similar to those more recently used in titles like *Crossy Road, Pacman 256* and *Shooty Skies*.

A highly skilled team of graphic artists sweated nights and days away to produce a small set of shiny voxel art just for your game. So, without further ado, please meet the cast of your next game:

From left to right:

• **Trees**: These three little tree types will be used to fill the charming park with lush vegetation. They'll also act as obstacles, so Mr. Pig will have to think on his hooves to move past them.

• **House**: What a pretty little house! This is Mr. Pig's residence, and is also the place where he stores all his found treasures.

• **Mr. Pig**: Meet the hero of your game – Pig, Mr. Pig that is. He's always on a mission to hunt for lost treasures in the nearby park. For a swine, he's rather nimble – you'll build in swiping gestures to make him jump around.

• **Vehicles**: These relentless gas guzzlers are known as Mini's, SUV's and School buses, and they couldn't care less about little pigs that cross the road. They've got places to go and certainly won't stop for our hero.

> **Note**: The voxel graphics were created with a very popular voxel authoring tool known as *MagicaVoxel*. You can download this awesome tool from voxel.codeplex.com for free and play around for yourself!

Working with your game project

> **Note**: Some of the steps in the next few sections are fairly basic, and are unrelated to the main subject of this chapter: Transitions. If you'd like to dive straight ahead into the meat of this chapter, feel free to skip ahead to the "Working with multiple scenes" section, where we'll have a starter project waiting for you.
>
> But if you'd like more practice with project setup, keep reading!

Its template time! As mentioned before, this time around you won't use the built-in Xcode Game template, but you'll make use of the Single View Application template instead.

By now you've made a game template the easy way and you're well acquainted with the steps involved. But you're in the final section. It's time to level up and play around with advanced methods and options to incorporate Scene Kit into existing applications.

Creating a Single View Application game project

Start Xcode and once started, press **Shift+Command+N** to create a new project. This'll launch the **Project Wizard**:

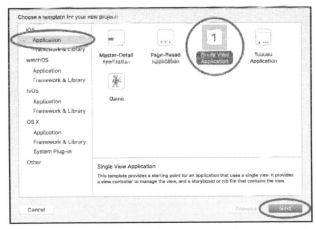

Choose **iOS\Application\Single View Application** template, and click **Next** to continue.

Next set some basic options for your new project.

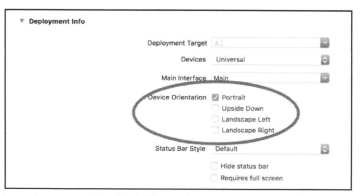

Make sure to set the following options:

- **Product Name**: Name the application **Mr.Pig**.

- **Organization Name**: You can make this whatever you choose.

- **Organization Identifier**: This is your reverse domain identifier.

- **Language**: **Swift** should be your preference by now. :]

- **Devices**: Make this **Universal** so that the application will run on an iPhone or iPad.

Leave the rest unchecked. The final step is to choose a convenient location to save your project. Pick a directory and select **Create**; Xcode will work its magic and generate your project.

Finally set the orientation for **Portrait** only under **Project Settings/General/ Deployment Info**.

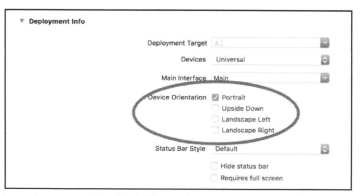

So far so good, nothing much really different from creating a standard game project. Well almost nothing changed, accept for the part where you had to choose **Single View Application**.

Select the Project Navigator to continue.

So what's the big difference? Take a closer look:

- **art.scnassets**: The first thing you might notice is that there are no **art.scnassets** folder. That bit is part of the game project template, so it wasn't created for you.

- **ViewController.swift**: This used to be **GameViewController.swift**, so the *Game* prefix fell away. The class still inherrits from UIViewController same as before. In this section, you'll reference the ViewController class instead of GameViewController.

> **Note**: You'll also notice that there's no boilerplate code to start the game. Fear not, you've been training for this, my apprentice.

Adding resources to your project

There are a whole bunch of resources ready to go for your game, you need to add them next.

Start by dragging and dropping the **resources\GameUtils** folder into your project. When prompted, make sure to add the folder as a **Group**:

Drag and drop the **resources\MrPig.scnassets** folder into the project next.

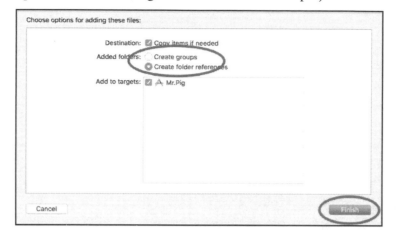

Finally, open the **File Navigator** to take a closer look.

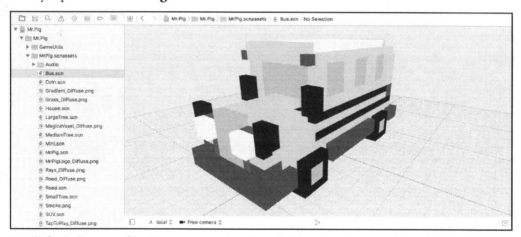

You'll find all sorts of hidden gems under these folders; here's a quick breakdown of what to expect:

- **GameUtils**: These are just a bunch of useful utilities you can use to make everyday tasks a little bit less taxing.

- **MrPig.scnassets**: This contains all the textures, 3D models, sound effects and even music your game will put to use.

> **Note**: Take some time to get yourself familiar with the content inside these folders. You'll be using them extensively in the coming chapters.

Setting up the app icon and launchscreen

You'll find a **LaunchScreen** and **AppIcon** folder under the **resources** folder. These contain a bunch of app icons and a launch screen image for you to use in your project.

Drag and drop the appropriate app icons into the **Assets.xcassets\AppIcon** container.

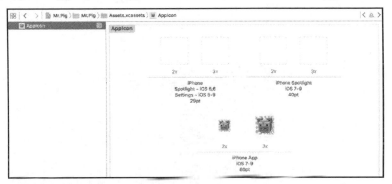

Next drag and drop the **MrPig_Launch.png** into the **Assets.xcassets** folder. This adds the image to your project, making it available from your **Media Library**.

Now you can set up the launch screen with the image.

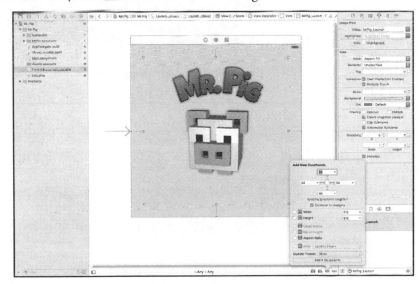

Here are a few things you need to do right now:

- Set the background color to a nice yellow.

- Drag and drop the launch image from the **Media Library**.

- Remember to add some pin constraints; pinning the image view horizontally and vertically in the container will do.

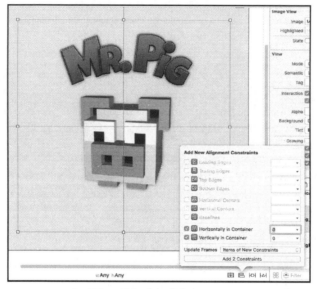

- Finally, make sure you set the **View Mode** of the image view to **Aspect Fill**.

Setting up the Scene Kit view

Now you need to set up the basic view controller, and then create the actual Scene Kit view for your game.

Setting up the View Controller class

Under the **Project Navigator**, select **ViewController.swift** then replace its contents with the following:

```
// 1
import UIKit
import SceneKit
import SpriteKit
// 2
class ViewController: UIViewController {
  // 3
```

```
  let game = GameHelper.sharedInstance

  override func viewDidLoad() {
    super.viewDidLoad()
    // 4
    setupScenes()
    setupNodes()
    setupActions()
    setupTraffic()
    setupGestures()
    setupSounds()
    // 5
    game.state = .TapToPlay
  }

  func setupScenes() {
  }

  func setupNodes() {
  }

  func setupActions() {
  }

  func setupTraffic() {
  }

  func setupGestures() {
  }

  func setupSounds() {
  }

  override func didReceiveMemoryWarning() {
    super.didReceiveMemoryWarning()
  }

  override func prefersStatusBarHidden() -> Bool {
    return true
  }

  override func shouldAutorotate() -> Bool {
    return false
  }
}
```

Let's have a quick look at what happens in here:

1. This part imports the usual suspects, but did you notice that you're now importing **SpriteKit** too? What's up with that? If you'll recall, this chapter actually deals with Transitions, and Scene Kit relies on Sprite Kit functionality to make the transitions. So for now, just make a mental note of this incredibly important import.

2. The class is now known as the `ViewController` that simply inherits from the `UIViewController` with a game template.

3. This declares the `game` object that retrieves the shared instance of the `GameHelper` class. This contains some basic helpful functionality that you'll use throughout the game.

4. The `viewDidLoad()` function is the first to execute once the application starts. Here you're simply calling a whole bunch to stubs that'll set up all the important aspects of your game later on.

5. Finally, you set the game into an initial state of `TapToPlay`.

Setting up the Scene Kit view

Now to tackle the big hole you made for yourself by making use of a **Single View Application** template. You ned to manually create an `SCNView` instance and will start by creating the property that will hold your `SCNView`.

Add the following property to top of `ViewController`:

```
var scnView:SCNView!
```

This is to hold the instance of the SCNView for quick access later on.

Add the following to `setupScenes()`:

```
scnView = SCNView(frame: self.view.frame)
self.view.addSubview(scnView)
```

This creates an instance for `SCNView` by passing in the `view.frame`. Then the key part is to add the Scene Kit view as a sub view of the current view with `addSubView()`.

Feel free to build and run if you'd like, but note you'll end up with a blank white screen because you still need to present a scene in the view.

Working with multiple scenes

> **Note**: If you skipped ahead from earlier in this chapter, you can pick up at this point with the starter project in **projects\starter\Mr.Pig**.

There will be no fun with transitions between scenes until you set some up. You'll create the two main scenes for your game: a splash scene and a game scene.

Create the game scene

The game scene is where all the action will take place. You'll build the entire level inside the game scene. To create a new scene, drag and drop a **SceneKit Scene File** from the **File Template library** into the root of your project.

Name the scene **GameScene.scn**, choose **MrPig.scnassets** folder as destination and click **Create**.

Make sure the **MrPig.scnassets\GameScene.scn** is still selected then drag and drop a **Floor Node** into the scene from the **Object Library**. Select its **Node Inspector** to continue.

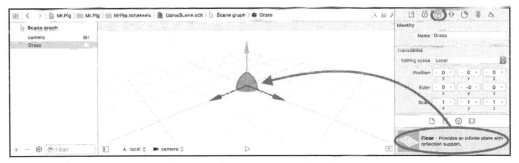

Name the node **Grass**, and zero out the **position** and Euler **rotation**.

Select the **Attributes Inspector**.

Set the **Floor Reflectivity** to **0**, you definitely don't want the grass to be reflective because, well, grass isn't glass!

Move on to the **Materials Inspector**.

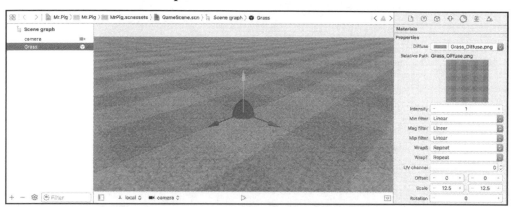

Select the **Grass_Diffuse.png** as the **Material Diffuse** map, then scale it down to 12.5 units vertically and 12.5 units horizontally. This should make a nice repeated grass pattern all over the floor node. It's so realistic you can almost smell the freshly cut grass.

Create the splash scene

The splash scene will be the front scene where Mr. Pig will introduce himself with some some serious dance moves. He's patient, energetic and will keep on rocking until your player initiates a game.

Drag and drop another **SceneKit Scene File** from the **File Template library** into the root of your project.

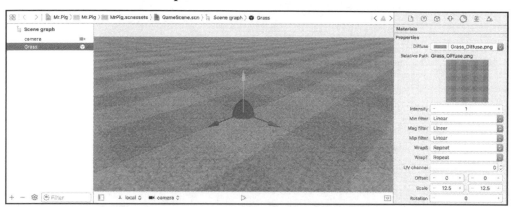

Name the scene **SplashScene.scn**, choose **MrPig.scnassets** folder as destination then click **Create**.

With the **SplashScene.scn** scene still selected, drag and drop a **MrPig** reference node into the scene from the **Media Library**.

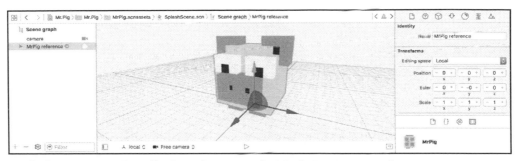

With the **MrPig** node still selected, go into the **Node Inspector** and zero out its position and rotation. Mr. Pig is in position now.

Next you'll give the splash scene an aesthetically pleasing gradient background – solid colors are *so* 2002.

Make sure you still have the **MrPig** reference node selected then select the **Scene Inspector**, the very last inspector. Drag and drop the **Gradient_Diffuse.png** file from the **Media Library** into the **Scene Background** property.

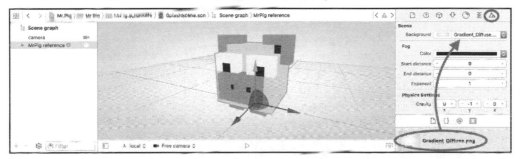

The whole scene background should change to the gradient image. Yes, Mr. Pig loves bright colors. :]

> **Note**: Since you're using a single square image for the background, Scene Kit does something special by stretching it so that it fills the whole scene at all times. Just another cool way you can use some of the hidden features of Scene Kit.

Now to create some sun rays behind Mr. Pig. Drag and drop a **Plane** node into the scene from the **Object Library**.

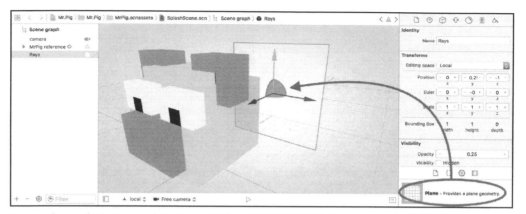

Name the node **Rays**, and set its position to (x:0, y:0.25, z:-1) and make sure it has a zero rotation. Also set **Visibility Opacity** to 0.25 to make the plane almost entirely transparent.

Now move on and adjust the plane dimensions under the **Attributes Inspector**.

Set the **Size** to (x:5, y:5), and just for the fun of it, make the plane a disc by setting the **Corner Radius** to 2.5, essentially half of its size.

Now you need to make the plane look like actual rays, and to do that you need to give it a nice little diffuse texture. Select the **Materials Inspector**.

Select the **Rays_Diffuse.png** for a diffuse map. You should notice the plane changing into glorious rays, but there's bound to be a power struggle between the rays of light and your scene lighting.

To fix that, you need to scroll down to the Materials Inspector **Settings** section.

Settings		
Transparency		
Mode	A One	
Value	— 1 +	
Lighting model	Constant	
	☐ Lit per pixel	
Visibility	Cull front	
Blend mode	Subtract	
	☑ Double sided	

You first need to set the **Lighting Model** to **Constant**. This ensures lighting will have no effect on the rays. Yes, you'll add those to the scene shortly

Set **Blend Mode** to **Subtract**, which will then darken the scene by using the blend diffuse map by means of subtraction.

Set up camera and lights

What makes the eyes recognize dimension? Lighting, of course. And if you're adding lights you need cameras. Lights, cameras, action!

By default, the splash scene already has a camera. You'll use it *mostly* as-is.

First make sure nothing is selected under your **Scene Graph** tree then click the + button to add an **empty node** into the root.

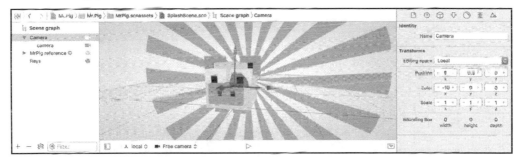

Name the empty node **Camera** and drag the original camera node under it, making it a child node. With the outer **Camera** node selected, use the **Node Inspector** to set its position to (x:0, y:0.3, z:0) and its euler angle to (x:-10, y:0, z:0). This will tilt the camera view downwards and aim it straight at the dancing swine almost as if he's holding a selfie stick.

Select the inner **camera** node, so you can set some properties on it too.

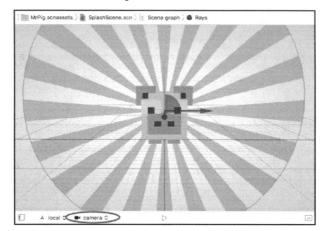

You want to pull the camera back a bit on that selfie stick, but not too far, just far enough to see Mr. Pig, so set its position to (x:0, y:0, z:3) and make sure its Euler rotation is (x:0, y:0, z:0).

To make sure the camera is configured correctly, select the **camera** in the dropdown in the bottom left of the scene editor to preview the view:

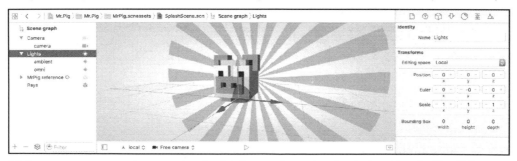

Now add another empty node into the root of the **Scene Graph**, and name it **Lights**. Drag and drop an **Ambient** and an **Omni** light into the scene from the **Object Library**.

Make sure you move them under the **Lights** node under the **Scene Graph**. You'll leave the attributes as-is, but you need to position the omni light properly, so select it, then select its **Node Inspector**.

Position the light at (xL–5, y:5, z:5). Looking very dapper! :]

Mini challenge

You're almost done with the entire splash scene, there are just two more components to be added: the logo and tap to-play nodes. But you're more than capable of handling these two tasks all on your own. :]

Your little challenge is to produce the same results as below. Take special note of the **Scene Graph** structure with the added **Logo** and **TapToPlay** nodes and obviously the precious pink Mr. Pig logo and Tap To Play writing in front of the pig in the scene.

These two nodes are plane nodes with simple diffuse maps on them. Here are a few tips to reference if you need a helping hand:

- **The Logo node**: It uses a basic **plane** node with the **MrPigLogo_Diffuse.png** applied, set to a **size** of (width:1, height:0.5). Make sure to position it in front and above our hero at position (x:0, y:1, z:0.5). Also make sure it's not affected by any light, just like the **Rays** at the back.

- **The TapToPlay node**: Also uses a basic **plane** node with the **TapToPlay_Diffuse.png** applied, set to a **size** of (width:1, height:0.25). Position it in front and below the pig at **position** (x:0, y:-0.3, z:0.5). It also should not be affected by any light.

> **Note**: You can find the solution to this little mini challenge under the **projects \challenge\Mr.Pig** folder.

Load and present the splash scene

Finally you've got your splash scene setup, and the game scene is on its way. What's left now is to load them up and present the splash scene.

You first need objects to hold your scenes, so add the following properties to ViewController:

```
var gameScene:SCNScene!
var splashScene:SCNScene!
```

Add the following code to setupScenes():

```
// 1
gameScene = SCNScene(named: "/MrPig.scnassets/GameScene.scn")
splashScene = SCNScene(named: "/MrPig.scnassets/
SplashScene.scn")
// 2
scnView.scene = splashScene
```

Let's take a closer look:

1. This loads both the **GameScene.scn** and the **SplashScene.scn** into memory from the **MrPig.scnassets** folder.

2. This part sets the splash scene up as the initial scene for your game. So once everything is loaded up and the game is started, the splash scene is shown first.

You can do a quick build and run just to make sure all is well.

You're all good if your game started up and showed the splash scene. Oh, yes!

So how do you get from the splash scene to the game scene? Well, if you've just asked yourself that question, then hurry to the next part, because it will show you exactly how.

Creating transition effects

Finally you're ready to learn more about transitions. So what exactly are transitions? To understand this better you'll have to go watch all seven episodes Star Wars again. See you back here in about 14 hours.

Why the Star Wars reference? Well, George Lucas, in all his brilliance, mastered the art of using wipes to transition between scenes. One could even go as far as to say that without these classic sweeping effects, the movies would loose some of their magic. There are many more kinds of transitions, including dissolves, cross fades and cuts.

Scene Kit leverages Sprite Kit's SKTransition object for transition effects, and that's precisely why you imported Sprite Kit. So, if you come from a Sprite Kit background, you should feel right at home with these effects.

The SKTransition object will help you animate your transition from the active scene to the scene you want to present next by using various transitioning effects.

There's quite a few out of the box transition effects at your disposal:

- **crossFadeWithDuration**: Cross fades from current scene into the new scene.
- **doorsCloseHorizontalWithDuration**: Presents the new scene as a pair of closing horizontal doors.
- **doorsCloseVerticalWithDuration**: Presents the new scene as a pair of closing vertical doors.
- **doorsOpenHorizontalWithDuration**: Presents the new scene as a pair of opening horizontal doors.
- **doorsOpenVerticalWithDuration**: Presents the new scene as a pair of opening vertical doors.
- **doorwayWithDuration**: The current scene disappears as two doors opens up, presenting the new scene from behind opening doors.
- **fadeWithColor**: The current scene first fades into a constant color then presents the new scene by fading into it.
- **fadeWithDuration**: The current scene first fades to black then presents the new scene by fading into it.

- **flipHorizontalWithDuration**: Presents the new scene, flipping away the current scene horizontally.

- **flipVerticalWithDuration**: Presents the new scene, flipping away the current scene vertically.

- **moveInWithDirection**: Presents the new scene by moving it on top of the current scene.

- **pushWithDirection**: Presents the new scene by pushing out the current scene.

- **revealWithDirection**: The current scene moves out, revealing the new scene underneath it.

- **transitionWithCIFilter**: Presents the new scene by making use of Core Image Filters for the transition effect.

Add a transition effect

In this part you're about to kill two birds with one stone.

Poor birds...

Relax, that's just an old expression; you're not really going to kill any birds! :]

But Mr. Pig better watch his step!

about to add some basic functions that will control the three game states **WaitForTap** and **GameOver**) your game will go through. Along with that you'll also add some code to do the actual transition from the one scene to another.

The first function will switch your game into the **Playing** state. It will also transition into the game scene.

Add the following function to `ViewController` class:

```
func startGame() {
  // 1
  splashScene.paused = true
  // 2
  let transition =
SKTransition.doorsOpenVerticalWithDuration(1.0)
  // 3
  scnView.presentScene(gameScene, withTransition: transition,
incomingPointOfView: nil, completionHandler: {
    // 4
    self.game.state = .Playing
    self.setupSounds()
    self.gameScene.paused = false
  })
}
```

Let's see what happens in here:

1. You're assuming that the game can only start from the splash scene. So the first thing you're doing here is manually pausing the splash scene by setting the pause property to true. This will stop all actions and any active physics simulations.

2. Here's how you create a transition effect using the `SKTransition` object. This part simply presents the new scene while the current scene slides away as two vertical doors opens up.

3. You the make a call to the SCNView's `presentScene()` function by passing in the freshly created transition effect. You can also specify which point of view should be used for the transition, but because all your scenes will only have one camera you simply leave this `nil`. Then you have a completion handler kick in once the transition effect completed.

4. This bit executes after the transition completes and officially sets the game state to **Playing**. It also loads up the correct sounds for the scene and pauses the scene.

The following function switches the game into a GameOver state. This will typically happen once Mr. Pig gets hit by one of the evil gas-guzzling vehicles.

Add it to `ViewController` class:

```
func stopGame() {
  game.state = .GameOver
  game.reset()
}
```

It simply makes sure the game state is set to **GameOver**, and it also resets the scores, readying up for the next game.

The last function switches the game into **WaitForTap** state. This is where the splash scene is presented, and the game waits for the player.

Add the following function to `ViewController`:

```
func startSplash() {
  // 1
  gameScene.paused = true
  // 2
  let transition =
SKTransition.doorsOpenVerticalWithDuration(1.0)
  scnView.presentScene(splashScene, withTransition: transition,
incomingPointOfView: nil, completionHandler: {
    self.game.state = .TapToPlay
    self.setupSounds()
    self.splashScene.paused = false
  })
}
```

Now for a closer look at what's happening here:

1. This simply pauses the game scene, essentially preventing all physics simulations and actions from running.

2. Again as before, this creates a transition effect then performs the actual transition to the splash scene. Once the transition completes, the game state is officially set to WaitForTap, the splash scene sounds are re-configured, and the scene is un-paused.

So, now you have all the basic functions to control the flow of your game setup. There's still one little function left to add, and that's the one that kicks off your game once the user taps to play. Add the following function to `ViewController` class:

```
override func touchesBegan(touches: Set<UITouch>, withEvent
event: UIEvent?) {
  if game.state == .TapToPlay {
    startGame()
  }
}
```

The `touchesBegan()` event will fire once the player taps on the screen. You're only interested in tap events while in a **WaitForTap** state. Once the event fires, you know the player wants to play the game, so you trigger the `startGame()` function.

Time for a build and run to test that transition.

Note: Be sure to test this on a device, not the simulator, as the simulator may be too slow to show the transition.

The game starts up with the splash scene and when you tap to play, the scene transitions into the game scene. Perfect!

Where to go from here?

As usual, you can find the final project for this chapter under the **projects\final\Mr.Pig** folder.

To top it off, you just earned yourself a gold star for completing the first chapter in this section, and your game is already looking mighty fine. :]

Here are some key takeaways from this chapter:

- **Single View Application:** You've now learned how to add Scene Kit to basically any type of application. No more do you need to rely on the Game Template.

- **Transitions:** You've learned that Scene Kit relies on Sprite Kit for transitions, and you added a basic transition effect for your game.

Take a quick break, but hurry back because things will get more interesting in the next chapter where you'll start building the game scene.

Chapter 17: Advanced Scene Creation

Chris Language

Your game is off to a great start. In the previous chapter, your main focus was creating the basic project for your game. Not only that, but you also created the two main scenes for your game - the splash and game scenes. The rest of your focus was on adding making the splash scene pop and setting up a basic transition to the game scene.

In this chapter, your focus will shift towards building out the game scene.

You've already created a massive grass plane that forms the basis of the lovely park in which Mr. Pig lives and collects coins.

There are, of course, some missing details: those two nasty highways filled with traffic running through the park, a whole bunch of trees and the star of the game.

> **Note**: This chapter continues where the previous one left off, so if you followed along you can continue using the same project. Otherwise, you can load up the starter project for this chapter from **projects\starter\Mr.Pig**.

Adding the pig

You'll start off by adding our hero, Mr. Pig, to your game scene so you have a good reference point for where to place the rest of the objects.

Add Mr. Pig

With your Project Navigator open, navigate down and select **MrPig.scnassets \GameScene.scn**.

Drag and drop a **MrPig** reference node from the Media Library into the scene.

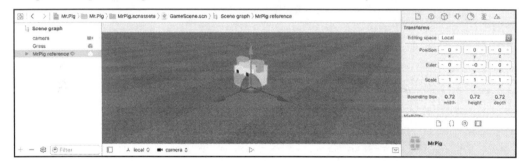

Make sure you zero out his position and rotation. Sweet, that was almost too easy.

Quickly jump over to **ViewController.swift** and add the following property to `ViewController`:

```
var pigNode: SCNNode!
```

This property will hold the instance of Mr. Pig in the game scene. Later on, if you want Mr. Pig to jump, you'd run an action on this node.

Add the following line of code to `setupNodes()`:

```
pigNode = gameScene.rootNode.childNodeWithName("MrPig",
recursively: true)!
```

This method is called after **GameScene.scn** loads, so this line of code is safe to use as a means of binding `pigNode` to the actual object in your game scene.

> **Note**: Although **MrPig** is a reference node, you still access the node in the game scene as if it was a non-reference node.

Set up camera and lights

Now that you have something more than just a massive grass field to look at, it's time to set up a camera and some lights for your scene. Again, you'll make use of the selfie-stick principle by creating an empty node that will act as the focus point for the camera or light – this approach simplifies and eliminates a whole bunch of mathematical issues I'm sure you won't mind skipping. :]

Create the follow camera node

Go back to **MrPig.scnassets\GameScene.scn** to set up the camera.

First, make sure nothing is selected under your scene graph, then click the **+** button to add an empty node into the scene graph. With the node selected, rename it **FollowCamera** under the Node Inspector, zero out its position and set **Euler** to (x:-45, y:20, z:0) to adjust the rotation.

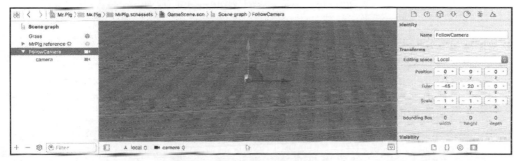

Next, drag and drop the existing **camera** node under the newly added **FollowCamera** node. With **camera** still selected, change its position to (x:0, y:0, z:14) and zero out rotation.

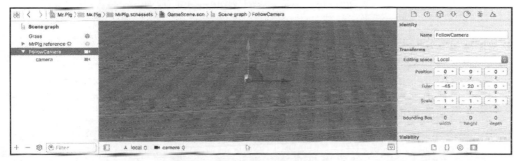

Select **camera** to be your view point at the bottom of the Scene Editor, and then your scene should resemble the image above.

At this point, you're almost done playing around with the camera, but you still need to add some code for it. Select **ViewController.swift** and add the following properties to

`ViewController`:

```
var cameraNode: SCNNode!
var cameraFollowNode: SCNNode!
```

These will hold instances of **camera** and **FollowCamera** in code.

Now add the following to `setupNodes()`:

```
// 1
cameraNode = gameScene.rootNode.childNodeWithName("camera",
recursively: true)!
cameraNode.addChildNode(game.hudNode)
// 2
cameraFollowNode =
gameScene.rootNode.childNodeWithName("FollowCamera",
recursively: true)!
```

What's going on in there?

1. This attaches `cameraNode` to **camera** in the game scene. Then you add `hudNode` as a child node to it, which will keep the HUD in view of the camera at all times. You use the game helper to create `hudNode`, and in turn, it will be used to display information to the player.

2. This attaches `cameraFollowNode` to **FollowCamera** so that when you want the camera to follow the pig around the scene, all you'll need to do is update the position for `cameraFollowNode` to be the same position as the pig.

Create the follow light node

You'll follow a similar process to create the lights for your game scene as you did to set up the camera. This scene will make use of two basic lights: an ambient light, and a directional light to mimic sunlight and cast hard shadows for everything in the view.

First make sure nothing is selected under your game scene scene graph then click the **+** button to add an empty node. Name it **FollowLight** and zero out both the position and rotation.

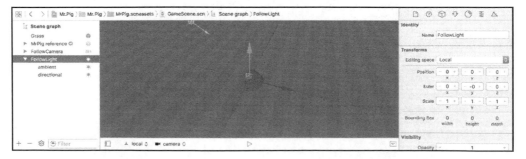

Drag and drop an **Ambient light** and a **Directional light** into the game scene from the Object library. Make sure both lights are children of **FollowLight**.

Select the **ambient** light, and zero out its position and rotation in the Node Inspector.

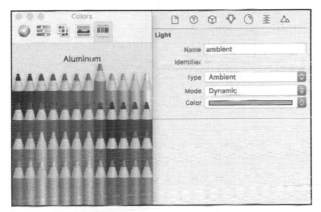

Then, move on to the Attributes Inspector and give the ambient light a mid-grey color by clicking the colored bar next to **Color** to bring up the color picker. Go to the crayons tab, and find the **Aluminum** color to use for the light – this will brighten up the scene a little more.

Now select the **directional** light, and bring up its **Node Inspector** again. Set the **Position** to (x:-5, y:5, z:5), and adjust the rotation by setting **Euler** to (x:-45, y:-60, z:0).

This places the directional light above and to the left of the scene, lighting up everything nicely.

Move on to the Attribute Inspector to configure **Light** and **Shadow** properties.

This next list will both tell you what to changes and give you some detail about the properties:

- **Behaviour**: Check this to make the light cast shadows.

- **Sample radius**: Set this to 0 so the edges of shadows cast by this light are not blurred. For this game, which is set outdoors, you want the directional light to mimic the sun and the kinds of crisp shadows it produces.

- **Near/Far clipping**: Specify a value of −1 for **Near clipping** and 15 for **Far clipping**: Only surfaces between the range of the near and far clippings can have shadows cast upon them. Limiting this range is important for performance, and you calculate how large it will be based on the light source's position.

- **Scale**: Set this to 11. This sets the extents of the orthographic projection for the directional light, large enough so that the casted shadows fills the entire view.

- **Sample count**: Set this to 0. Again, you want the light to cast a hard shadow. A higher sample count produces softer shadows, so you want to set this to as low as possible.

Once you configure both lights, you should end up with the following result.

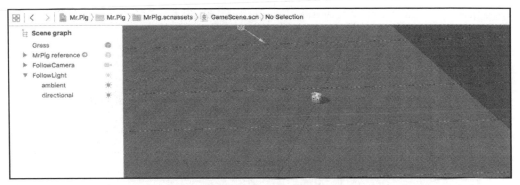

Wait a minute, why on Earth would you want the light to follow the pig around the scene anyway? The answer is simple – performance!

You've already limited the directional light's shadow clipping range, but that range is based on the light's position. When you start panning around the scene, you'll run into parts of the scene that fall outside of the clipping range, and those parts will look very strange without any shadows.

To overcome this issue, you simply set the light to follow the camera view, allowing the shadow clipping region to come along. In short, this approach contrains the task of casting shadows for objects within the camera's *current* point of view.

The alternative is rather expensive and would make this game slow – all in the name of producing shadows the user can't even see. That's why you want the light to follow the pig around the scene.

The only bit left now is to write some code. Start by adding the following property to `ViewController`:

```
var lightFollowNode: SCNNode!
```

This will hold the instance of **FollowLight**.

Add the following code to `setupNodes()`:

```
lightFollowNode =
gameScene.rootNode.childNodeWithName("FollowLight", recursively:
true)!
```

This attaches `lightFollowNode` to **FollowLight**. Now you can move this node to the same position as **FollowCamera** to make sure that the objects in view always cast pretty shadows for the player to see. :]

Do a quick build and run to review what you've done so far.

The game should start up and show the splash scene. Start a game and watch as the scene transitions to the game scene, revealing a very lonesome little pig standing on massive, open grass plane.

Notice that the effect of the hard shadow cast by the sun makes it look hot on that grass. You can almost smell sizzling bacon! :]

Adding highways and traffic

Now to do the bidding of the big bad wolf who built the mall down the street. It seems that his deal included an easement for a new highway straight through Mr. Pig's lovely green park.

Unfortunately, traffic is extremely dangerous for little park-strolling pigs.

Put on your hard hat, it's time to build some highways and a nice big traffic jam while you're at it!

Add the highways

First make sure nothing is selected in your scene graph, then click the + button to add an empty node into the scene. Name it **Highway**.

You'll use this as a container node for the two highways.

Next, drag and drop two **Road** reference nodes from the Media Library into the scene, and make sure to place both of them under **Highway** node.

Select the first road, position it at (x:0, y:0, z:-4.5) and zero out the rotation.

Now select the second road and position it at (x:0, y:0, z:-11.5), placing it slightly further away from the first one. Make sure to also zero out the rotation for this road.

Once you're done positioning both the roads, select **camera** as your point of view in the Scene Editor. You should see something like this:

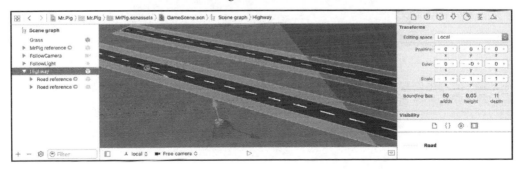

Add the traffic

Build it and they will come, they say. Sure enough, you've built the road and will now make the traffic come. :]

Once again, make sure nothing is selected in your scene graph and add another empty node to the scene to serve as the container node for all the traffic in your game scene. This time around, name it **Traffic**.

Now drag and drop a **Bus** reference node into your scene from the Media Library. Make sure you move the **Bus** node under the **Traffic** node, then set its position to (x:0, y:0, z:-4) and give it a rotation of (x:0, y:-90, z:0).

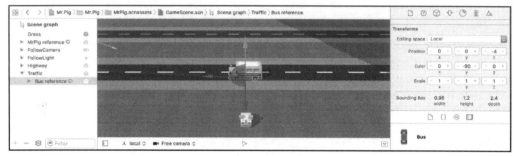

This places the bus nicely on the left lane of the first highway, facing left. Great!

Drag and drop a **Mini** reference node from the Media Library into the scene, and make sure to place it under the **Traffic** node as well. This time, place the Mini on the right lane, at position (x:3, y:0, z:-5), and rotate it to (x:0, y:-90, z:0) so that it also faces left, like so:

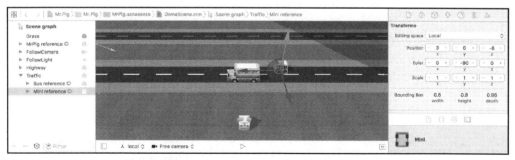

Now drag and drop a **SUV** reference node from the Media Library, and also place it under the **Traffic** node. Place the SUV on the right lane as well – slightly ahead of the Mini – at position (x:-3, y:0, z:-5) and rotate it to (x:0, y:-90, z:0).

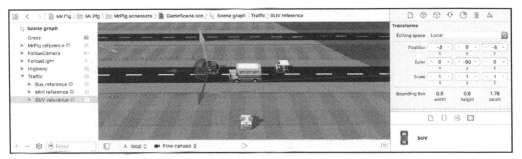

Great job! Now for the coding bit. Select **ViewController.swift** and add the following property to ViewController:

```
var trafficNode: SCNNode!
```

This time, instead of making a property for each reference node in traffic, you're going to simply use one container node that holds all the vehicles.

Add the following to setupNodes():

```
trafficNode = gameScene.rootNode.childNodeWithName("Traffic",
recursively: true)!
```

This attaches trafficNode to the **Traffic** node in the scene, so now you can easily access all the children of this node to make them drive.

The traffic challenge

Time for a little fun with traffic – no need to drive anywhere for this experience!

Since the vehicles are in place, you should know exactly how to get this challenge done. The challenge is to fill up those highways with even more traffic – lots more.

The final result should look something like this:

Here are some guidelines to follow while adding more traffic:

- Make the left lane a bus lane, and keep the right lane for the smaller, faster vehicles.

- Make one highway's vehicles drive left and the other side's go right.

- To make your life easier, use the **Option** key to make quick copies of something already placed in the scene.

- Also make sure to hold the **Command** key when positioning the cars so they snap to nice round numbers.

- Remember to leave enough space between vehicles for a little pig to run through. You don't want to make the game too difficult.

- Once you've finished the one highway, select all its vehicles and drag them to the other highway while holding **Option** to make a copy. Then, simply rotate them 180 degrees so that they face the other direction.

- Again, while you are rotating the vehicles, hold the **Command** key so that the angles snap into place.

CHALLENGE ACCEPTED

Once you're done adding all the traffic, you can do another build and run just to do a quick sanity check.

Poor little pig is lonely no more! He now shares the once lovely park with two massive highways filled with traffic. :]

> **Note:** If you struggled a bit or want to push ahead, you'll find the completed project after this challenge under **projects\challenge\Mr.Pig**.

Adding trees

At the moment there's one critical element still missing — those cute little trees! It looks like someone built a massive highway across a soccer field, not a green park at the moment.

In this section, you'll create two different groups of trees: a tree line and a tree patch. You'll use the tree line as a border around the whole park, essentially boxing Mr. Pig in.

Then you'll use tree patches to create a few groups of trees to fill in give the scene a park-like look.

Create the tree line

Instead of planting little trees one by one, take a smarter approach and create reusable scenes comprised of a bunch of trees, and then use those as reference nodes in your game scene.

Start off by dragging an empty **Scene Kit Scene File** from the File Template Library into the root folder of your project under the Project Navigator. Name the new scene **TreeLine** and place it under **MrPig.scnassets**:

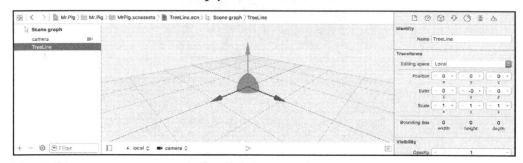

Inside **TreeLine.scn**, create an **empty** node and name it **TreeLine**.

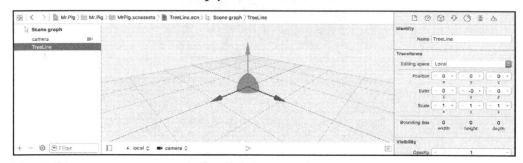

This will be your container node for all the trees in this scene.

Use the following grid pattern to build the tree line.

		-5	-4	-3	-2	-1	0	1	2	3	4	5
	-1	S	M	S	M	S	M	S	M	S	M	S
Z	0	M	L	M	L	M	L	M	L	M	L	M
	1	S	M	S	M	S	M	S	M	S	M	S

What exactly does that grid mean? Each cell holds a tree element and indicates what size of tree to place there.

- **Columns**: indicates the x position for where you'll place the tree element
- **Rows**: indicates the z position for where you'll place the tree element
- **S**: represents a **SmallTree** reference node
- **M**: represents a **MediumTree** reference node
- **L**: represents a **LargeTree** reference node

Thus, as an example, for row 1 and column 1 you need to drag and drop a **SmallTree** reference node from the Media Library into the scene and position it at (x:-5, y:0, z:-1).

To speed things up you can hold the Option and Command keys as you drag to quickly create duplicates that snap to the grid.

Once you're done, your tree line should look something like this:

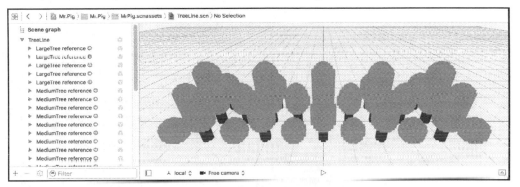

Make sure all the trees are placed under the **TreeLine** container node, and remember to remove that default **camera** because you're going to use this scene as a reference node.

Create the tree patch

You are going to repeat the same steps to create a patch of trees that you can use as a reference node.

Drag another empty **Scene Kit Scene File** from the File Template Library into your project. Name this one **TreePath**, and make sure you place it under **MrPig.scnassets**.

Create an empty node and name it **TreePatch**. This will be your container node for all the trees in this scene.

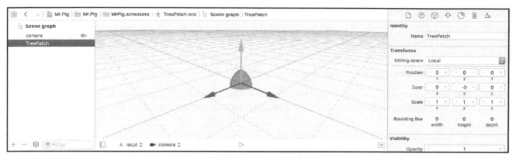

Use the following grid pattern and build the tree patch.

		-2	-1	0	1	2
Z	-3			S		
	-2		S	M	S	
	-1	S	M	L	M	S
	0	S	M	L	M	S
	1	S	M	L	M	S
	2		S	M	S	
	3			S		

This works exactly the same as before.

Once done, your tree patch should look something like this:

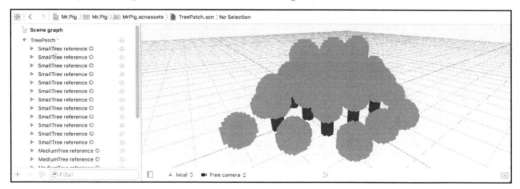

Make sure all the trees are placed under the **TreePatch** container node, and also remember to remove **camera** once you're done because you'll use this scene as a reference node too.

Add the tree line

Now that you got those tree reference nodes ready, you'll need to add them into your game scene so that the lovely park can look and smell like a real park with just a hint of fresh exhaust fumes hanging in the air. :]

Select **MrPig.scnassets\GameScene.scn**, make sure nothing is selected under your scene graph and create an empty node named **Trees**.

This will be the container node for all the trees you're about to add to the game scene, so make sure you drag all the tree nodes under this container node.

The next bit it going to be somewhat of a challenge, but with settings detailed out all the way through. I think that you're ready for less detail by now. You're about to add the tree lines and you can use the following image as a reference:

The orange highlighted trees should give you a good indication of the desired result.

Start off by dragging and dropping a single **TreeLine** reference node from the Media Library into your scene. Copy the rest of the tree line from this first reference node by holding Option as you drag. Then use the following positions and rotations to place each one at the correct location and orientation in the game scene.

The tree lines in the front, near Mr. Pig:

- **Position**: (x:0, y:0, z:7), **Euler**: (x:0, y:0, z:0).
- **Position**: (x:-7, y:0, z:3), **Euler**: (x:0, y:90, z:0).
- **Position**: (x:7, y:0, z:3), **Euler**: (x:0, y:90, z:0).
- **Position**: (x:-14, y:0, z:-1), **Euler**: (x:0, y:0, z:0).
- **Position**: (x:14, y:0, z:-1), **Euler**: (x:0, y:0, z:0).

The tree lines between the highways:

- **Position**: (x:-14, y:0, z:-8), **Euler**: (x:0, y:0, z:0).
- **Position**: (x:14, y:0, z:-8), **Euler**: (x:0, y:0, z:0).

The tree lines in the back:

- **Position**: (x:18, y:0, z:-19), **Euler**: (x:0, y:90, z:0).
- **Position**: (x:-18, y:0, z:-19), **Euler**: (x:0, y:90, z:0).
- **Position**: (x:-11, y:0, z:-23), **Euler**: (x:0, y:0, z:0).
- **Position**: (x:0, y:0, z:-23), **Euler**: (x:0, y:0, z:0).
- **Position**: (x:11, y:0, z:-23), **Euler**: (x:0, y:0, z:0).

> **Note**: Remember to put all the copied nodes under the **Trees** container node.

Add the tree patches

Now follow the same process as before to recreate the orange highlighted **TreePatches**.

Start off by dragging and dropping a single **TreePatch** reference node from the Media Library into your scene. Then copy the rest from this node as needed, using the following positions and rotations:

- **Position**: (x:10, y:0, z:-17), **Euler**: (x:0, y:0, z:0).
- **Position**: (x:-10, y:0, z:-17), **Euler**: (x:0, y:0, z:0).
- **Position**: (x:0, y:0, z:-17), **Euler**: (x:0, y:90, z:0).

Again, make sure to move these new tree patch reference nodes under the **Trees** container node you created earlier.

Adding coins

Everybody knows that little piggies are avid coin collectors. Mr. Pig is no different. He even takes his obsession to the next level by risking his own life daily to search for lost coins in the park.

Your mission now is to prevent major disappointment for the little pig by adding some coins to your game scene. :]

Start off by creating an empty node and name it **Coins**. As before, this will be the container node for all the coins you'll add to the scene.

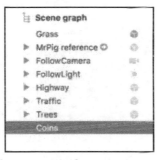

Now drag and drop a **Coin** reference node from the Media Library into the game scene. Make three other copies of this node, and use the following positions for the coins:

- **Position**: (x:0, y:0.5, z:-8).
- **Position**: (x:0, y:0.5, z:-21).
- **Position**: (x:-14, y:0.5, z:-20).
- **Position**: (x:14, y:0.5, z:-20).

Make sure all the coins are under the **Coins** container node. Your scene should now look like this:

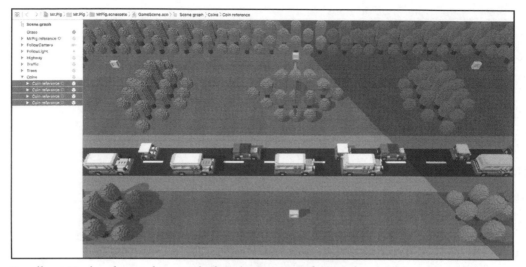

Excellent! You're almost done with this chapter, save for one last build and run that should look like this:

The game now starts up with the splash scene; once the player taps to play, the scene transitions into the game scene, which now has traffic, trees and most importantly, coins for Mr. Pig. :]

Where to go from here?

Good job! You've reached the end of this chapter. You can find the final project for this chapter under **projects\final\Mr.Pig**.

There are a few things in this chapter that you should take away, so let's review:

- You're now starting to apply your skills in a methodical approach when creating complex scenes. This will become second nature – if not already.

- You've learned the importance of using reference nodes inside of reference nodes to turn hard work into child's play. Think back to how you planted a whole bunch of trees in a matter of minutes.

- You've also learned about boosting your game performance by restricting the cast of your shadows. There's also the lesson of moving the light source with the active camera view while keeping the shadows in view.

The game is adorable but still pretty boring at this point because there's nothing to do.

In the next chapter you'll learn all about actions and how to use them within Scene Kit to make traffic move, coins bounce and Mr. Pig jump! So hurry back after a well deserved break. :]

Chapter 18: Actions

Chris Language

Your game is looking great, but seems to be frozen in time because there isn't any movement. In this chapter, you'll learn all about **actions** in Scene Kit and how to use them to make the nodes in your game move, thus creating a dynamic 3D environment.

You'll start off by making Mr. Pig twerk like *Miley* and head-bang like *Ozzy*! :] Once Mr. Pig has his groove on, you'll add some gestures and actions to make him jump on command so he can navigate to pick up coins as well as bob and weave through traffic.

You'll also make all that traffic flow from one side to another. Then finally, you'll close out this chapter by making shiny coins that spin and bounce.

> **Note:** This chapter picks up where the previous one left off, so if you followed along, you can continue using the same project. Otherwise, you can load up the starter project for this chapter from **projects\starter\Mr.Pig**.

Actions

Actions allow you to manipulate a node's position, scale, rotation and opacity within a scene. For example, when the player swipes left, Mr. Pig should do a leftwards turn while jumping one space to the left. A right swipe should do the opposite.

These basic movements are accomplished by running actions in sequences and groups on the pig node.

You can build action sequences within the Scene Kit editor by dragging and dropping actions from the Object Library into the Secondary Editor, just below the Scene Editor, when you have a node selected. From a coding perspective, you first need to create an

SCNAction object, optionally setting its timingMode if you want, and then you can execute that action on any SCNNode instance by using the runAction(_:) method on the node.

There are four basic categories of actions at your disposal for manipulating a node's behaviour in the scene: **Move**, **Scale**, **Rotate** and **Fade**. There are two more special actions used to either run actions in a **Sequence** or as a **Group**.

> **Note**: Think back to when you first learned about physics bodies, and you found out about the three types of physics bodies, which are **dynamic**, **kinematic** and **static**.
>
> If you want the physics engine to take control over a node's movement and rotation, you'd set its physics body to **dynamic**. If you want the node to never move, but still participate within the physics simulation, you'd set its physics body to **static**. When you want to take control of a specific node's movement and rotation, while letting it participate within the physics simulation, you'd to set its physics body type to **kinematic**.

Move actions

When you want to move a node from one point to another point in 3D space, **Move** actions are just the thing to use.

Take a closer look at the two types of move actions:

• **Move Action**: This moves the node by an offset from the node's *current position*.

• **MoveTo Action**: This moves the node to a *specified location* in 3D space *regardless* of the node's current position.

The following image illustrates how you'll use the **Move** action to make Mr. Pig bounce up and down:

For example, the above **Move** action moves the pig to by an offset of (x:0, y:1, z:0) from his current position over a period of time, thus moving it upwards along the y-axis. To get the pig back on the ground, you'll have to run another **Move** action, but this time you need to reverse the offset to (x:0, y-1, z:0) to get him back on the ground. Awesome! :]

You'll use the same **Move** action to make him move left, right, forward and backward.

Scale actions

Maybe Mr. Pig is extremely allergic to bee stings and you'd like to spice up the game with some bee swarms. :] You could use the **Scale** actions to make him swell up after he becomes a repository for some bee's stinger.

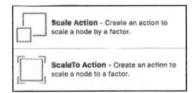

Scale actions work pretty much the same as the move actions.

- **Scale Action**: This scales the node by a factor from the node's current scale.

- **ScaleTo Action**: This scales the node to a specified scale factor, regardless of the node's current scale.

The following image demonstrates how Mr. Pig grows-up from a little piglet to the massive porker he is today:

Did somebody say bacon?

You can also use these **Scale** actions to make nodes wobble by scaling each axis independently. Doing so will distort the geometry, creating an effect that you might want to use when the pig gets stung by a bee, or when he picks up a power-up – like good old Mario after he picked up that magic mushroom! :]

Rotate actions

When Mr. Pig jumps left or right, it makes sense to have him turn towards the same direction; to do that you'll use **Rotate** actions.

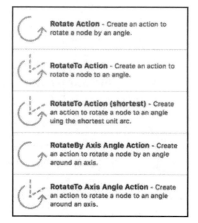

There are a few more options for rotation than there are for move or scale actions:

- **Rotate Action**: Rotates the node by an angle offset from the node's current rotation angle.

- **RotateTo Action**: Rotates the node to a specified angle regardless of its current rotation.

- **RotateTo Action (Shortest)**: Rotates the node to a specified angle, regardless of the node's current rotation, and it'll take the shortest possible rotation to get to the specified angle.

- **RotateBy Axis Angle Action**: This rotates the node by an angle offset on a specified axis from the node's current rotation on that axis.

- **RotateTo Axis Angle Action**: This rotates the node to a specified angle on a specified axis, regardless of the node's current rotation on that axis.

The following image shows how Mr. Pig turns from frontward to backwards by means of using the **RotateTo Action (Shortest)** over a period of time.

From left to right, Mr. Pig spins around, showing you his very cute curly tail. Awww! :]

You can also use **Rotate** actions to make the pig look up or down or even topple over onto his back. Yes, with these controls, Mr. Pig and his world are at your command.

Fade actions

Rarely does a little pink pig fare well when struck by a vehicle. In this scenario, he goes where all pigs go when they die – piggie heaven, where there are countless coins to collect, a never-ending supply of tea, pretty flowers to smell and *no* traffic.

But there's a transition that happens when he leaves this mortal existence. You'll need to represent this with a visual so that the player knows he just killed Mr. Pig.

To turn our hero into a ghost, you'll use the **Fade** actions to make him turn translucent.

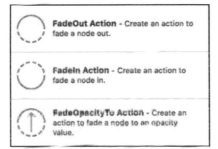

There are a few fade actions at your disposal – take a look:

- **FadeOut Action**: Fades the opacity from its current setting to completely *invisible*.

- **FadeIn Action**: Fades the opacity from its current setting to completely *visible*.

- **FadeOpacityTo Action**: Fades the opacity to a specified value.

The following image demonstrates how Mr. Pig turns into a ghost then vanishes into thin air. From left to right, Mr. Pig fades out from vibrant visible to non-existent. Rest in peace, pig. You lived a good life...

You can also use the **Fade** actions to make nodes pulsate from visible to invisible while they are in a certain state, such as when a spaceship respawns in a shoot-em-up game.

Sequenced and grouped actions

Once you've created a bunch of basic actions, you can combine them together in sequences and groups to make actions run one after another, or together at the same time.

The following diagram shows the relationship between a few basic actions that will play out over a period of two seconds:

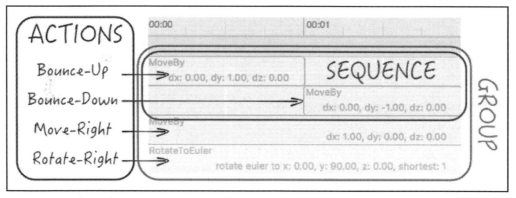

Let's take a closer look:

- **Actions**: The left simply names the four basic actions: bounce-up, bounce-down, move-right and rotate-right.

- **Sequence**: Inside the blue rectangle, you'll see two actions in a *sequence*. So when you move down the timeline, the time cursor will first start the bounce-up action for one second, and once that finishes, it starts running the bounce-down action. This is called a sequence of actions.

- **Group**: Inside the red rectangle is the blue sequence of actions, along with two other actions of *move-right* and *rotate-right*. As you move down the timeline, the time cursor will start bounce-up, move-right and rotate-right at the same time, in parallel. When the timeline reaches one second, the bounce-up action completes and the bounce-down action starts. At the same time, move-right and rotate-right are still running and halfway done at that point. When the timeline reaches the two-second mark all the actions are complete. By grouping actions together, you can run them all in parallel.

The image below shows the actual animation, as it plays out over time:

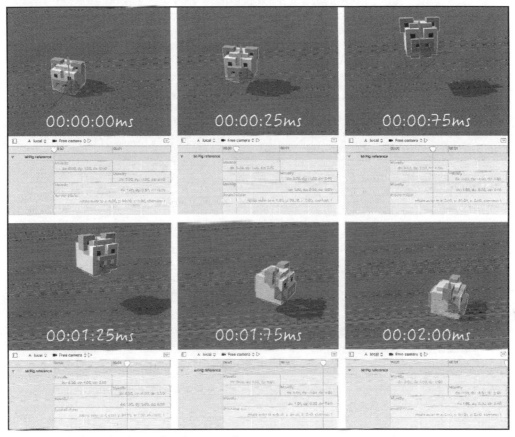

Let's take a closer look at what happens here:

1. First, by running the bounce-up and then the bounce-down actions in a sequence, you make the pig starts on the ground then leap up into the air, only to drop back to the ground again.

2. Although he starts off in one position, over time he moves one space to the right of where he started, by means of the move-right action.

3. At the same time, our hero starts off facing forward, but over time rotates so that he ends up facing right, by means of the rotate-right action.

Action timing functions

Scene Kit provides some basic timing functions you can use to control the progression of the action over time. When Mr. Pig jumps into the air it has to look realistic, and you have some work ahead to make that happen.

At the moment, bounce-up is merely a move action to some defined point in the air, and bounce-down is another move action that takes him to a point on the ground. If you played out these actions in a linear fashion, it would strange because the pig would move up and down in the air in a robotic manner.

This simply is not true when you consider what happens when you toss an egg into the air.

Take the following steps into consideration when you toss an egg into the air:

1. When the egg leaves your hand it's at full velocity, traveling upwards into the air.

2. It continues upwards, but because of gravity's unavoidable pull, its velocity is reduced with time.

3. At some point in time, the egg reaches a point where it comes to a complete stand still in mid-air.

4. It then starts its journey to splatterdom on the ground, falling back to earth with a starting velocity of zero.

5. It continues downwards, all the while its velocity increases thanks to gravity's relentless pull.

6. Eventually it reaches maximum velocity, or would if it there wasn't some force acting on it to stop it, like the ground – a collision that is inevitable. Lastly, it shatters to make a terrific mess, which is another physics lesson for another day.

To simulate this bevavior in actions, Scene Kit gives you four basic timing functions to make use of:

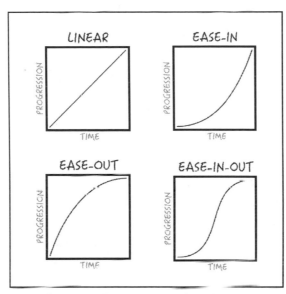

- **Linear**: This is the default timing function used for all actions. The action will play out at the same speed throughout its duration.

- **Ease-In**: This timing function gives the action a slow start, eventually accelerating to its full speed for the rest of the duration.

- **Ease-Out**: This starts the action at its speed and slows as it reaches the end.

- **East-In-Out**: This gives the action a slow start that reaches full speed at its halfway mark. Then it slows as it approaches the end.

To accurately simulate gravity for Mr. Pig's jump action, you'll use a combination of these timing functions.

> **Note**: You can make use of the `timingMode` property on an `SCNAction` to set it's timing function in code.

The action editor

Now that you know all about actions, it's time to see them in action! :]

Xcode has a hidden little feature known as the **Secondary Editor**. In the case of the Scene Kit editor, this secondary editor is the **actions editor** for nodes in a scene.

Take a look at the following image:

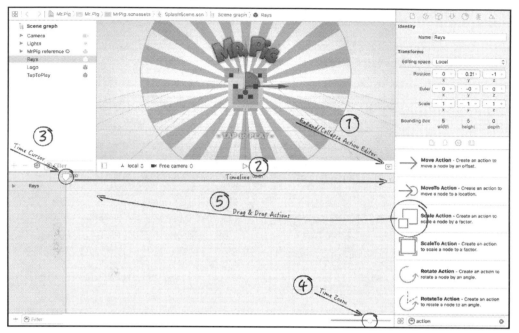

There are a few numbered points to go through:

1. **Expand/Collapse Action Editor**: This is the secondary editor button that you need to press to expand or collapse the actions editor.

2. **Timeline**: This is the timeline, and there's a grid below it that shows when actions take place. Time progression increases as you move to the right.

3. **Time Cursor**: Drag this cursor across the timeline to see the resulting actions running on your nodes in the scene.

4. **Time Zoom**: Use this slider to zoom in or out on the timeline to make editing easier for yourself.

5. **Drag & Drop Actions**: To add actions to a node, you simply drag and drop them from the Object Library into the action editor.

> **Note:** At the time of writing this chapter, there appear to be a few bugs in the Scene Kit Editor relating to actions. Sometimes, when you go back and try to edit existing actions on a node, things can go horribly wrong, and Xcode might even crash on you. If you run into this problem, you may find it best to rather delete the actions and re-create them from scratch.

Animate the rays

Now it's time to apply your knowledge and make the rays spin. :]

Start by opening your project and select **MrPig.scnassets\SplashScene.scn** to bring up the Scene Kit editor. Select the **Rays** node in the scene graph and open up the actions editor for it.

Drag and drop a **Rotate Action** from the Object Library into the actions editor. Make sure to drop it so that the action starts off at time 00:00:

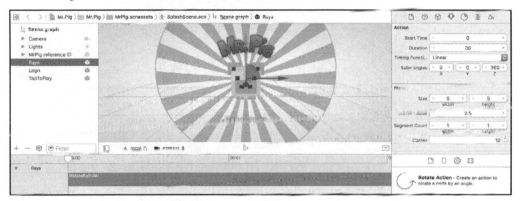

With the action still selected, select the Attributes Inspector:

Here you set the properties available for both the action and the node. Let's take a closer look at the available properties you can adjust for this action:

- **Start Time**: This sets the starting point when the action starts to run. Leave this at its default of 0.

- **Duration**: This sets the duration of how long the action will run for. Set this to 30 so this action runs for 30 seconds in total.

- **Timing Function**: This sets the timing function to use while running the action. Leave this at its default of Linear.

- **Euler angles**: This sets the offset of the node's current once the action completes. Leave **X** and **Y** at 0, but be sure to set the **Z** value to 360, or else nothing will happen.

Now you want to loop the action so that it runs forever, effectively keeping those rays spinning for an eternity. Right-click on the action and select **Create Loop**:

This will show another little **Looping** pop-up:

Click the ∞ (infinite) so that it turns blue and then click outside of the menu to close it. Don't click the **X** button because it'll cancel your loop option selection.

You're all done! Try dragging the time cursor to the right and left to see a preview of your rays spinning:

> **Note**: You can access the looping options again by simply right-clicking on a looping action and selecting **Edit Loop**.

Animate the coins

Another fun little animation you'll add is one that makes the coins in your game scene spin and bounce up and down, making them easy for our hero to see! :]

First select the **MrPig.scnassets\Coin.scn** reference node, then make sure you have the **Coin** node selected and the actions editor open. Drag and drop two instances of **Move Action** one after another. Then, drag and drop a **Rotate Action** parallel in there by placing it below the move actions you added:

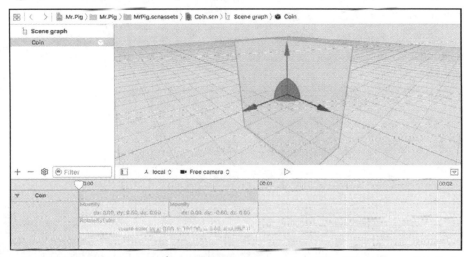

Select the first **Move Action** and set the **Start Time** to 0, with a **Duration** of 0.5. Set the **Timing Function** to **Ease In, Ease Out**, and set the **Offset** to (x:0, y:0.5, z:0):

This move action will move the coin upwards, easing in and out as it reaches the end of the action.

Select the next **Move Action**. This time, set its **Start Time** to 0.5, starting as soon as the previous action ends. Also set its **Duration** to 0.5, its Timing Function** to **Ease In, Ease Out**, with an **Offset** of x:0, y:-0.5, z:0:

This will move the coin downwards, first easing in then out again as it reaches the end of the action.

Now select the **Rotate Action**. It starts at the same time as the first move action and runs for the same duration as both move actions combined. Set its **Start Time** to 0 and **Duration** to 1.

Leave its **Timing Function** to **Linear** so that it spins at a constant rate. Finally, set the **Euler Angle** to (x:0, y:360, z:0) so that the coin does a full 360 degree spin in one turn of animation:

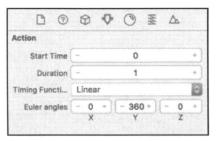

Now to make the coin spin forever.

First, make sure you've got all the actions selected; do this by pressing the Shift key while clicking on each action. Now do a right click to reveal the list of options available.

Select the **Create Loop** option:

Another little pop-up will appear with the **Looping** options:

Select the ∞ (infinite) button, which will turn blue. Click outside of this box to confirm your selection. If you click the **X** button, you will delete the loop. This infinite selection means the actions in the loop run forever.

Again, feel free to use the time cursor to preview your work so far.

Challenge!

Now here's a fun little challenge to test yourself — the twerk challenge! Hey, where are you going? I didn't mean *you* have to twerk. (But kudos if you're one of the select few who can actually do it without looking silly.)

The idea here is to make Mr. Pig twerk and show off that curly little tail, not for you to show off *your* sweet dance moves. :]

Go into **MrPig.scnassets\SplashScreen.scn** to start your challenge. You don't want to make the reference node twerk or else Mr. Pig will be constantly twerking during the game scene and that might be considered obscene.

Twerk it, pig!

Relax, it's much easier than one would think. First, select the **MrPig** reference node in the splash scene and bring up the actions editor.

Next, read through these tips if you need help figuring out how to achieve a twerking pig!

1. Connect 7 **Rotate Actions** in a sequence, and set all of them to a duration of 0.25s.

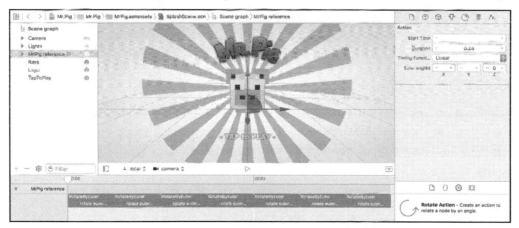

2. Start off by setting the first rotate action to tilt the pig forward by rotating it 30º on its x-axis.

3. Then set the next rotate action to tilt the pig backward by rotating it −30º on its x-axis.

4. Repeat steps two and three for all the following actions except the last one.

5. For the very last rotate action, you want the node to do a full 180º turn so that the pig shows you its tail-end. Do this by rotating it 180º on the y-axis.

6. If you scrub the time cursor along the timeline, the pig will head-bang, and then flip around to show you his tail. Perfect! :]

The next bit is easy. Simply select all the actions, right-click and select the **Create Loop** option.

7. Make sure to select the ∞ (infinite) loop option when you see the **Looping** options.

> **Note:** You can find the solution for this little challenge under **projects\challenge \Mr.Pig**.

It's a good time for a build and run.

Your splash scene should look much more attractive now, with the spinning rays and a very energetic twerking Mr. Pig! :]

Now you see that it's really easy to to give your characters a whole lot of attitude with just a few, simple animations.

Coding actions

So now that you know how to create and use actions using the built-in Xcode actions editor, this section will focus more on how to create and use actions in code. That's right, you're getting into the thick of it now!

You'll start by creating two actions that will ultimately make the traffic move. Then you'll create a few basic actions for making the pig jump around the scene using gestures.

Finally, you'll create a game over action to use when Mr. Pig meets his fate against the moving traffic.

Animate the traffic

There are two highways, one with traffic flowing left and another with traffic flowing right.

A **Move Action** should meet the need to make the cars and buses move, as this will move the traffic a certain distance over a period of time.

Remember there's also a bus lane filled with slower moving vehicles. Instead of creating multiple actions for the two speeds, you're simply going to run the same action on the different vehicles and adjust the action's speed.

> **Note:** If you are an Extreme Home Makeover fan, you might find fitting to take a break at this moment and shout: "Move that Bus! Move that Bus! Move that Bus!" :]

In code, actions are represented by instances of the `SCNAction` class and there are, of course, class methods to create all the various actions you looked at in the Object Library.

For instance, **Move Action** can be created in code using the `SCNAction.moveBy(_:duration:)` class method.

Open **ViewController.swift** and add the following action properties to `ViewController`:

```
var driveLeftAction: SCNAction!
var driveRightAction: SCNAction!
```

These two properties will store the move left and move right actions so you can reuse them at will.

Add the following to `setupActions()`:

```
driveLeftAction =
SCNAction.repeatActionForever(SCNAction.moveBy(SCNVector3Make(-2
.0, 0, 0), duration: 1.0))
driveRightAction =
SCNAction.repeatActionForever(SCNAction.moveBy(SCNVector3Make(2.
0, 0, 0), duration: 1.0))
```

The `SCNAction.repeatActionForever(_:)` class method creates a special action that will simply loop, or rather repeat, another action forever. The `SCNAction.moveBy(_:duration:)` class method creates an action that will move the node by a specified vector over a certain duration.

Now put these two new actions to good use by adding the following code to `setupTraffic()`:

```
// 1
for node in trafficNode.childNodes {

  // 2 Buses are slow, the rest are speed demons
  if node.name?.containsString("Bus") == true {
    driveLeftAction.speed = 1.0
    driveRightAction.speed = 1.0
  } else {
    driveLeftAction.speed = 2.0
    driveRightAction.speed = 2.0
  }

  // 3 Let vehicle drive towards its facing direction
  if node.eulerAngles.y > 0 {
    node.runAction(driveLeftAction)
  } else {
    node.runAction(driveRightAction)
  }
}
```

The `setupTraffic()` method is already being called from `viewDidLoad()` so you don't need to worry about that, but let's take a closer look at what the actual code does:

1. At this point, `setupNodes()` has already initialized `trafficNode`, which is attached to the **Traffic** node in the game scene. The `childNodes` property of `SCNNode` returns a list of child nodes for you to iterate through. This will essentially be a list of all the vehicle nodes on the highways.

2. If the node is a bus, you set the `SCNAction.speed` to be `1.0`, otherwise you set it to `2.0` to run the action for the smaller vehicles twice as fast.

3. Based on the assumption that you only have traffic moving left and right, this does a crude check to see which direction the vehicle currently faces. It then executes the correct facing drive action on the node.

Do another build and run, then start the game by tapping on the splash scene:

The traffic is moving, oh goody! :]

But wait there's a problem, all of the traffic drives off the screen leaving a safe, empty road for Mr. Pig to cross. At this rate, crossing the road hardly qualifies as heroic.

Don't worry, this is a small little problem that you'll tackle when you're handling updates within the game render loop. That won't be in this chapter, so for now, just accept the current state.

Animate the pig

Your next focus point is to make that pig jump like a little flea. Mr. Pig will need to be quick on his feet, able to jump forwards, backwards, left and right.

To accomplish this, you'll create a whole bunch of little, basic actions that you'll sequence and group together.

Add the following action properties to `ViewController`:

```
var jumpLeftAction: SCNAction!
var jumpRightAction: SCNAction!
var jumpForwardAction: SCNAction!
var jumpBackwardAction: SCNAction!
```

These are the four resulting actions that will perform the jump action in the various directions.

Add the following to bottom of `setupActions()`:

```
// 1
let duration = 0.2

// 2
let bounceUpAction = SCNAction.moveByX(0, y: 1.0, z: 0,
duration: duration * 0.5)
let bounceDownAction = SCNAction.moveByX(0, y: -1.0, z: 0,
duration: duration * 0.5)

// 3
bounceUpAction.timingMode = .EaseOut
bounceDownAction.timingMode = .EaseIn

// 4
let bounceAction = SCNAction.sequence([bounceUpAction,
bounceDownAction])

// 5
let moveLeftAction = SCNAction.moveByX(-1.0, y: 0, z: 0,
duration: duration)
let moveRightAction = SCNAction.moveByX(1.0, y: 0, z: 0,
duration: duration)
let moveForwardAction = SCNAction.moveByX(0, y: 0, z: -1.0,
duration: duration)
let moveBackwardAction = SCNAction.moveByX(0, y: 0, z: 1.0,
duration: duration)

// 6
let turnLeftAction = SCNAction.rotateToX(0, y:
convertToRadians(-90), z: 0, duration: duration,
shortestUnitArc: true)
let turnRightAction = SCNAction.rotateToX(0, y:
convertToRadians(90), z: 0, duration: duration, shortestUnitArc:
true)
let turnForwardAction = SCNAction.rotateToX(0, y:
convertToRadians(180), z: 0, duration: duration,
shortestUnitArc: true)
let turnBackwardAction = SCNAction.rotateToX(0, y:
convertToRadians(0), z: 0, duration: duration, shortestUnitArc:
true)

// 7
jumpLeftAction = SCNAction.group([turnLeftAction, bounceAction,
moveLeftAction])
jumpRightAction = SCNAction.group([turnRightAction,
bounceAction, moveRightAction])
jumpForwardAction = SCNAction.group([turnForwardAction,
bounceAction, moveForwardAction])
jumpBackwardAction = SCNAction.group([turnBackwardAction,
bounceAction, moveBackwardAction])
```

Quite the screen full, so how about a breakdown?

1. Using a variable for the duration will simply make your life easier once you start tweaking action animation times. You'd typically work in fragments of a specific duration, and this simplifies it so that you can use simple math to specify a fragment of the original duration.

2. This creates the two basic actions that bounce the pig up and down, similar to the visual examples demonstrated in the beginning of this chapter.

3. This updates the timing functions for the bounce actions so that when they run in a sequence, the pig will have a realistic jump animation with some hang-time! :]

4. This creates `bounceAction` by using the bounce up and bounce down actions in sequence.

5. This creates four move actions using `SCNAction.moveByX(_:y:z:duration:)` to move in every direction.

6. This creates four rotation actions using `SCNAction.rotateToX(_:y:z:duration:shortUnitArc:)`, one for rotating to each direction.

7. Finally, this creates the four jump actions by combining the turn, bounce and move actions into a group, which will run all three actions in parallel.

Add gesture controls

All the actions are now ready to go. What's left now is to get Mr. Pig to respond to some gestures so that you know what actions to run.

Create four basic gestures for your game by adding the following to `setupGestures()`:

```
let swipeRight:UISwipeGestureRecognizer =
UISwipeGestureRecognizer(target: self, action:
#selector(ViewController.handleGesture(_:)))
swipeRight.direction = .Right
scnView.addGestureRecognizer(swipeRight)

let swipeLeft:UISwipeGestureRecognizer =
UISwipeGestureRecognizer(target: self, action:
#selector(ViewController.handleGesture(_:)))
swipeLeft.direction = .Left
scnView.addGestureRecognizer(swipeLeft)

let swipeForward:UISwipeGestureRecognizer =
UISwipeGestureRecognizer(target: self, action:
#selector(ViewController.handleGesture(_:)))
```

```
    swipeForward.direction = .Up
    scnView.addGestureRecognizer(swipeForward)

    let swipeBackward:UISwipeGestureRecognizer =
    UISwipeGestureRecognizer(target: self, action:
    #selector(ViewController.handleGesture(_:)))
    swipeBackward.direction = .Down
    scnView.addGestureRecognizer(swipeBackward)
```

This registers the `handleGesture(_:)` method as the event handler for the swipe up,
down, left and right gestures, so that when the player does a swipe gesture,
`handleGesture(_:)` will trigger further action.

> **Note**: You're sending all the gestures to the same handler. You'll filter out the exact
> details of the gesture within the handler method itself, which is up next.

Now add `handleGesture(_:)` to `ViewController`.

```
// 1
func handleGesture(sender:UISwipeGestureRecognizer){
  // 2
  guard game.state == .Playing else {
    return
  }
  // 3
  switch sender.direction {
    case UISwipeGestureRecognizerDirection.Up:
      pigNode.runAction(jumpForwardAction)
    case UISwipeGestureRecognizerDirection.Down:
      pigNode.runAction(jumpBackwardAction)
    case UISwipeGestureRecognizerDirection.Left:
      if pigNode.position.x > -15 {
        pigNode.runAction(jumpLeftAction)
      }
    case UISwipeGestureRecognizerDirection.Right:
      if pigNode.position.x < 15 {
        pigNode.runAction(jumpRightAction)
      }
    default:
      break
  }
}
```

Take a deeper look at exactly what happens here:

1. This defines a typical gesture handler and receives a `UIGestureRecognizer` as an
   input. You'll need to inspect this element to determine the exact gesture details.

2. This keeps the game state in mind. Typically you're not interested in any gestures

unless the game is in a .Playing state, so ignore all gesture events when the game state is something else.

3. This inspects direction of the gesture recognizer to determine the direction the player swiped in. Then, it executes the correct jump action on the pig node, which will make the pig jump in the direction of the swipe. There's also a small check when jumping left and right to prevent Mr. Pig from jumping out of the play area.

Do a build and run and go test out the gesture control system:

Once your game starts, you should be able to swipe in any direction, and Mr. Pig will follow your every command. Excellent! :]

But wait there's another problem, the camera isn't following the pig, so he's able to jump out of sight. Don't worry, this is just another small little problem to sort out when you're handling updates within the game render loop.

Create game over action

You're almost done with this chapter. There's just one more action you need to create that you'll use a little bit later on: the triggerGameOver action!

This little action comprises a few sub-actions that will send our beloved hero to piggie heaven, and then finally trigger a call to startSplash() to show the splash scene again.

Start off by adding the following action property to ViewController:

```
var triggerGameOver: SCNAction!
```

This stores the final action you'll run to trigger the game over sequence.

Add the following to the bottom of `setupActions()`:

```
// 1
let spinAround = SCNAction.rotateByX(0, y:
convertToRadians(720), z: 0, duration: 2.0)
let riseUp = SCNAction.moveByX(0, y: 10, z: 0, duration: 2.0)
let fadeOut = SCNAction.fadeOpacityTo(0, duration: 2.0)
let goodByePig = SCNAction.group([spinAround, riseUp, fadeOut])
// 2
let gameOver = SCNAction.runBlock { (node:SCNNode) -> Void in
  self.pigNode.position = SCNVector3(x:0, y:0, z:0)
  self.pigNode.opacity = 1.0
  self.startSplash()
}
// 3
triggerGameOver = SCNAction.sequence([goodByePig, gameOver])
```

Here's what happens in here:

1. This creates a few basic actions: one to spin the pig 720 degrees, one to move him up into the sky and another to fade him into nothingness. All three actions are put together under a single action group, fittingly named `goodByePig`. This is the animation sequence to make poor Mr. Pig go to the heaven's gate when he meets his fate. :]

2. The `SCNAction.runBlock(_:)` class method creates a special action that allows you to inject code logic into an action, which then can be executed just like any other action. This specific code block simply resets Mr. Pig to his original position and opacity level and then triggers `startSplash()` to bring you back to the splash scene.

3. This creates the final `triggerGameOver` action sequence that first executes the `goodByePig` action, and then once completed, it executes the `gameOver` run block action.

To finish off this chapter, add the following to the bottom of `stopGame()`:

```
pigNode.runAction(triggerGameOver)
```

This will insure that what ever makes a call to the `stopGame()` function will trigger the `triggerGameOver` action sequence, ultimately ending the game. So sad... :[

To test this, add the following temporary code to the top of `handleGesture(_:)`:

```
stopGame()
return
```

Build and run, start the game, then swipe in any direction to trigger the death animation. Poor pig!

Be sure to delete or comment the test code before you continue on:

```
//stopGame()
//return
```

Where to go from here?

Your steller performance has brought you to the end of yet another chapter! Your game is in fantastic shape and there's not too much left to do.

To recap what you've learned in this chapter:

- **Actions**: You learned about actions and how to combine them to build intricate animation sequences.

- **Actions Editor**: You learned all about Xcode's built-in secondary editor for SCNNode, aka the actions editor.

- **Timing Functions**: You learned about timing functions that manipulate the progression of an action over time and allow you to simulate realism in action-packed animation sequences.

- **Coding Actions**: You also got your hands dirty by manually creating a whole bunch of different actions for your game in code.

There are a few things that still needs to be addressed, one of the more hilarious being that our hero is unstoppable – neither tree nor car nor bus can stop him. Did you mean to make some kind of mutant pig? :]

The next chapter will focus on solving all that by means of collision detection.

Chapter 19: Advanced Collision Detection

Chris Language

Your game is almost done. It has a vibrant splash scene complete with spinning sun rays, a twerking pig and a game scene that hosts a beautiful park filled with lovely trees, coins and two massive traffic-filled highways.

To top it off, you've added animations to bring the whole thing to life.

In this chapter, your target will be to solve a few problems:

- Nothing can block the little pig right now. Typically obstacles like the trees would fence him in. This poses a little secondary challenge: proactively block movement so that there is no way for the pig to even collide with the tree.

- Traffic isn't a threat, which makes for a most unchallenging game. You'll change all that. The next time the little pig runs in front of a bus it will be his last! .]

- Your poor little pig can only look at the pretty, shiny coins – he can't pick them up. Don't worry, you'll solve that too.

Well, the game isn't to finish itself! Wake up and smell the bacon. It's time to get to it!

> **Note**: There's a starter project for you available under **projects\starter\Mr.Pig**, it continues exactly where the previous chapter left off.

Hidden geometry for collisions

You've already covered basic collision detection and are familiar with collision masks and how they work. To proactively block the little pig's movement before he even collides with an obstacle like a tree, you'll use some ultra-cool, advanced collision detection techniques.

The secret is to make use of hidden geometry that would actually cause an active collision with nearby obstacles, essentially giving Mr. Pig a sixth sense.

He can only move one space forward, backward, left or right. By creating four boxes placed around the pig for each one of those directions, you'll be able to keep track of every box that might find itself in an active collision with an obstacle.

You simply need to block jumps in the direction(s) where these boxes are actively in a collision. Mind blowing stuff, right?

In the below scenario, you can see four boxes placed around the pig, and none are currently in an active collision. For now, Mr. Pig can freely jump in any direction.

Now consider the next scenario. In this instance, the box to the right finds itself currently in collision with an obstacle. Now you have something substantive to use to prevent the pig from jumping to the right.

Create a hidden collision node

Now that you know how the hidden geometry collision technique will work, you need to create the collision node for your game that will contain the four boxes you'll use for the purpose of collision detection.

Create a collision node

Create a new empty scene by dragging and dropping a **Scene Kit Scene** into the root of your project folder. In the creation wizard, name the new scene **Collision.scn**, and make sure you save it under **MrPig.scnassets**.

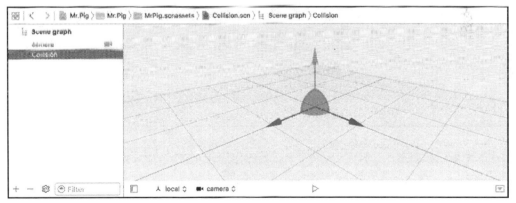

With **Collision.scn** selected, add an empty node to the scene graph and name it **Collision**.

This will be the group node for the collision boxes. Now to create those boxes, drag and drop a **Box** into the scene, and make sure to place it under the **Collision** group node.

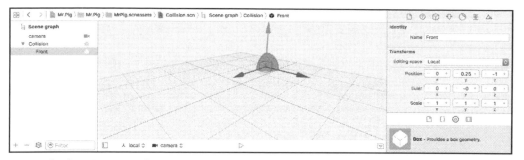

Name the box **Front** and position it at (x:0, y:0.25, z:-1) to offset it a bit from the center. Bring up the Attributes Inspector and set the size to be (x:0.25, y:0.25, z:0.25), a bit smaller than default.

Now simply press the Option key along with Command to drag out three quick copies of the front box for the back, left and right. Make sure that all the new copies are placed under the **Collision** group node, just like the front box node you created.

Once you have three copies of the node, you need to position them correctly. Start off with the back box. Name it **Back**, and position it at (x:0, y:0.25, z:1).

Next, select the node that will be your **Left** box. Name it **Left** and position it at (x:-1, y:0.25, z:0):

Finally, select the remaining node, name it **Right** and position it at (x:1, y:0.25, z: 0):

At this point, your scene editor should look like this:

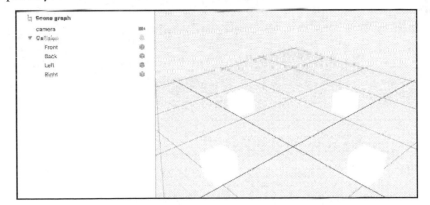

You're halfway done with this part and will play around with physics next.

Enabling physics

Each box needs a category bit mask so that you can tell which one is involved in a collision with an obstacle.

You're about to do a cool little trick that the Scene Kit editor allows you to do – accessing and editing multiple node's attributes and physics properties at the same time. Say what? :]

Start by selecting all the boxes. One quick way to do this is by selecting the first box in the scene graph, and then holding the Shift key while clicking the last box.

With all the the nodes highlighted, bring up the Physics Inspector. Change the **Type** to **Kinematic**.

Since you have all four nodes selected, this change will apply to all of the boxes.

> **Note**: This cool little feature works for all the inspectors in the scene editor, so you can use the trick anytime you've got a group of nodes that should have similar properties – obviously, a box node will have different attributes than a sphere node.
>
> Another thing to point out here is that if all of the nodes have the same value for a specific property, then that value would be visible. If one of the selected nodes has a different value than the others, then you would see **Multiple Values** as a value. You can quickly synchronise properties by using this feature.

Here's another little trick to perform. Try licking your own elbow! Just kidding, stop trying, it's impossible. Seriously, stop now! :]

The *actual* trick is to hide the geometry so that your clever little collision trick is concealed from the player.

Besides, it would look pretty silly to have those four boxes showing.

With the four box nodes still selected, select the Node Inspector then scroll down to the **Visibility** section. Set **Opacity** to 0.5. You need to also disable shadows by unchecking the **Casts Shadow** checkbox, so that the boxes don't give themselves away with shadows.

For your purposes, you don't want them to be totally transparent because it'll be helpful to see them in action. In a final version of the game, you would be changing the opacity to 0 to make the boxes fully invisible to the player.

> **Note**: By setting a node's opacity level to 0, the node is physically still in the scene, it's just invisible. This means that if you have physics properties set on that node, it would still participate in collisions during the physics simulation.
>
> If you were to set the node's visibility to **Hidden,** you would completely remove the node from the scene to such a point that it wouldn't cause any collisions even if it has physics properties.

Things are about to get more granular.

You need to go to each box individually to set up category bit masks because each will have different values. Start with **Front**, bring up the Physics Inspector and set its **Category mask** to 8.

For **Back**, set its **Category mask** to 16.

Now for **Left**, set its **Category mask** to 32.

Then finally, set **Right** to have a **Category mask** to 64.

Remember to delete that default **camera**, and then you're all done.

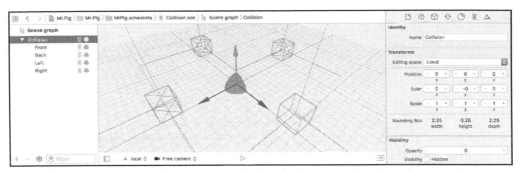

You should now have a **Collision.scn** with four little boxes placed nicely around the middle point of the scene.

Using the collision node

With **Collision.scn** created, what's left for you to do is to actually use this node as a reference node in your game scene.

Add collision reference node

Select **MrPig.scnassets\GameScene.scn**, then drag and drop a **Collsion.scn** reference node into the scene.

Be sure to position it exactly at position (x:0, y:0, z:0), smack bang on the pig.

Now you need to attach your code to the nodes. Add the following properties to ViewController in **ViewController.swift**:

```
var collisionNode: SCNNode!
var frontCollisionNode: SCNNode!
var backCollisionNode: SCNNode!
var leftCollisionNode: SCNNode!
var rightCollisionNode: SCNNode!
```

These are the properties you'll use to access the **Collision** group node as well as each individual collision box node: **Front, Back, Left and Right**.

To bind the code to the nodes in the scene, add the following code to the bottom of setupNodes():

```
collisionNode =
gameScene.rootNode.childNodeWithName("Collision", recursively:
true)!
frontCollisionNode =
gameScene.rootNode.childNodeWithName("Front", recursively:
true)!
backCollisionNode = gameScene.rootNode.childNodeWithName("Back",
recursively: true)!
leftCollisionNode = gameScene.rootNode.childNodeWithName("Left",
recursively: true)!
rightCollisionNode =
gameScene.rootNode.childNodeWithName("Right", recursively:
true)!
```

This will bind to all the different properties to the **Collision** group node and each collision box node.

Create the render loop

This collision node has to follow Mr. Pig around. The easiest way to do that is to simply update the position of the collision node to the same position as the pig inside the render loop updates.

First, you need to create a new method that will be responsible for updating the node's positions during the render loop of the game. Add the following method to ViewController:

```
func updatePositions() {
  collisionNode.position = pigNode.presentationNode.position
}
```

This will keep the position for collisionNode in sync with the position for pigNode.

Now that you have this method in place, you need to call it in your game's render loop. To do that, you're going to implement the renderer(_: didApplyAnimationsAtTime:) delegate method from the SCNSceneRendererDelegate protocol.

Add the following to the bottom of **ViewController.swift**:

```
// 1
extension ViewController : SCNSceneRendererDelegate {
  // 2
  func renderer(renderer: SCNSceneRenderer,
didApplyAnimationsAtTime time: NSTimeInterval) {
    // 3
    guard game.state == .Playing else {
      return
    }
    // 4
    game.updateHUD()
    // 5
    updatePositions()
  }
}
```

Take a closer look at that code:

1. This ensures that `ViewController` conforms to the `SCNSceneRenderDelegate` protocol. You use a class extension to organize code from the protocol so that it's separate from the rest of your `ViewController` code.

2. This injects your update game logic just after all the animation actions completed inside the render loop. This way you know exactly the position of each object in your scene, after the applied actions.

3. Again, keeping game states in mind, you only want to do updates while the game is in a `.Playing` state. This `guard` statement will prevent the rest of the method from running if `game.state` is not `.Playing`.

4. This ensures that the HUD node gets updated whenever there is a render update. You added the HUD as a child node to `cameraNode` in a previous chapter.

5. Finally, you make a call to `updatePositions()`, keeping the `collisionNode` position in sync with the `pigNode` position.

Remember to set `ViewController` as the delegate for the view by adding the following line of code to the bottom of the `setupScenes()`:

```
scnView.delegate = self
```

Do a quick build and run and move the pig around to verify the render loop is actually functioning.

If you used an opacity of 0.5 for the boxes, you should see the four boxes follow Mr. Pig wherever he goes, like his own personal security detail. You should also now notice updates that happen in the HUD showing at the top of the screen. Excellent!

> **Note**: Quick clarification of the contents of the HUD: The pig snout shows the total amount of coins collected, and the little house shows the total number of coins banked.

Configure the physics

Define bit masks

Continuing with granular tasks, you'll define a bunch of collision masks next. In ViewController, define the following constants:

```
// 1
let BitMaskPig = 1
let BitMaskVehicle = 2
let BitMaskObstacle = 4
let BitMaskFront = 8
let BitMaskBack = 16
let BitMaskLeft = 32
```

```
let BitMaskRight = 64
let BitMaskCoin = 128
let BitMaskHouse = 256
```

Now you have a good idea of all the elements in the game that will play an important role within the collision detection space.

Enable physics

With the bit mask constants defined, you get to move on to a fun little exercise where you'll enable physics for all the important elements of your game, starting with the *most important* element, our hero, Mr. Pig.

Select **MrPig.scnassets\MrPig.scn** to open up the reference node for Mr. Pig. Select the **MrPig** node in the scene graph and open up the Physics Inspector. Change **Type** to **Kinematic** because you'll be running actions on the pig node to change its position.

Under the **Bit masks** section, change **Category mask** to 1. Then finally, under the **Physics shape** section, change **Type** to **Bounding Box** and set **Scale** to 0.6 to shrink the bounding box down to a smaller size.

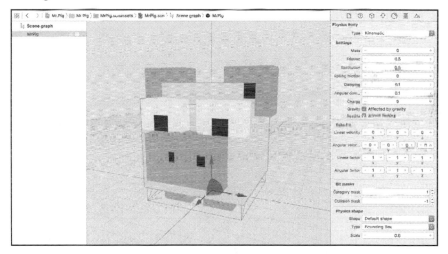

> **Note:** When your game reaches its final stages, you might want to come back and tweak the bounding box size to give the collisions a bit of leeway.

Vehicles are up next, so select **MrPig.scnassets\Bus.scn** and follow the same process as before. Select the **Bus** node in the scene graph, and open the Physics Inspector. Remember that there is already a move action running on the bus node, so you have to change the **Type** to **Kinematic**.

Next, change the **Catergory mask** to 2, which is the same bit mask you'll use for all the vehicles. Then finish off by scrolling down to **Physics shape** and setting **Type** to **Bounding Box** and **Scale** to 0.8:

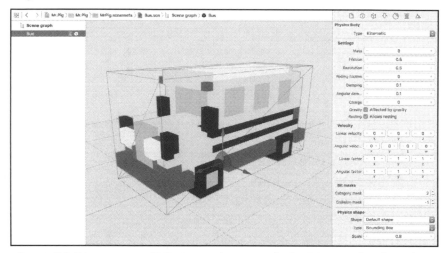

Next in line is **MrPig.scnassets\Mini.scn**. Again, with the **Mini** node selected, set **Type** to **Kinematic** in the Physics Inspector, then set the **Category mask** to 2.

Finally, under **Physics Shape**, set the **Type** to **Bounding Box** with a **Scale** of 0.8:

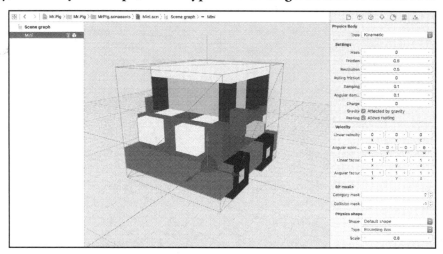

Select the last vehicle, **MrPig.scnassets\SUV.scn**. The SUV will be exactly like the Bus and Mini, so select the **SUV** node and open the Physics Inspector. Set the **Type** to **Kinematic**, then set the **Category mask** to 2.

Finally, under **Physics shape**, set **Type** to **Bounding Box** and **Scale** to 0.8:

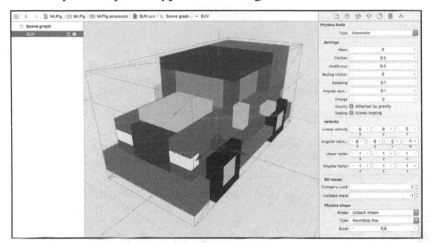

Let's see. Pig? Check. Vehicles? Check. Trees? Not set up yet.

To keep you on your toes, instead of enabling physics on each individual tree, you're going to enable physics on the reference nodes you created in an earlier chapter, **MrPig.scnassets\TreeLine.scn** and **MrPig.scnassets\TreePatch.scn**.

First, select **MrPig.scnassets\TreeLine.scn**. Make sure you have the **TreeLine** node selected and the Physics Inspector open. Trees don't need to move around – unless you're planning to create some kind of fantasy world – so you're going to set the **Type** to **Static**.

Set the **Category mask** to 4, indicating that the trees are all obstacles. Under **Physics shape**, set **Type** to **Bounding Box** and leave the **Scale** at 1.

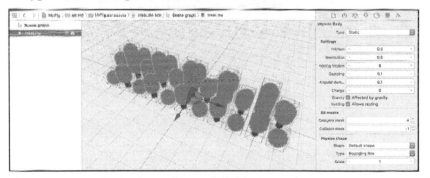

Because the TreeLine node consists of several child tree nodes, you're saving yourself a ton of work once again. The children will inherit the parent's physics properties, saving you from enabling physics on each and every little tree.

Select **MrPig.scnassets\TreePatch.scn** next. This one will work exactly the same as the TreeLine node. With the **TreePatch** node selected, along with the Physics Inspector, set the **Type** to **Static**, **Category mask** to 4. Under **Physics shape**, set the **Type** to

Bounding Box and leave the **Scale** at 1:

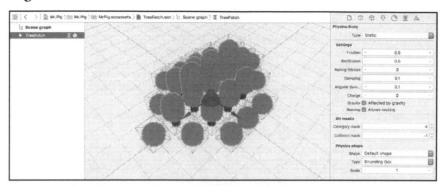

Looks like you're just down to playing around with the coins. Find the **MrPig.scnassets \Coin.scn** reference node.

As it was before, there are actions running on the coin, so you need to set the **Type** to **Kinematic**. Set the **Category mask** to 128, then change the **Type** under **Physics shape** to **Bounding Box** with a **Scale** of 0.8.

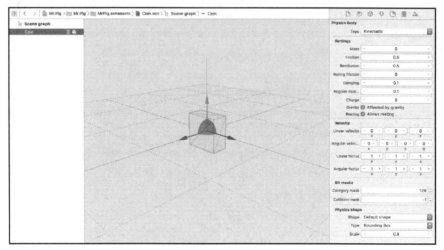

You're finally all done with that. Phew! :]

Set contact bit masks

Now you're back to one of your original objectives: actually blocking the pig when there are obstacles in his way. For this, you'll make use of the contact test between physics bodies.

Oddly enough, the Scene Kit Editor doesn't allow you to modify to the contact test bit mask property yet, so you'll have to manually set that up in code. Fortunately, you don't have to figure it all out on your own!

The following snippet of code has you covered – just open up **ViewController.swift**, add this to the bottom of `setupNodes()` and you're all set:

```
// 1
pigNode.physicsBody?.contactTestBitMask = BitMaskVehicle |
BitMaskCoin | BitMaskHouse
// 2
frontCollisionNode.physicsBody?.contactTestBitMask =
BitMaskObstacle
backCollisionNode.physicsBody?.contactTestBitMask =
BitMaskObstacle
leftCollisionNode.physicsBody?.contactTestBitMask =
BitMaskObstacle
rightCollisionNode.physicsBody?.contactTestBitMask =
BitMaskObstacle
```

There are a couple of things to note:

1. This sets up the contact test bit mask for `pigNode`. From this, you now know that the pig itself will be able to make contact with vehicles, coins and the house.

2. This sets up the contact test bit mask for all the box nodes inside the **Collision** node. The boxes are interested in any object that's an obstacle.

Handle collisions

Collisions with obstacles

As you learned in Chapter 10, "Basic Collision Detection", you set the `contactTestBitMask` of a physics body so that you get notified whenever it touches another physics body with a category mask that matches that mask value.

To keep track of the active collisions in your game, you'll create a special property called `activeCollisionsBitMask`. When one of the four collision boxes makes contact with an obstacle, the `physicsWorld(_:didBeginContact:)` delegate method will be triggered.

You can then use the affected box's category bit mask and add it to the `activeCollisionsBitMask` by means of a bitwise OR (|) operation. This will essentially keep track of all active collisions. Then, the gesture handler can inspect `activeCollisionsBitMask` and ultimately block the gestures based on the active collision directions.

Once the collision ends, the `physicsWorld(_:didEndContact:)` delegate method will be triggered. At that point, you can remove the affected box's category bit mask from `activeCollisionsBitMask`.

This is done by means of first performing a bitwise NOT (~) operation on the category bit mask and then performing a bitwise AND (|) on the result.

Add the following property to `ViewController`:

```
var activeCollisionsBitMask: Int = 0
```

This is the bit mask that will keep track of all the active collisions. Now you need to implement the methods from the `SCNPhysicsContactDelegate` protocol. Add the following code to the bottom of **ViewContoller.swift**:

```
// 1
extension ViewController : SCNPhysicsContactDelegate {
  // 2
  func physicsWorld(world: SCNPhysicsWorld,
    didBeginContact contact: SCNPhysicsContact) {
    // 3
    guard game.state == .Playing else {
      return
    }
    // 4
    var collisionBoxNode: SCNNode!
    if contact.nodeA.physicsBody?.categoryBitMask ==
BitMaskObstacle {
      collisionBoxNode = contact.nodeB
    } else {
      collisionBoxNode = contact.nodeA
    }
    // 5
    activeCollisionsBitMask |=
      collisionBoxNode.physicsBody!.categoryBitMask
  }
  // 6
  func physicsWorld(world: SCNPhysicsWorld,
    didEndContact contact: SCNPhysicsContact) {
    // 8
    guard game.state == .Playing else {
      return
    }
    // 8
    var collisionBoxNode: SCNNode!
    if contact.nodeA.physicsBody?.categoryBitMask ==
BitMaskObstacle {
      collisionBoxNode = contact.nodeB
    } else {
      collisionBoxNode = contact.nodeA
    }
    // 9
    activeCollisionsBitMask &=
      ~collisionBoxNode.physicsBody!.categoryBitMask
  }
}
```

Here's a section-by-section breakdown:

1. This adds a class extension to `ViewController` and makes the class conform to the `SCNPhysicsContactDelegate` protocol.

2. This defines a handler for when a `physicsWorld(_:didBeginContact:)` event gets triggered.

3. You only want to keep track of collisions while the game is in a `.Playing` state.

4. This is a familiar bit of code where you determine whether `nodeA` or `nodeB` is the obstacle, which means that the other node is the collision box.

5. This does a bitwise OR operation to add the colliding box's category bit mask to `activeCollisionsBitMask`.

6. This defines a handler for when a `physicsWorld(_:didEndContact:)` event gets triggered.

7. Again, you only want to keep track of these events while the game is in a `.Playing` state.

8. Again, this is used to determine which node in the contact test is the collision box.

9. Finally, this first does a bitwise NOT operation followed by a bitwise AND operation to remove the collision box category bit mask from the `activeCollisionsBitMask`.

Now you can add code that will inspect the `activeCollisionsBitMask` to block gestures inside the gesture handler.

Add the following code inside `handleGestures()` right after the block, making sure you're in a `.Playing` state:

```
// 1
let activeFrontCollision = activeCollisionsBitMask &
BitMaskFront == BitMaskFront
let activeBackCollision = activeCollisionsBitMask & BitMaskBack
== BitMaskBack
let activeLeftCollision = activeCollisionsBitMask & BitMaskLeft
== BitMaskLeft
let activeRightCollision = activeCollisionsBitMask &
BitMaskRight == BitMaskRight

// 2
guard (sender.direction == .Up && !activeFrontCollision) ||
  (sender.direction == .Down && !activeBackCollision) ||
  (sender.direction == .Left && !activeLeftCollision) ||
  (sender.direction == .Right && !activeRightCollision) else {
    return
}
```

Let's look at the code you just added:

1. This uses a bitwise AND to check for active collisions in each direction stored in `activeCollisionsBitMask` and saves them in individual constants.

2. This `guard` statement makes sure that you only continue on to the rest of the gesture handler code when there is no active collision in the direction of the gesture. For example, if the gesture direction is up and there is an active collision, the entire condition will evaluate to `false` and code execution will go to the `else` clause of the `guard` statement which will end the gesture handler.

One last thing you need to do is to set your `ViewController` up as the contact delegate for your game scene's physics world by adding the following line of code to the bottom of `setupScenes()`:

```
gameScene.physicsWorld.contactDelegate = self
```

This sets `self` as the `contactDelegate` for `gameScene.physicsWorld`.

Time for a quick build and run to test things out.

Try and jump as far down as possible. If all sanity is intact, then Mr. Pig will not be able to jump into the tree anymore. Yay!

Collisions with vehicles

The next bit is easy. You need to make sure that he doesn't survive when he throws himself in front of a bus.

Add the following code to bottom of `physicsWorld(_:didBeginContact:)`:

```
// 1
var contactNode: SCNNode!
if contact.nodeA.physicsBody?.categoryBitMask == BitMaskPig {
  contactNode = contact.nodeB
} else {
  contactNode = contact.nodeA
}

// 2
if contactNode.physicsBody?.categoryBitMask == BitMaskVehicle {
  stopGame()
}
```

1. You should now be very familiar with how this snippet of code determines which node is the pig and which is not. Once done, you know for a fact that the `contactNode` is not the pig.

2. If the node the pig made contact with is indeed a vehicle, then it's the end of the game.

Build, run and throw that pig under a bus!

If you're fast enough, you can catch some traffic. Once the bus collides with the poor little pig, he flies off to heaven and the game transitions back to the splash scene, exactly as it was designed to do.

Collisions with coins

Next up, Mr. Pig needs to be able to actually collect those coins.

Add the following code to the bottom of physicsWorld(_:didBeginContact:):

```
// 1
if contactNode.physicsBody?.categoryBitMask == BitMaskCoin {
  // 2
  contactNode.hidden = true

  contactNode.runAction(SCNAction.waitForDurationThenRunBlock(60)
  { (node: SCNNode!) -> Void in
    node.hidden = false
  })
  // 3
  game.collectCoin()
}
```

Let's look at the code:

1. You check if the node the pig made contact with is a coin.

2. If it is, you hide the coin node, then run an action on it that will unhide the coin after 60 seconds.

3. Then you call the collectCoin() method on game, which will update the score.

Build and run and go grab that coin!

Be careful though – Mr. Pig is a mere mortal now. Watch out for that bus! :]

If you manage to cross the road, you'll see coins disappear once Mr. Pig jumps on them. You should notice the score increase as well. Excellent!

Where to go from here?

You've now conquered the hardest tasks of your game, and the end is in sight! Reaching this point means you deserve a pat on the back.

You can continue to administer said back-patting for yourself as I'm stuck behind the print here; feel free to sneak in another attempt to lick your elbow while you're at it. :]

Understanding how to use hidden geometry to assist your game with collision detection is the primary concept to take away from this chapter.

It's a technique that can be applied to many use cases, including these:

- In an FPS game, it can be used to determine if your hero was stabbed from the front or back.

- In a platform game, it can be used to flip a nearby switch or check if your hero is standing close to the edge.

- You can also use hidden geometry for particle systems, like a campfire for example, so you can respond accordingly when someone steps into it.

There are quite a few bits that are left unattended, so in the next chapter you'll add those much needed finishing touches. For now, go and take a well deserved break, but hurry back!

Chapter 20: Audio

Chris Language

This is the final chapter in which you'll conclude the 3D Scene Kit game you've been building since Chapter 16 – Mr. Pig. Don't worry, that light at the end of the tunnel isn't a bus about to hit you, it's success barreling down on you!

The main focus of this chapter will be on audio and Scene Kit. Along the way, you'll get to put some final touches on the game too.

Only a few more steps to go before all is done. Good luck! :]

> **Note:** There's a starter project for you available under **projects\starter\Mr.Pig**, it continues where the previous chapter ended.
>
> There is one small difference: the opacity of the collision boxes are now set to 0 to make them invisible to the player. If you want to continue using your current project, just make that same change before continuing.

Adding finishing touches

Mr. Pig's habit of jumping out of the camera's view is pretty annoying, and where the heck is all the traffic disappearing to?

Don't worry. You're about to resolve all these little annoyances by working with render loop updates for your game.

Update camera position

It's time to unleash Big Brother and follow that little pig's every move. Surely the authorities are wondering where on earth he gets all his money, and you need to keep a sharp eye on him so you can usher him and his coins safely across traffic. Killing off that darn static camera is the best thing for all parties involved.

Open up **ViewController.swift** and add the following code to bottom of `updatePositions()`:

```
let lerpX = (pigNode.position.x - cameraFollowNode.position.x) *
0.05
let lerpZ = (pigNode.position.z - cameraFollowNode.position.z) *
0.05
cameraFollowNode.position.x += lerpX
cameraFollowNode.position.z += lerpZ
```

In the previous chapter, you already created the `updatePositions()` method, which gets called 60 times per second as part of your game's render loop update.

So the first two lines calculate a linearly interpolated x and z value between `pigNode` and `cameraFollowNode`, with a factor of `0.05`. The results are then added to the position of `cameraFollowNode`. In turn, this moves the camera towards the pig's position over a period of time.

Instead of simply updating `cameraFollowNode` to the same position as that of the `pigNode`, this technique creates a smooth, lazy camera tracking effect.

> **Note**: To make the camera less lazy and more responsive, you can tweak the factor. Setting the factor to `1.0` will make the camera tracking 100 percent real-time.

Do a build and run and see if you can get the little pig to escape the eye in the sky.

At last, the camera follows the pig everywhere, and now he can explore the entire park under your watchful eye. Hey, did Mr. Pig just discover another coin? Awesome! :]

Hang on, after moving Mr. Pig around the park for a bit, did you notice something odd with the scene?

Is that large shadow on the top-right an alien mothership about to land? And why the heck does that coin have no shadow? Is it impervious to sunlight?

Relax, there are no aliens in this game and the shadow mystery will soon be resolved. All will be revealed in the next little section.

Update light position

In order to make your game as efficient as possible, one of the applied techniques was tweaking your light settings so that only the visible areas in view cast shadows.

And this is the culprit for all those weird things you noticed. Specifically, it's because of the shadow clipping range that you configured on the directional light that you configured earlier.

Now that you know the problem, the fix is elementary: just make the light follow the camera around. Thank goodness, sanity restored! :]

Add the following line to the bottom of `updatePositions()`:

```
lightFollowNode.position = cameraFollowNode.position
```

This simply updates `lightFollowNode`'s position to the exact same position of `cameraFollowNode`, thus keeping the light in sync with the camera's point of view.

Do another build and run to see if the shadow issue has been resolved.

Hey, that coin is still there, and everything now has shadows. It looks like you successfully foiled an alien invasion too.

What a lovely, sunny day indeed!

Update traffic bounds

On to your next problem – where is all that traffic going? Something is seriously wrong here; traffic never just disappears, unless there's a black hole in the road ahead. :]

What you really want to accomplish here is the effect of endless traffic with only a few cars. Fortunately, the solution is quite simple.

By introducing a bounds check for each moving vehicle, you can actively monitor for when a vehicle drives past a defined boundary and then reset the vehicle's position to the opposite side of the scene.

Once you do that, the vehicle has to travel from the beginning again, thus driving through the scene in an endless loop of madness.

Add the following updateTraffic() method to ViewController:

```
func updateTraffic() {
  // 1
  for node in trafficNode.childNodes {
    // 2
    if node.position.x > 25 {
      node.position.x = -25
    } else if node.position.x < -25 {
      node.position.x = 25
    }
  }
}
```

1. You are iterating through all the vechicle nodes placed under trafficNode group node.

2. Once the node's x-position crosses the 25 unit mark, you reset it to −25 and vice versa for nodes moving in the opposite direction.

Don't forget to actually call the updateTraffic() method inside the render loop update. Add the following code to the bottom of renderer(_:updateAtTime:):

```
updateTraffic()
```

Build and run, and review the changes.

Wow, look at that traffic flow. It just never stops, as you'd expect. How on earth did the poor little pig manage to get himself trapped on that island between the highways? Now the traffic flows forever and ever, just like in real life! :]

Challenge!

Why did the little pig cross the road? Because he got *boared*!

Granted, that was pretty weak, the real answer is because he wanted to *score*...points.

Speaking of scoring, it's time to reward yourself by proving you've got the skills to crack this challenge. What? Huh?

That's right, it's challenge time, and this one is specifically designed to give your game some *purpose*.

When you think about it, what happens if Mr. Pig runs across the road, then simply stays in the park, never to cross the road again? He's a smart little pig; he would totally try to do something like that just to avoid a run-in with an SUV.

But, there's an incentive for him to make that dangerous trek across the highway: points.

Once the little pig has collected a few coins, in order to actually score, he has to bank them somewhere. Plus, they get heavy after a while.

Back in Chapter 16, you read about how Mr. Pig banks coins in his house (most likely under the mattress) and that he's got a kettle of tea on the ready.

Your challenge, dear reader, is to build that home.

Fear not, most of the hard work is done and you won't have to pick up a hammer. All you need to do is build a small reference scene with a little house, car and garden in it. Doesn't that sound like fun?

Here's a high level look at the steps ahead:

1. Start by creating an empty Scene Kit scene named **Home.scn** and deleting the default camera.

2. Add a little **House.scn** into the scene, right in the middle.

3. Create an empty group node named **Obstacles**. Make sure you place all the rest of the objects for this scene under this node.

4. Add a few trees – big, medium and small. (See reference image below)

5. Add a little **Mini.scn** too.

You can use the following reference image for building Mr. Pigs little **Home.scn**:

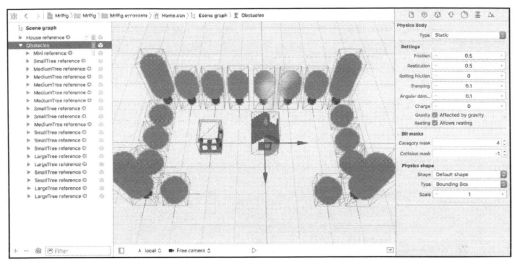

7. You need to set up the physics for all **Obstacles** too; make sure they are static physics bodies with a category bit mask of 4. For the little **House**, use a category bit mask of 256. Remember to change their physics shapes to a bounding box as well.

8. Once you're done with the home scene, you have to add a reference to it in the game scene.

9. Finally, you can use the following code inside of `physicsWorld(_:didBeginContact:)` to make sure all the game correctly credits Mr. Pig when he brings coins into his little house.

```
if contactNode.physicsBody?.categoryBitMask == BitMaskHouse {
  if game.bankCoins() == true {
  }
}
```

Once a collision with a house occurs, you use the provided `game.bankCoins()` function to tally all the collected coins and add them to the actual score.

Audio in Scene Kit

Mr. Pig is nearly done, but there's one crucial missing element. Where are the sound effects? The worst thing a game developer can do is to underestimate the power of audio.

Sound is so powerful that the scariest movie ever made would turn into a comedy of note. Go ahead, put in a classic suspense film like "Rear Window" and mute it. Tell me how long you manage to stay interested. Three minutes – five, maybe?

In particular, ambient sounds create atmosphere, giving your game environment life. Sound effects bring actions to life by letting your audience experience every little jump, bump or crash. Music taps into that deep, dark, scary place inside all of us, just as easily as it pulls out the happy, giddy inner child.

In fact, even before there were games and movies with elaborate audio tracks, the screening of silent movies were accompanied by a lovely little ivory-tickling piano player.

Thank goodness the good folks at Apple also realized the importance of sound because they added some really cool sound capabilities into Scene Kit for you to use.

Here are a few important elements in Scene Kit you can use for audio:

- **SCNAudioSource**: An *audio source* is an object that represents an audio file such as music or a sound effect. It can be preloaded into memory or streamed in real-time.

- **SCNAudioPlayer**: With an *audio player* you can play back an *audio source* as 3D spatialized audio using the position of an **SCNNode** object.

- **SCNAction.playAudioSource(_:waitForCompletion:)**: Is a special action you can run on an **SCNNode** that will play back an *audio source*.

Add music

To start your exploration of sound, the first sound element you'll add is music to set the overall tone for your game.

Scene Kit puts a few special objects at your fingertips, especially for playing music.

In **ViewController.swift**, add the following code to setupSounds():

```
// 1
if game.state == .TapToPlay {
  // 2
  let music = SCNAudioSource(fileNamed: "MrPig.scnassets/Audio/
Music.mp3")!
  // 3
  music.volume = 0.3;
  music.loops = true
  music.shouldStream = true
  music.positional = false
  // 4
  let musicPlayer = SCNAudioPlayer(source: music)
  // 5
  splashScene.rootNode.addAudioPlayer(musicPlayer)
}
```

Take a deeper look at what this code does:

1. This makes sure that the music only plays while on the splash scene.

2. This creates an SCNAudioSource object from **MrPig.scnassets/Audio/Music.mp3**.

3. What follows are a few properties that configure the audio source.

- volume: Controls the volume at which the audio source is played back.

- loops: Controls whether the audio source is played back in a loop or not.

- shouldStream: This controls whether the audio source is streamed from its source or preloaded into memory. Typically music and large audio files should be streamed, but for small sound effects it's better to preload them into memory for faster playback.

- positional: Controls whether the audio source will make use of 3D spatialized playback.

4. This section creates an audio player that will make use of the music audio source for playback.

5. By adding the audio player to the rootNode of the scene, this will start the audio player, and the music will start to stream from its audio source.

Do a build and run, and this time around look *and* listen.

Hey, it's really hard to visualize music, but you get the idea. Now you also know why Mr. Pig's been twerking his little tail off! :]

Add ambiance

Do you really think a park with two massive highways through its heart could be so peaceful?

Add the following `else if` block to the bottom of `setupSounds()`:

```
// 1
else if game.state == .Playing {
  // 2
  let traffic = SCNAudioSource(fileNamed: "MrPig.scnassets/
Audio/Traffic.mp3")!
  traffic.volume = 0.3
  traffic.loops = true
  traffic.shouldStream = true
  traffic.positional = true
  // 3
  let trafficPlayer = SCNAudioPlayer(source: traffic)
  gameScene.rootNode.addAudioPlayer(trafficPlayer)
  // 4
  game.loadSound("Jump", fileNamed: "MrPig.scnassets/Audio/
Jump.wav")
  game.loadSound("Blocked", fileNamed: "MrPig.scnassets/Audio/
Blocked.wav")
  game.loadSound("Crash", fileNamed: "MrPig.scnassets/Audio/
Crash.wav")
```

```
    game.loadSound("CollectCoin", fileNamed: "MrPig.scnassets/
  Audio/CollectCoin.wav")
    game.loadSound("BankCoin", fileNamed: "MrPig.scnassets/Audio/
  BankCoin.wav")
  }
```

Here's what's happening in there:

1. This time around you check if the game is in a .Playing state.

2. This sets **MrPig.scnassets/Audio/Traffic.mp3** as a streaming audio source.

3. Then you start to play the audio source as soon as it's added to the rootNode.

4. This preloads a whole bunch of sound effects that you'll use in the next section.

Build and run, start a game and then look and listen.

Suddenly the park springs to life. You can hear the traffic with sounds of little cars, big cars and even those noisy old squeaky buses too. Yippee!

Add sound effects

For your final act, you just need to unlock the sound effects so the player can hear every jump, bump and crash.

Start off by giving life to every jump. Add the following line to the bottom of handleGesture(_:):

```
game.playSound(pigNode, name: "Jump")
```

This will play a nice little *boing* sound effect every time a valid gesture is handled.

> **Note:** This uses a helper method found in GameHelper to play a sound. Under the hood, all it does is simply run a playAudioSource(_:waitForCompletion:) action on the node you pass it by using a preloaded audio source. You can take a look at how it does this by browsing **GameHelper.swift**.

What about when Mr. Pig stumbles into an obstacle? To solve that, add the following sound effect code inside the second guard statement that will block gestures matching the activeCollisionBitMask at top of handleGesture(), just before the return statement:

```
game.playSound(pigNode, name: "Blocked")
```

Now blocked gestures will make a short little *thump* when the player tries to jump into an obstacle.

Coins need sound too! Add the following line just after the call to game.collectCoin() inside of physicsWorld(_:didBeginContact:):

```
game.playSound(pigNode, name: "CollectCoin")
```

Collecting coins certainly sounds much cooler, but the sound effect is somewhat muted. The reason is because the player hasn't really scored yet; he needs to bank that coin in order to get the full audio experience.

Add the following sound effect to that moment when the pig makes contact with the little house.

You'll go back into physicsWorld(_:didBeginContact:), where there's an if statement checking the return value of game.bankCoins(), so that you only play a sound if there are actual coins available to bank:

```
game.playSound(pigNode, name: "BankCoin")
```

Ah, yes! Once the pig jumps into his little house, that familiar, yet satisfying coin sound effect lets the player know that some valuable points were just added to the score board.

Cha-ching! :]

Last but not least is the moment of impact when pig meets bumper and fades away on his way to piggie heaven.

Still inside of `physicsWorld(_:didBeginContact:)`, add the following line of code inside the `if` statement that handles the moment when `pigNode` makes contact with a vehicle, but place the code just before the call to `stopGame()`:

```
game.playSound(pigNode, name: "Crash")
```

Do a final build and run, and enjoy the full Mr. Pig experience, now with music, ambiance and sound effects!

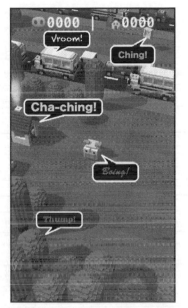

And with that, you just finished your last game and this book. Congratulations! :]

Where to go from here?

The final project for this chapter can be found under the **projects\final\Mr.Pig** folder.

In this chapter, you've learned the value and impact of sound. Thanks to Scene Kit, it's easy to add sounds to all of your future titles.

Mr. Pig certainly has so much unexplored potential just waiting for you to discover, here are a few ideas for you to consider:

- **Voxel Graphics**: Voxel graphics look sharp and are super easy to create. It's the perfect style for someone who's wanting to make something in 3D but not ready to go into great detail.

- **More characters**: You should definitely add more characters to your game. Mr. Wolf, the menacing figure behind that atrocious mall and traffic, is a big bad bully, and he would love nothing more than to troll Mr. Pig from time to time. Rumor has it that he's got his eyes on the park and cute little house. He could be a good motivator to stay away from certain parts of the park or take on the role of an evil boss Mr. Pig must defeat.

- **More obstacles**: Go and explore a nearby park and see what else you could add into the park. There could be a fountain, some park benches and even birds!

- **More actions**: Use actions to add juice to your game. The more elaborate and fun the animations, the more players will enjoy playing it.

- **Go big**: At the moment it's such a small little park – surely you can think up some other clever designs to make the park bigger and more interesting. Why not add power-ups and traps to keep our hero on his hooves?

Now for your final challenge; free your mind, think outside the box and unleash your newly found Scene Kit powers onto the world! :]

Conclusion

We hope you've enjoyed your journey through this book. If you followed it from top to bottom, you've created four epic games from scratch using SceneKit and Swift — from colorful, exploding geometry, to a shiny paddle with a bouncing ball; a beautiful maze, up high in the sky, right down to a cute little pig that twerks.

You now have the knowledge to make your very own hit game. Why wait any longer?

Got a great idea? With SceneKit, prototyping your app is child's play. Share it with your friends, then use their feedback as inspiration to keep on improving it. Don't forget about adding juice: music, sound effects and stunning graphics. Keep on pushing, until you make that final push and publish your game for the whole world to enjoy!

We can't wait to see what you come up with! Be sure to stop by our forums and share your progress at www.raywenderlich.com/forums.

You might also be interested to know that we have a monthly blog post where we review games written by fellow readers like you. If you'd like to be considered for this column, please visit this page after you release your game: www.raywenderlich.com/reviews

Thank you again for purchasing this book. Your continued support is what makes the tutorials, books and other things we do at raywenderlich.com possible. We truly appreciate it.

Best of luck in all your iOS adventures,

— Chris L., Ken, Wendy, Toby, Chris B. and Ray

The *3D iOS Games by Tutorials* Team

Made in the USA
Lexington, KY
21 May 2016